BEAUTY IN CHAOS
A NOVEL

NACOLE STAYTON

PRAISE FOR BEAUTY IN CHAOS

"Nacole Stayton stuns with her beautiful prose in this captivating story about survival, acceptance, and falling in love." -**E.K. Blair,** New York Times Bestselling Author

"Nacole Stayton's *Beauty in Chaos* is a dramatic portrayal of the powerful depths of love."- **Jennifer Foor,** Author of The Mitchell Family Series & Love's Suicide

"*Beauty in Chaos* is the come-back book I've been waiting for! Nacole seamlessly weaves all of the intricate pieces of this book together with such delicate ease. And showcases true love and determination to rise through life's obstacles despite adversity." **Erika Ashby,** Bestselling Author of Broken Wings

"Nacole has a way of writing that makes you feel like you're reading poetry."- **Goodreads** Reviewer

"This book broke my heart in the first chapter and then put me back together. It was such an emotional and heart-warming story." -**Mari's Lit Corner**

"*Beauty in Chaos* is a compelling novel that keeps readers on the edge of their seats until the very end. Nacole Stayton's storytelling prowess shines through, making this book a must-read for fans of emotional and heartfelt narratives."- **Yami's Bookshelf**

DEDICATION

To my mom, Cameron, for being the ultimate confidant, teaching me the definition of being a self-sacrificing mother and for *now* being my guardian angel.

Cameron Colleen Cannon

1966-2021

OTHER TITLES BY NACOLE STAYTON

The Upside of Letting Go

In the Lyrics

A Graceful Mess

Savaged

Bad Intentions

PLAYLIST

Cruel Summer Taylor Swift

Ghost Town Benson Boone

Lucky Elle King

Wreckage Nate Smith

I Don't Go Back Kassi Ashton

The Wolves Madeline Edwards

Butterflies MAX

Everybody Hates Me The Chainsmokers

How to Love Cash Cash

Part of Me Cian Ducrot

CHAPTER
ONE

RORY

"The sky is a fucking liar," I announce before sliding my threadbare curtains over the windowpane. My eyes rake over the horizon as I take in the clouds. Diverse in shapes and sizes and color, their soft pink haze sweeps across the skyline of buildings framed outside. The pigment beckons and tempts my cold, black heart to thaw with the strength of their exquisiteness. There is an illusion in the way the clouds drift over us, tethering our worlds together, and unifying those who reside under their sheer beauty.

I can't help but appreciate these hues of lavender and ginger that dance across the sky, weaving together like some priceless masterpiece.

Screw the sky and her pretty tones.

Taking one last look at the cityscape, I survey the tops of the stone and brick buildings as a black silhouette catches my attention in my peripheral. With ears flattened in forewarning, my nemesis, a black cat, glowers. The cat kneads at the blanket, twirls, and then flops down staking her claim on my twin-sized bed.

"By all means, knock yourself out." The silence is broken by an angry hiss from my adversary.

The impending dread of Miranda, my umpteenth social worker, barging through my bedroom door to whisk me away to another foster family, pulls me from my standoff with the cat that never gave me a chance in the first place. Even though I was the only one who remembered to feed her, she still loathes me. Which is precisely why cats cannot be trusted.

With a quick flash of my eyes around the small room, an unnatural stillness comes over me. A shabby four-drawer dresser sits next to the window. Its drawers are so hard to pull out that I just laid my clothes on top of it. I remember the first night I got here. The unfamiliarity of this room engulfed me as I curled up under the stained quilt atop the twin bed. The ear-splitting bangs and noises that echoed from outside this window kept me up for weeks until the chilling noise became routine.

A couple stitches and a year later and here we are. *Sayonara.* As much as I detest this place, the home I'm headed to next could be worse. That probability is greater than the musty drafts and kitty litter odor that linger here. It's doubtful, but I may end up longing for the comfort that the peeling wallpaper brings me tonight when we arrive, wherever it is I'm going.

I've become too numb to the life I've been given. The constant shuffling from one foster home to the next has left me so detached that I didn't even flinch when Lloyd, our piece of shit foster father, was hauled off in handcuffs after the incident a couple nights ago.

Even with the uncertainty that leaving this place brings, no tears fall from my eyes. The only emotion coursing through my veins is hopelessness. Not even being removed from this apartment after the incident and placed in a temporary home helped. If anything, it only made things worse because it reminded me that I have many more months until I turn eighteen. My existence is like a giant avalanche. I keep sliding down the slippery slope of life, hoping that one day I just propel over the edge of the mountain.

"Aurora!" The front door rasps on its hinges, Miranda's high-pitched voice echoing down the hall.

I eye the black fur-ball who is observing me with caution. A hiss slithers down my spine. The last thing I want is to be attacked. If Lloyd and Jean forget about their foster children like houseplants, left to wither and fade, you can bet your bottom dollar that the cat will surely not last long without me feeding it. Squaring my shoulders, I take a step toward the door stealing a small glance backward. "I hope no one feeds you and you starve to death."

The cat hisses just as my door swings wide. "Grab your bag and let's go. I just loaded Lonnie's. We need to get on the road."

I'm a captive to the State of Kentucky, and unlike the clouds, rich in their color and allure, the only thing tethering me to this dump of an apartment and the system, is my distant eighteenth birthday.

Another home.

Another family.

Another disappointment.

Miranda gives me a nudge. "We've got about an hour drive."

Everything I own has been stuffed into the black trash bag sitting by the door. Grabbing my worldly belongings, I follow her into the hallway, eager to get away from the walls coated in tar residue, thanks to my foster parents' cigarette addiction.

I hope the next tenants don't have asthma.

Lloyd's dependence on bad substances and hitting

minors, and whatever the fuck I walked in on the other night, should finally land him some time behind bars.

The sight of Lonnie, my seven-year-old foster brother, makes my chest tighten. His arm bears a neon-green cast, and in it, he clutches a worn teddy. His honey-colored eyes are void of any emotion, aside from the all too familiar fear.

I've only known him since we were both placed with Lloyd and Jean a year ago. At the ripe age of six, he was placed here with one stuffed animal and the clothes on his back. He needed someone to protect him, and luckily, doing just that gave me a purpose I didn't know I needed. For the last year, it's been us against this cruel world. To say our trauma bond runs deep would be an understatement. We also share a love for reading. Thanks to our weekly trips to the public library. Which is about the only free and accessible form of entertainment that there is for kids like us. He immersed himself in learning as an escape, and I immersed myself in protecting him at all costs. There isn't anything in this world I wouldn't do to keep him safe. Including tackling our unhinged foster dad without a second thought.

"Hey buddy," I rest my hand on his shoulder and give it a small squeeze. The already cramped hallway feels much tighter as I notice another figure. He reaches for my foster brother. I don't care that he's a cop; instinctively, I slide in front of Lonnie, guarding his petite frame with my own. Living in a constant state of fight or flight will do that to a person.

I don't necessarily trust cops.

Or anyone for that matter.

"She's...Miranda...kick out." Lonnie's words form a lump in his throat as he struggles to get out a full sentence, a look of dread on his face. I've witnessed the cruelty of this world far too many times in my seventeen years. Nothing is worse than seeing a seven-year-old break at the thought that his sister is leaving him.

Alone.

Vulnerable.

Exposed to the harsh reality that foster care entails.

The world deserves a big middle finger salute.

With her bleached hair pulled into a bun at the nape of her neck, Miranda clears her throat. "I had to cash in some favors with the judge to place you two in a home together. Luckily," she pauses and makes eye contact with the officer I forgot was privy to this private moment. "A family came forward that is open to taking in two children and had an up-to-date background check. They live on the outskirts of the city in a small town called Bardstown. It's known as the bourbon capital of the world." Her manner indicates she's familiar with the town we're headed to. For some reason, Miranda reminds me of a cheap bottle of whiskey, diluted to a sensitive palate. The thought makes me beam on the inside. Even knowing she's just doing her job as a social worker doesn't mean I have to be fond of her.

"She's not kicking *just* me out. *We're* going to live somewhere else for a little while, buddy." My gut twists knowing that we're leaving and most likely headed to another shoddy facility that smells like mildew, or with another foster family that will take us in until I turn eighteen. Then I'll scrape up enough money to retain a lawyer and try to adopt Lonnie myself. He deserves more than the hand he's been dealt. "You and me. Until the end." To my dismay, my voice breaks. I smile tenderly trying to regain his confidence and attempt to hide the unease in my tone as I bend down until our foreheads meet. "I will never leave you. Ever." I'm not a liar, unless that means painting a picture that this next family is as welcoming as The Brady Bunch.

Lonnie's tiny arms circle around my neck, and the edge of his cast scrapes across my skin. "I love you, Rory," he says. "I know you will keep me safe from the monsters." Innocence radiates in his declaration.

A flash of the image of what Lloyd could have done to Lonnie if I didn't interfere when I had causes a fury to stir within me. The thought of us being separated coils my stomach. There was no way in hell I was going to allow Miranda, or the state of Kentucky, to separate us. Even if that meant doing something brash and running away. As my pulse quickens, we walk down the narrow hallway filled with memories that will undoubtedly plague us both forever.

I once read a quote from a painter in a magazine I found on a sidewalk. I think her name was Frida Kahlo. She said, "Not fragile like a flower, fragile like a bomb." Her words resonated with me and remained my own personal mantra. I'm not weak. The system might have failed me time and time again, but this world has another thing coming if it thinks I'm not a force to be reckoned with.

Passing by the mirror hanging by the front door, I push a straw-colored lock behind my ear and grab Lloyd's baseball hat from the back of the sofa. Sliding it onto my head, I inhale his musty scent. It's repulsive. Ever since I can remember, it might have even been my first placement, I've kept or *stolen* a piece of something from the house. A trinket. I'm not sure what possesses me to do it. If anything, I wish I could forget the awful places I've had to stay, and the things I've had to do to survive. Maybe the knick-knacks are reminders of what I've endured and conquered.

Maybe, I'm just screwed in the head.

Inhaling the stale air of the city, I glance over my shoulder and send a silent goodbye to the buildings towering over us. We have a lot in common, the buildings and me. They, too, have seen better days.

Some neglected.

Some restored.

Both, resilient to the storms we've weathered.

With every foster family, I lost a little of myself and gained a piece of the person I am now. The girl who resides in my five-foot-two-inch frame is a collection of weary souls, ones that I've encountered and left over the years. Like a vase that's been shattered and haphazardly glued back together, I've managed to piece together an emotionally scarred zombie. Our cracks may be hidden from the surface, but they're still there, barely holding us together inside.

Uneven and jagged.

Acres of greenery and a handful of farms pass by our windows on the hour-long drive into the suburbs. I've been to a couple parties outside of the city before. Never have I traveled this far into the countryside though. The first thing I notice as Miranda turns into a subdivision are perfectly trimmed bushes lining the paved driveways as they lead up to impressive houses. You can almost count the blades of grass. The lawns are so well-maintained. Either lawn care is a budding empire or the residents in this place have a bad case of obsessive-compulsive disorder.

"You two might just be the luckiest kids I've ever placed in a home before." The loud sound the muffler makes as it rattles on its hinges, even after the ignition is killed, is bothersome. The state really should provide better vehicles to its employees who haul children around all day. Miranda turns in her seat and gives me a smoke-stained smile, and I notice her exposed midriff as she repositions her charcoal-colored blouse.

Agitated by her assertion, a fury unleashes in my chest. I know I should bite my tongue, but it's a futile attempt. "Lucky? I hope you're joking."

"Stop, Rory," Lonnie pleads from the back seat. He's grown accustomed to my defiance. "I don't want to go to a group home."

"He's right. If this doesn't work out, that's where you're

both headed again. Dr. Greenwell is the physician who treated you and Lonnie after the incident with Lloyd. This is the best-case scenario here, Aurora. I suggest you don't mess it up. We don't have many open homes right now. It will be hard to keep you *together* if this family doesn't work out."

Placating is a trait I keep in my arsenal. "I'll behave." I give her a forced smile before turning and finally allowing myself to take in the house where we're parked. My first thought is, it's a little extravagant for two people. I assume physician's make a lot of money, as I take in the size of the house. She might as well own the hospital to afford this place.

Miranda unbuckles her seat belt and slithers out of the car like a serpent. The fact that she believes either Lonnie or I are lucky is mind blowing. I can't help but marvel that this may be the last home we'll be forced to reside in until my eighteenth birthday.

"I'll make the best of it." I prod Lonnie's side. Pressing the latch, I unbuckle his seat belt and undo his booster. "Home sweet home," I lie, silently pleading that my nerves are hidden enough for him to believe my web of deceptions as warning bells sound like boulders rolling off a cliff in my brain. By the looks of the manicured lawn, I know that this place is too good to be true.

A flicker of movement catches my attention as a child on a yellow bicycle rides by the car waving vigorously. The sight may seem ordinary. Not to me. The fact a child can safely be alone and ride his bike on the sidewalk reminds me that we're not in the city anymore. I turn toward the front porch, following the line of the boy's smile.

It's then that I notice Dr. Bernadette Greenwell. I don't know what I was expecting. This house, for starters, threw me for a loop. She's petite and older than I remember when we met in the emergency room. Truthfully, Harry Styles could have stitched me up and set Lonnie's arm, and I probably wouldn't have noticed. I was high on adrenaline and fury.

Dr. Greenwell's hair is hanging over her shoulder in a loose braid. Her cheeks look worn like they've smiled more than they've frowned in her lifetime. Her wide, pleasant smile seems genuine. I've been fooled too many times to count, playing it safe and not expecting too much from anyone is the only route I'm used to. I smile back, not wanting to get off on the wrong foot so early in our new placement.

After saying goodbye to Miranda, Dr. Greenwell leads us into the foyer of her home. Lonnie's small hand intertwines with my own. "Do we need to take off our shoes?" I've never stepped foot in a house with a fancy foyer or a chandelier like the one hanging above our heads.

"Please, child, these floors have seen better days." Her voice is calm. She leans forward and for a split second, I think she's going to fold me in a hug.

I retreat a step. "I don't like when people touch me without warning."

"I was just going to shut the door all the way behind you. We get a lot of June bugs this time of year." I feel like a complete idiot. "With what you've both been through recently, I don't blame you for being a little jittery. Let me show you guys around."

Biting my tongue, I follow as she gives us a tour of the first floor of the house. She doesn't act like someone who'd live in a place with ceilings this high. She seems traveled and more carefree than an emergency room physician would be. Which explains the paintings that hang on almost every wall. Some of them are enormous. I stop at one that catches my eye.

"Do you like horses?" She notices my marvel.

"I like art."

"I grew up riding. I had this painting commissioned."

There's something so satisfying about taking a canvas and turning it into something, anything you want it to be. I don't have the means to do a lot of pieces, but sometimes when I'm able to save enough extra money, I'll buy a couple canvases at the store and a small paint set. Creating art sets my mind free and liberates my soul. It's something where I can control the outcome. I once even earned a hundred bucks by doing face paintings for a kids' birthday party at Lonnie's school.

"We have a small art gallery in town. I know the owner. I can arrange a visit for you if you'd like." An expression of satisfaction glimmers in her hazel eyes at my nod, she continues guiding us into the kitchen. When we enter the massive kitchen, she explains that her husband, Officer Greenwell, is on duty and won't be home until dinner time.

Imagine my surprise to learn that the officer who rearranged our previous foster dad's face is married to the emergency department physician who pieced us back together.

Fate is a fickle hellion like that.

"I'm delighted that you're both here." Laugh lines bracket her lips. "Please call me Bea though. Bernadette is too formal. No one calls me that other than Russell, and even I think he does it to get under my skin." Her features become animated.

"Okay, Bea." Lonnie and I both say quietly as we turn a corner.

The house resembles a mansion or what I've envisioned one looking like. There is a grand staircase in the middle of the room. It reminds me of those stuffy prom pictures girls take and post all over social media. Whenever I could find access to free Wi-Fi, I would browse their social media pages. I looted an iPad mini last year that someone left on the bus, and had it reset, but Lloyd broke it in a drunken rage not too long afterward.

Add social media stalker to my resume. Even though I've never created my own profile before.

As we follow Bea around the house, something Miranda said to me floats to the surface of my mind. "They have money. They're not into fostering for a paycheck." She said while boring holes into my head as she stared at me. "Give the Greenwells a chance. Surely you can survive the next year without having to be moved again. On your eighteenth birthday you're free." In a twist of luck, Miranda might be onto something. We may have just been handed a blessing on a silver platter.

"This here is your room, Aurora." Bea opens a set of white double doors, and I immediately smell flowers. Long gone is the musty smell of the apartment. She faces me, looking for approval of my new digs.

"It's Rory."

"Understood." She nods. "I'll make sure to let the school know as well. Anyway, it's been a while since we've had a child in the house." Her gaze lowers like she is reminiscing. I use the time to step through the door. My feet shuffle on the soft carpet and I regret not removing my tattered shoes in the foyer.

"I wasn't sure what you were into. Most of our family and friends have boys. I always wanted a little girl."

In my seventeen years in the system, no one cared about our living conditions. If there was running water and food on the table when the social workers came for their visits, my foster parents' monthly stipend checks kept rolling in. The reality is, I've been a paycheck for far too many adults in my lifetime.

My eyes sweep the room in front of me. There's a huge, four-poster bed with a see-through canopy with lights attached to it. It has more pillows than I've ever seen on a bed in person, and they're placed in picture-perfect order. Absent-mindedly, I glide my hand along the duvet. It's soft, and the floral smell wafts up once again. This is surely an upgrade to how I was greeted at the last home. Honestly, I don't recall even having a pillow on my bed when I first arrived.

My mind is blank as I run my fingertips over the throw blanket, perfectly folded and perched at the bottom of the bed. I'm at a loss for words, which doesn't happen often.

"Is this heaven?" Lonnie's small voice breaks my stupor. He hops onto the bed and burrows his tiny frame in the mass of pillows. "Did you and Officer Greenwell win the lottery or something?"

A small glimmer of hope dances across Bea's face as the significance of his question jars us both. "I wish we won the lottery, little man. I sincerely hope you like it here, Rory. And you, too, Lonnie. Wait until you see your room." She grabs his hand and guides him back into the hallway. Much to my surprise he willingly takes it.

As nice as my bedroom is, it would be foolish not to see right through this situation. Can you doubt someone like me? Being alert has saved my ass too many times to count. Warning bells ring in my head as I recall her statement about not recently having a child in their home. *What happened to their last placement?*

Every foster family must go through rigorous training and background checks. With a system that is loaded down with too many kids and not enough families, mistakes like approving Lloyd and Jean happen. More often than not. My gut tells me this isn't the same scenario, but I'd be stupid to let my guard down.

"Look at this, Rory!" Lonnie shouts from the room adjacent to mine. There is a strict rule in foster care that only members of the same sex can sleep in the same room, and they must be the same age. I catch him sliding his frayed shoes off and jumping onto the bed. His eyes beam with a happiness I've never seen before.

The elation on his face is mimicked in my own. This whole day has been a lot to take in. It's been me against the world for so long, I'm not used to the feeling of being dependent on somebody else for anything. I make sure Lonnie is comfortable with Bea and his new surroundings before I excuse myself for some much needed air.

CHAPTER
TWO

RORY

The first few nights in a new home are the worst. You don't have a clue about the family's dynamics and where you fit into them. I've been in homes where families pray together before meals, and homes where joints are rolled on the counter next to frozen Salisbury steak dinners.

For a moment, I miss being at Lloyd and Jean's in the apartment I've called home. At least there, there were no surprises. I knew where I stood and what two pieces of trash held my fate in their hands.

With permission from Bea to go explore the neighborhood, curiosity urges me onward as I round the exit of the subdivision that I'll call *home* for the next several months. The town's unfamiliarity makes me nervous. Dark foliage dances on the limbs of trees lining the road as I make my way across it. I appreciate the lush greenery. It's something I'm not used to, having lived in the city my whole life. Everything looks so crisp and alive. Even the air smells different here. It's not coated with odors from car exhaust or rotting garbage.

Paved sidewalks line the street. I choose one and amble forward, trying to recall the direction of the quaint little town Miranda drove through on our way to the Greenwell's. I'm used to the bustle of the big city, so if the suburbs have anything resembling a town, no matter how minuscule, my interest is piqued.

As the sun begins to recede, the sky takes on an ambient orange glow, casting a shadow over an old three-story brick building, that rests in the middle of a turn-about where vehicles move around it. A breeze whistles by, signaling that summer is almost over. I briefly close my eyes and inhale for what feels like the first time in years. The aroma of flowers blooming, and barbecue cooking keeps me shuffling forward.

A steady warning bell signaling that I'm a tourist in this small town, rings loudly in my head as I trot onward. I hate the feeling of always being an outsider. My eyes rake over a slew of storefronts all nestled together down the main drag. The road is lined with vehicles parked on either side. I amble forward, weaving between other spectators, maybe tourists, as they stroll through the bourbon capitol of the world. I pass through a small crowd hovering outside a bar and make my way to the end of the block, noticing the attractiveness of the town is amplified by a heap of traditional-style houses sitting beside one another. Most have American flags waving from their porches, and several have brightly colored front doors beckoning to people like a pair of open arms.

The historical main street with its splendor of architecture is charming. You can tell there's a rich culture based on the variety of shops on the main thoroughfare. No wonder people come here to visit and shop. I bet it's just as breathtaking around the holidays.

With summer on its last leg, people must be trying to get as much outdoor time as possible. I try to blend in while taking in the shops and bustling shoppers trying to get their items before the stores close. On the corner, I notice a small crowd of girls around my age posing by a brick arch adorned with a wall of flowers behind it. It amazes me how carefree they all look. Their parents are probably loaded and gave them a hundred dollars to blow as they parade down the street, stopping at every boutique they see.

With some hesitation, I think about senior year. I'm sure they're out shopping to make a statement on the first day of school, while I don't even know where I'll be going yet. I didn't give Bea much time to fill me in on the details of our stay with them before I fled to get some air.

Brushing by the group of girls, I dip into a drugstore nestled on the corner. A giant clock chimes outside as I pull open the creaky door. The benefit of being a nobody is that it's easy to blend in. Which is exactly what I plan to do while I restock on allergy medication. I'm not great with asking anyone for anything. Even if being a foster parent comes with the responsibly of supplying medication. I've learned to just take care of myself, which is just what I'm doing.

Get in and get out has been a motto I've come to live and survive by. The air is stale, which leads me think that this necessities store has been around for a while. I wander aimlessly, looking around trying to blend in. It's usually less suspicious if I appear to be browsing in search of an item rather than hovering over one section of the store.

I make my way to the aisle I'm in search of and quickly spot what I need. I grab the small box and pretend to stretch my neck, craning it to the side and make a quick sweep of the store. Its other patrons are oblivious to my presence.

Once invisible. Always invisible.

I slide the item up my sleeve and grip my hand at the opening, ensuring nothing falls out and lands me in a detention center until my eighteenth birthday. With adrenaline coursing through my veins, I turn the corner of the aisle and slam straight into a hard chest. I freeze as a thin layer of sweat coats the nape of my neck and anxiety floods my body. I hear a faint thump and look down as a pack of cigarettes slides out of the hem of said hard chest's T-shirt, bouncing off the worn toe of my shoe.

Disoriented from the collision, I struggle to plant my heel on the stained linoleum in an attempt not to fall backward and fail miserably. The person who I struck catches me by the elbow keeping me upright.

"What the hell?" I growl, my reaction violent. "Watch where you're going." My body goes rigid when my eyes rake in the Adonis staring back at me, teeth clenched.

"Excuse me? You ran into me. Why don't *you* watch where you're going?" His words are clear and cool like ice water, except they don't extinguish the annoyance that has pitted in my stomach.

My mission, when I noticed this little store, was to get in and out, and this…birdbrain, for lack of a better word, is preventing that from happening. "Screw you, dude." I match his energy swallowing down a sliver of panic. What if he works here and tells his boss he caught me stealing?

Smooth. Real smooth, Rory.

"Wouldn't you like that?" I notice the firm grip he still has on my arm.

"To what? Screw you? You're delusional and shouldn't think that highly of yourself. I've seen more attractive men on ads for toothpaste." I lift my lashes and look up only to find a sliver of laughter in his amber glare.

"Riddle me this. How did I become the bad guy when I saved *you* from falling on your ass and making a fool of yourself? I'm your knight in this scenario."

"I'd say that, but I'm not a damsel who needs saving, and I suggest you remove your hand before you regret it." I'm not fond of people touching me without my permission, even though his embrace doesn't send off warning bells like it usually does. That fact alone sends a shiver up my spine. My eyes slowly drag upward from his clasp still holding my arm, past his broad chest clad with a black shirt. A pine scent invades my senses from our proximity. It's a deep, lovely smell. I inhale as the intruder of my personal bubble arches an eyebrow. "Let go and move. I have some place I need to be."

Dark tendrils of hair stick out from under a baseball cap. *Maybe's it's his shampoo that smells of pine.* His face is reserved. Rugged almost, and I've never seen eyes so dark, like two chocolate orbs with hints of gold creating a warm honey gaze before. His brutal and unfriendly stare cuts deep, and I *almost* want to be scorched by his stare.

I don't move.

Hell.

I don't think I breathe.

Right now, I'm speechless as he and I remain glued staring at one another for an inappropriate amount of time before he unfolds his fingers from my arm and bends to grab the pack of cigarettes lying on the linoleum floor. The black T-shirt he wears tightens around the arms as he reaches forward and grips the pack of cigarettes, crushing it gently in his steady clasp. I peep down to shake off the unsettling glare staring back at me, surveying me in the same way I am him.

Eyes are the key to everything that makes someone themselves. A portal to the truth that lingers in someone's soul. Your past leaves your eyes haunted. I've learned not to look people in their eyes. From judges, the numerous social workers I've had the joy to encounter, and my many foster parents.

Until now.

His are like a blank canvas waiting to be painted and I'm the artist deciding if he's worth the subtle glow of his irises or if they should be mired like a summer lightning strike ruining everything in its path.

Is it a compliment to notice how full and thick a guy's eyebrows are?

"Can you give me a hand?" A man with winter-white hair

and a gruff voice cuts through our peculiar exchange and provides me an out. Using the split second, the man, who resembles Colonel Sanders in overalls, seizes the attention from me, I scurry by, making wide strides toward the door.

I rush by incoming patrons and corner the building, stumbling into an alleyway lined with brick as I attempt to gather my bearings. My chest rises and falls rapidly as I lean against the wall steadying myself. The day's humidity has melted into an even muggier summer night, leaving the air so thick my top sticks to my skin. I can't distinguish if it is the thrill of shoplifting or his eyes that leave me feeling breathless. Knowing damn well it's the latter.

He made me feel alive. Something I haven't felt before with just one torrid glance from a stranger. Maybe I'm delirious. I haven't been sleeping well since Lonnie and I had to go to a temporary foster family for a few days following the incident. Thanks to being in a new place, I barely slept a couple hours at a time.

"Did *you* steal something?" A condescending voice demands.

Hello juvie.

How am I going to lie my way out of this one?

Wordlessly, I organize my thoughts before I open my mouth in protest. I'm a master thief. Something that I shouldn't be proud of, but it's a trait that has kept me fed too often to care about how it sounds. I survey the alley around me debating on making a break for it, but I contemplate too long because a small rock skirts by my foot.

Huffing, I turn to find cigarette boy with his devastatingly beautiful eyes standing behind me, smug delight etched onto his mouth. Who is *he* to accuse me when he was literally doing the same thing? I don't care how captivating his eyes are, this guy is a hypocrite, and an asshole. His nervy eyes bore into mine, awaiting an answer.

"And you're one to talk?" I retort coolly. He was caught

red-handed, but I get the feeling that he doesn't care that he was just outed for smuggling stolen cigarettes in the hem of his T-shirt. Guys like him only care about placing blame on others. Deflection is a superpower, and he's wielding it.

A string of lights dangles from a post above us, making it bright enough in the alleyway that I can see his haunting eyes staring back at me. Their glare is insolent and empty. I notice his tan skin has been kissed by the summer sun. His striking features have me convinced that his sharp chin is made of iron. I'm lost in a daze of cheek bones and heart-shaped lips.

"I don't know what you think you saw. I wouldn't steal from Freddy. He's an old family friend." His voice is smooth, yet assertive. Cigarette guy certainly thinks he's persuasive. I bet if you put him on an infomercial, he'd be rid of whatever he was selling in a jiffy. He has that much appeal, even though I know he's lying through his teeth.

"If you steal from your friends, I'd hate to see how you treat people you actually care about."

He tilts his head back and laughs, brushing off my comment. This dude has the nerve to laugh at me. Even the gruff sound he chokes out is condescending. "There's an optometrist down the block. You might want to get your eyes checked…and watch where you're going next time."

The audacity of this guy.

My lips stay taut. We are two wild animals from different packs, sizing the other up. He's the first person around my age I've encountered, other than the Barbie squad, and he's equally as ominous. "Possession is nine-tenths of the law, is it not?"

"You're a little young to have sat for the bar."

"My age is irrelevant. I saw you steal those cigarettes. It's a disgusting habit by the way."

"So is eye-fucking a stranger. People still do that." I can almost feel the smugness rolling from his tongue. He slides a hand into his pocket. My eyes follow his movements as the denim fabric tightens. Such a simple movement, yet I bite my lip as I watch him lean back against the brick wall. If there was a photographer near, he'd be the perfect model with his perilous swagger.

Damnit, get your head on straight. He's just a guy. I scold my inner thoughts as soon as my brain fires them off.

"What a charmer you are. I hope I see you… never again." He's not the first or last moron I'm bound to encounter, and if I'm being honest, today has been taxing enough. Standing in a dark alleyway arguing with a stranger is likely to push me over the edge. Luckily, sarcasm is like punching people in the face with words and no repercussion.

"By all means," he gestures with a hand. "It's okay if you don't like me. Not everyone has good taste." He replies matter-of-factly and turns on his heel. Carelessly strolling back onto the busy sidewalk, he glances over his shoulder at me and then vanishes into the crowd.

I slide my stolen allergy meds out of my sleeve and stuff the small box into my pocket. Launching forward, I hope to get lost in the crowd as well.

Senior year hasn't even started, and I've already made an enemy.

My life is a magnet for disaster.

My stomach growls. I can't recall the last time I ate, which means Lonnie is probably starving too. I'm sure he is anxiously wondering about my whereabouts.

Retracing my steps, I head back to my new foster home.

CHAPTER
THREE

CREW

Straw-colored, wavy hair cascades over her petite shoulders and frame. I'm convinced that baseball caps on women should be a crime. She watches me warily, almost as cautiously as I watch her. There isn't an ounce of wavering in her emerald eyes as they bore into mine, holding me hostage. This stranger sees straight through the disguise I wisely crafted.

That does not appeal to me.

From the moment her lips part and she spews her venomous words back at me, I'm a goner. Like the sacrificial lamb, I'm at her mercy. Something clicks inside like lights flickering back on after a bad thunderstorm, and it blinds me. Her spirit is a sliver of reprieve that calls out to me.

My pulse beats violently. I'm almost positive I'm still breathing, although, for the life of me I can't seem to muster up enough air in my lungs to say anything suave after we collide. I usually have a lot more game than I'm showing.

Time ceases, and never once do I yield to think about the predicament we're in. Standing toe-to-toe, breaking the law without a hint of remorse in either of our eyes. For a minute, I forget about all my life's drama—and trust me, there's a truckload full of it. Just ask my court-appointed therapist. I choke out a short slur about watching where she's going, casting the blame on her for our inopportune crash.

Everyone blames their mistakes on me. It's about time I deflect a little too.

The truth is, Freddy, the store owner, is as old school as they come. He doesn't even keep the cigarettes behind the counter like most convenience stores, and he still has a manual cash register. He's the definition of an old-timer. I'm over eighteen and legally able to buy cigarettes. But Freddy plays golf with my dad and is almost as ruthless as the women in this town are with gossip. The rumor mill won't let anyone forget my tarnished name. My parents still care about their social status, so instead of buying a pack and having to hear the wrath of my dad about the dangers of smoking, I slide the small square pack of cigarettes under my shirt and try to make a beeline for the exit.

Only I don't quite make it. The blonde with worn shoes, and legs that a runway model would kill for, literally stopped me in my tracks. *Who the hell is she?* I tilt my head to the side with curiosity, taking notice of her pouty lips. Which so happens to be my kryptonite.

Mystery girls' mouth is one even I don't recognize, and I've kissed a lot of mouths. I slide my lower lip between my teeth and bite in a feeble attempt to jump start my brain. It doesn't work because as I bite down, her lips separate, and she inhales a sharp breath. My brother, Trice, would have croaked already seeing me speechless with a woman as breathtaking as the one in front of me. Hell, he'd already be pining for her attention.

He's a greedy bastard.

My pulse quickens seconds before she shoves by me and storms outside. Doing what any sensible guy with raging hormones would do, I follow her and ignore Freddy's request for help. Surely, he can get someone else to lend him a hand. I'm occupied suddenly.

Commotion from the street surrounds me as I walk outside. A faint buzz of fireflies swirl toward a dark alleyway. I round the corner and spot her. She looks like she may need a paper bag to hyperventilate into.

Like some sort of creep, I quietly draw closer to her from behind.

I am totally off my game today.

Even in faded shorts, shoes that look like they need to be retired to the Goodwill, and a plain shirt, she looks better than any female I've ever laid eyes on in this town. When I open my mouth, a heap of derogatory accusations passes my lips.

She doesn't cower.

Surprisingly, she barks back.

I don't believe in nirvana. My sheer inability to produce manners would never allow me to feel real peace. Blondie matches my banter, leaving me feeling schooled like a dog whose owner told him to heel.

No one has ever called me obedient.

Determined, yes, and I want to know *her*.

If I didn't need a cigarette before, I sure as hell do now.

CHAPTER
FOUR

RORY

The last time I lived in a house that didn't have garbage spewed across the lawn, or cracks in the windows that were duct taped back together, was when I did a stint in the orphanage. It wasn't elaborate by any means. It provided me with a bed to sleep in and a hot shower, which is a luxury a lot of people take for granted. The place did, however, reek of decay and unanswered prayers.

It's ominously dark when I reach the Greenwell's front porch. Luckily, I was able to make the short distance from town square to their house running solely on the butterflies in my stomach, and the revulsion toward the dude from the store.

Stone pavers and small solar lights illuminate my way to a set of wooden double doors. A worrisome thought comes over me as I near the entrance. *Do I knock or just walk in?* Before I can reach up to knock, a deep male voice catches me off guard.

"You don't have to knock, ya know." I turn to see Officer Greenwell.

"Isn't that what guests are supposed to do?"

"Aurora...Rory, I mean." He clears his throat. "You're not a guest in this house. This is your home now. Like it or not, we're your family for a while." He opens the door and ushers me inside.

"Rory! Rory!" Lonnie yells as we cross the threshold. Grazing by Officer Greenwell, I anxiously push forward, only to find Lonnie nestled on the kitchen island looking exuberant. "Look what Bea taught me!" With flour on his nose and hands, he's rolling what appears to be a noodle on the counter. "Bea said spaghetti noodles shouldn't come from a box." He smiles from ear to ear. Spaghetti is his all-time favorite food. I once scrounged up enough money to buy us both kids meals at Olive Garden. He was in heaven and talked about it for an entire month.

"You are an excellent sous chef. Why don't we go upstairs and get washed up for dinner?" I help him off the barstool and turn to follow.

"Rory, here," Bea wipes her hands on a maroon apron and pulls something out of the pocket. "I know you're used to being independent, but our job is to keep the both of you healthy and safe. I don't mind if you explore, but please keep this on you so we know you can be reached." She puts a cell phone in my hand. "I've already programed my number and Russell's, as well as Miranda's—should you ever need to reach her."

With my mouth ajar, I nod. I've never owned a cell phone in my entire life. No one has ever cared enough to need to get a hold of me, much less keep tabs on my whereabouts. "Um, thanks. I can do chores, or whatever, to pay you back."

"Nonsense. It's a gift. We will have some ground rules to go over after dinner, though," she brings her attention back to the pot of homemade noodles in front of her, stirring as a wave of steam engulfs her wooden spoon. "There's a laptop on your bed too. Senior year in a new place..." she pauses, and she and Officer Greenwell, or Russell, exchange a glance before she continues. "We figured you'd need it, and now you have the rest of the weekend to get organized before school starts on Monday."

I consider pinching my arm. In what alternate universe is Bea Greenwell from? Kindness seeps from her pores.

"Go ahead and get washed up. Dinner is almost ready."

Lonnie beats me upstairs, hollering for me to find him. I walk into his bedroom, and much to my surprise, it's incredible. I didn't look around much earlier, but now I wish I hadn't just taken off. No wonder why he looks so smitten. His room is incredibly suited for a child his age. "I know you're in here." I stifle a laugh, pretending to look around aimlessly for him.

"Boo!" Lonnie jumps out from behind the door, tackling me to the rich carpeted ground. His bedframe is a simple twin size. On it, a comforter with a detailed construction site woven into the fabric. I take in the large bookcase under the bay window that looks out onto the street. "Isn't it nice in here?" He gives me a wide grin. That's something I hadn't seen in a while, and now, he can't seem to stop smiling.

"It is pretty badass...nice." I brush my hand over his unruly caramel curls. Something as simple as having a bedroom without mold, and being able to sleep on clean linen, is exciting in his seven-year-old eyes. That sends a wave of emotion straight to my gut. I've grown accustomed to squatting in less than perfect conditions. He's just a kid. It's hard to remember back to when I was that age. I imagine I'd be squealing with delight like he is right now.

"Look," he grabs my hand. "I even have my own bathroom!" I didn't look around my room much earlier. I wonder if I have my own too. "It's like we're living in a hotel. Bea even said there are bubbles under the counter that I can use tonight."

"Just remember, we won't be here long, buddy. Don't get

too comfortable." I nudge his shoulder with mine. He saunters toward the bed and climbs onto it. His feet dangle over the side.

"I know the plan, Rory. It's okay to admit this place is sweet!" He leans backward and stretches before folding his small hand and cast under his head. He's much smarter than your average seven-year-old. He's had to be to remain alive. A wave of sadness pecks at my heart. Lonnie is the only person I care about, aside from myself, in this entire world. I'll be damned if he suffers the same life I was fated to.

"Wash your hands and meet me downstairs. Bea said dinner is going to be done soon." His infectious grin fills my heart as I make my way out of his room and into mine. Everything seems too good to be true. But instead of raining on his parade, I give him a faint smile and try to make the best of our situation.

The first thing I do is open a door opposite my bed. Much to my surprise, I, too, have an en suite, which I swear is bigger than my entire bedroom at the apartment. On the sink is an assortment of items sprawled out and arranged by color. An unopened toothbrush and tube of toothpaste, a brush, a pack of razors, a set of hair ties, a blow dryer, and a hair straightener. I feel like we've been cast in a movie, or we're living in an alternative reality. One where people care about one another's wellbeing.

I pinch the inside of my arm. Nope. I felt that. This is real life. I reach in my back pocket and take out the pack of allergy pills. I lay the box on the counter with the things Bea provided before washing my hands.

I scrub forcefully, washing and wringing at my thieving hands in the sink. Hands that have stolen much more than allergy medicine. Hands that have brawled with men twice my age from stealing my virtue, and hands that have held the mouths of small children as we hid in closets while our foster families fought.

No wonder Lonnie is enthralled with this place. With a doctor as a mom and a police officer as a father, it may be my safe haven, too, I think as I make my way downstairs for the first home-cooked meal I've had in years.

After dinner, Lonnie and I insist on washing the dishes. We get off easy because they have a dishwasher. I finish loading the last plate and excuse Lonnie to get ready for bed. It's been a long day and the small dark circles forming under his eyes are an indication he's spent. Using a damp rag to wipe off the counters and stove, I hear a noise behind me. Instinctively, my gut clenches.

"You're a natural caretaker." I look over my shoulder to see Bea leaning against the wall with a glass of red wine in hand, eying me interestedly, yet her mouth curves with a tenderness I've never really seen before in a person.

"You have no other choice when you're in my position." My harshness isn't directed toward her, but the hand I've been dealt in life. My thoughts flounder in the bleakness that has been my existence. Bouncing from place to place, enrolling and unenrolling in school. I'm a Tetris game that not even I know how to win.

My birthday is so close, yet so far from reach it's sickening. Making the best of the situation I add, "I really appreciate the dinner. We haven't had a home-cooked meal in a long while. Jean, our foster mother, worked a lot, and our old foster father, Lloyd, well," I gesture to my cut lip. "He was a worthless asshole."

"One thing you never have to thank us for is food or shelter, Rory." She steps forward until we're both staring out the window. "I was in foster care myself." Her admission makes my eyebrows shoot up in surprise. "I became a doctor to heal people. If we're having a heart-to-heart…" She pauses and takes a slow drink before sitting her glass with a clink on the countertop. "It's probably to heal myself, if I'm being honest. The thing is, the system doesn't define us. Neither does this world. It's *us*, how we carry ourselves, how we chose to love in a world that we don't deem significant to earn it. That's what defines us."

Russell enters the kitchen and wraps his wife in his arms from behind. "That's enough for tonight, don't you think, honey? I'm sure Rory is exhausted. I know I am." Public displays of affection usually make me want to hurl, but his grasp isn't possessive; it's tender. It's admirable.

"He's right. Go ahead and get cleaned up. Oh, before we forget. We have an alarm on the house. Here's your code," she slides a piece of paper toward me. "We can talk about rules and school tomorrow."

I trudge upstairs and give Lonnie a hug and tuck him in. The Greenwells really thought of everything. I flip the switch on a bulldozer lamp that illuminates small bulldozers on the wall. We'll see how long he lasts in his room tonight. Being in a new place with the torment that nighttime brings kids like us doesn't bode well. From night terrors to full-blown panic attacks, we've learned the hard way that the dark is not our friend.

Sliding into my room, I shut the door and reach for my black garbage bag on the floor. I sit down and spill out its contents. Remembering my new cell phone, I slide it out of my pocket. There isn't a passcode, so I hit the screen. Much to my surprise, it's already connected to Wi-Fi. I type in YouTube and then put on *Kings of Jupiter* while I unpack my clothes into the empty drawers in the dresser. I don't have much to unload, but as I slide open the first drawer my mouth hits the floor. A small stack of clothes already fills the space. Bea may be the most compassionate woman I've ever met.

I don't have to check the tag, knowing already that they'll fit me. When a child is assigned to a new home the foster parents usually get a quick rundown of information from medical needs to clothing sizes. Although monthly stipends are there to help foster families with housing expenses, food, and toiletries, the Greenwells must've already purchased these prior to our arrival. My hands rummage through the soft materials and pull out a black one-piece bathing suit. I hurry across the room and pull the curtain open.

Score.

The Greenwells must be filthy rich because outside the window is an inground pool. Without hesitation I lock my bedroom door and start to strip, sliding the soft black material over my body not thinking that it's night and the pool may very well be frigid. I grab my cell phone and the small paper that holds the code to the alarm system before quietly shutting my door, hoping to not alert anyone in the house. A quick dip is all I need to unwind after a day like today.

Unlike the city where horns and sirens chime twenty-four-seven, no one is arguing on the street corner in this neighborhood. The absence of gunshots shouldn't faze me, yet it does. I tiptoe through the house and make my way to the patio door. I slip outside and realize I forgot to grab a towel, but don't bother turning back. Crickets chirp in the moonlight as I step further onto the deck, the tense lines in my forehead relax. This is what the end of summer should sound like. Blissful harmony from nature, the echo of water as it cascades from the pool's grotto. The moon illuminates the retaining wall that has a lounge area with planters surrounding it. Although, the picturesque view is amazing, I notice the fenced perimeter around the pool. Another rule about foster care is that all bodies of water must be fenced.

I walk down the deck steps and onto cobblestone that leads me to the fence's entrance. Swinging it open, I perch on the side of the pool and remove my shoes before dipping one foot in. To my amazement the pool is still warm under the illumination of the moonlight. Without hesitation I dive in completely submerging myself in its warmth. A quiet snort leaves my mouth and ripples through the air. Maybe Lonnie was right, this place may just be Heaven after all. I swim a couple laps before noticing a small wooden building near the rear of the Greenwell's backyard. Hopefully, it's a pool house and there are towels in there.

Walking up the steps of the pool, I wring my hair. Water drips down my spine sending a shiver with it. I slide on my worn sneakers not caring that droplets of water slide down my legs as I step outside the gate with my new cell in tow. The building is very small in comparison to the massiveness that is their home, and it doesn't appear to be polished and manicured. It looks out of place. Instead, it's worn, and the shutters are faded, a clear indication that this shack has been severely neglected for some time. It's odd considering everything else is well cared for and groomed.

I'm drawn to its brokenness.

"It's probably just as empty as I am," I mumble as my feet glide over the lush lawn and guide me to the neglected structure.

Shifting on my feet, I catch a glimpse of Lonnie's window. A faint shadow of light escapes his curtains from what I assume is his bulldozer night light. It seems odd that there are no other children in the home, yet they're well equipped with an array of toys for all ages. It shouldn't be unexpected since foster kids come and go at a moment's notice. Lots of families keep a collection of toys and clothes on hand in preparation for their next house guest. What makes it odd, is recalling Bea saying a kid hasn't lived here in ages. Maybe their last placement was a long time ago. That happens often. Especially with placements of infants. People get attached, so when they're taken and placed in their forever homes, the foster families close their house down to new placements while they readjust to the void that they are left with.

Serenely, I make my way to the building's door. It screeches on its metal hinges as the eroded lock disintegrates to nothing with a gentle pull. Great. I'm already breaking shit.

A chill breaks out across my exposed body, and I wish I was wearing anything but my swimsuit right now. In the dim light of the moon illuminating off the pool's still water, I look around the small space. I frantically wave away cobwebs as I take a step inside. The stirring of dust causes a slew of sneezes to erupt from me. They echo in the small space as a cloud of dust fans around my ankles with every step. Hence my need to steal allergy meds earlier.

It's evident that this place has been vacant for some time. There is a bunk bed that is broken on top, the middle of its wood is cracked and hanging down sagging just a tad. Small white pebbles litter the floor like a pillow, or a bean bag, exploded decades ago. However, that's not what grabs my attention.

There's a tattered piece of paper hanging on the wall opposite me that catches my eye. Curiosity clings to my shoes as I trudge forward and click on a small table lamp. I have to squint and tilt the picture up to the window to make it out. "Boys Only," is scribbled across the length of the paper in a thick black marker.

It's a clubhouse.

I wonder if the Greenwells had a couple foster boys here previously. It had to have felt permanent for them to erect an entire building for them to play in. In the far-left corner, there is a Polaroid picture with frayed edges, barely hanging on by old tape. I grab the picture, using my hand to dust it off. Titling the picture, I spot three young boys whose arms are slung around one another in a childish embrace. Wide smiles speckle their innocent, tanned faces. It looks like they're standing in front of a lake in the background. A smile warms my heart. This is what childhood should be made of—laughter and friends. Something I've never really known either of.

"Who the fuck is in here?" A cavernous timbre breaks my intensity, startling me to my core. The photograph falls to the floor, along with the pit in my stomach, and my cell phone. I turn, timidly, and lock eyes with a guy leaning against the door. The cherry of his lit cigarette flares to life as he takes a long draw and holds it in. His eyes are dark and powerful, matching his physique.

Those eyes.

All the air leaves the small enclosure and makes it hard to breathe. My eyes deceive me as the guy from town raises his gaze to meet mine.

Cigarette guy.

"I thought you said you didn't steal anything." I stammer half questioning the guy in front of me. Suddenly the lack of space between us is suffocating. Never in a million years did I expect to see him again.

"I'm a liar."

"I can see that. Did you follow me? If it looked like I gave a damn about getting to know you back there in the store, please tell me. I didn't want to give you the wrong impression. Creeps who stalk girls aren't really my type."

"What is your type?"

"Judging by the whole stalking vibe you have going on, not you. Plus, you couldn't handle me even if I came with instructions. Now, why did you follow me?"

"You must really think highly of yourself if you think I'd follow you anywhere."

"What are you doing here lurking in the shadows then?"

"Lurking. That's a new one. I saw the lamp on through the window and came to check it out."

"You should know my dad's a police officer." A white lie between strangers never hurt anyone.

"You're in *my* old clubhouse. Let's be real, who's following who?" Confusion paints my face. "I live over there," he gestures to a house outside the window.

"Okay," is all I say, still curious as to why he's trespassing but then calling me out for it. To my recollection of the back-yard oasis, the clubhouse is on the Greenwell's side.

"I asked who *you* were," his voice hard, unnerving.

"No one," I grumble as if I'm guarding a secret.

He takes an abrupt step toward me, "First you ran into *me* and didn't apologize, and you expect me to believe you randomly stumbled into a building on private property that belongs to me?" His burning eyes hold me in place like a magnet yet again.

"I'm Aurora Bradshaw. Rory. I just moved in with the Greenwells," I answer as water drips off me onto the floor. Even under his hat with strands of opaque hair curling right below his chin, I can tell that his jaw is clenched. I watch as a swift hint of torment dances alongside his chiseled face along with the abrupt movement of his Adam's apple.

Realization of who I am seems to set in on his hooded eyes. Placing his hand across the back of his neck, his words come out flat, laced with cynicism. "You're the *foster* girl they told my parents about."

"In the flesh," I snap while shaking my head disapprovingly. I hurriedly brush past him. In my haste, I accidentally step on the photograph I had dropped. My shoe slides against the snapshot, sending it skating across the dust lined floor. Having nothing to keep me upright, I grab onto his black shirt in a feeble attempt to stay vertical but end up pulling us both down in a heap of exasperation and dust.

"Either you're awfully clumsy, or fate really wants you underneath me."

I'm momentarily stunned. Half because the way he's positioned on my petite build. I can feel the contour of his hard body, and half because I know destiny is evil and we're already on the outs. Not to mention he's apparently a pathological liar.

Ladies and gentlemen, we have ourselves our first red flag.

Anger washes over my face as I jolt upright into a standing position and clench my arms across my chest. I peer down at cigarette guy, who is still nameless. He doesn't blink. His eyes continue to lurk over me seductively. With each flutter of his lashes, I'm paralyzed to his unrelenting gaze. In a swift motion, they move downward, raking over my exposed body. My internal feminist snaps her fingers in front of my face bringing me out of my trance. I put the heel of my shoe on his stomach and press down not caring at all that he'll have a tennis shoe mark on his shirt.

Hearing the air expel from his heaving chest, tells me that I have the upper hand. Silence is most definitely not my best virtue. "If you ever put your hands on me again without my permission, I will unalive you." I spin leaving the dirtbag on the floor with the grime that he is.

"Wait." The shock of him calling out to me runs right through my body sending shivers down my spine. A knot forms in my chest as he gets up, not bothering to dust himself off. In one quick stride, he's standing right in front of me. "I think the only way you could possibly be more attractive standing there with the moonlight hitting your cheek, is if you let me get to know you."

I step forward until our chests collide. The dampness from my bathing suit may easily get his shirt wet, but I don't care. In a hurried intake of breath, I watch his tongue drift across his lips. Explosive fluttering hammers behind my ribcage for some reason as I prepare to shoot him down with one confident statement, "I'd rather eat glass than get to know someone who was stealing cigarettes and sneaking up on people in dark buildings."

His face pales, but he hastily regains composure. "Buildings owned by said cigarette smuggler. And I caught you stealing too. You're no better than me."

"You're right. I'm not. But I *know* better than to drop my standards for a guy that seems like he'll never rise from the bottom of the barrel. I have more respect for myself than that." I straighten my back knowing that tonight I'll be able to bask in the euphoria of putting this guy in his place and make a beeline for the door. I flee from the building, racing across the lawn toward the house.

Quietly, I open the back door and make my way back upstairs and into the shower. I went into that stupid club-house looking for a towel and left with questions I may never find the answers to, like why this guy is such a prick and who were the three kids in that photograph. I can't help but feel like I already know who one of them is.

I quickly brush my hair and make my way into my new room. I have never felt safe enough to sleep in a new house on the first night before but lying down on the plush bed in clean cotton pajamas, with the lock on my door latched, sleep quickly consumes me.

CHAPTER
FIVE

CREW

Aurora is an enigma.

This is more than just an instant attraction for a stranger. What I feel from the nearness of her could teeter on infatuation, and it just so happens that I've never been one to back down from a challenge. I'm the spelling bee champion of my middle school after all and was voted most likely to survive the *Hunger Games.*

I could feel her judging me. The version of myself she had the pleasure to meet, isn't the same version I was back in high school. Back then, I cared a lot more. Now, there isn't much I do care about.

"Shit," I groan while dusting my hands on my jeans. The scarcely habitable building is blanketed with filth. A clear sign of its neglect. I huff through my annoyance that it took me two years to step foot in here while pinching the bridge of my nose. I could have kept my hiatus going if I hadn't seen a light when Della and I pulled into my driveway. I unlocked the basement door in a frenzy and told her to wait for me inside before stalking toward the old clubhouse that rests between the Greenwell's property and my parents'.

Never in a million years would I have imagined running into *her* again so soon especially after our initial confrontation. Not reading too much into the nameless beauty who caught my attention earlier, I picked up Della, an old friend. Any company is better than none.

Who am I kidding?

The entire car ride to Della's house and back home, I'd wondered where the mysterious girl had run off to after she rolled into town like a tumbleweed. Della's a senior now, and already eighteen. Lucky for me. Not so lucky for her that the entire ride to my house my mind was preoccupied by the girl I now know as Aurora, with her wealth of blonde hair and defiance that shook me to my core.

I kick the edge of our old, matted rug underneath my shoe. Of course, she's Russell and Bea's new foster kid. Why did she have to be so sexy trespassing in a little black swim-suit that left *too* much to my imagination? Her assertiveness mixed with her lack of clothes, is really doing something to me. I adjust my junk and notice a cell phone on the floor. She must have dropped it. There's no lock code needed to open the device, which is odd. *Who doesn't have a lock pin?* Scrolling through it there are only two contacts I recognize, Russell and Bea's and someone named Miranda. At least I know she's not a liar. She really is who she claims to be.

Getting to know Aurora has just become my new favorite hobby. I pocket her phone and swivel my head realizing that I haven't been in here in far too long. No wonder it looks like The Addams Family has taken up residence in the small space. Cobwebs drape from the rafters. Dust is at least an inch thick, coating every surface. I should be ashamed. No, *both* Trice and I should be ashamed, if I'm being honest.

My phone dings.

A picture of Della laying daringly on my bed pulls my feet forward. Despite my sudden interest in my new neighbor, I'm not a fool or blind, and the emoji of an eggplant that chimes next sends my feet scampering home for obvious reasons.

39

CHAPTER
SIX

RORY

The dew is still clinging to the blades of grass when I awake and peer outside my window. I pull myself out of bed and tie a robe around my body and venture from my room. In the long hallway, I notice a painting of a sunrise coming up over a mountain. It's incredible and captures my attention instantly, reminding me that Bea is also an art enthusiast.

There is a stillness and peace that occurs when dawn slowly gives way to the day that centers me. It always has, even at a young age. No matter the turmoil of the previous day, the sun's luminescence, its yellow orb peeking through the horizon, glistening against everything it touches, makes me feel alive. It's my preferred time of day and I bet whoever painted this piece felt a connection to the sunrise as well.

Like a goliath-sized paintbrush, the sun strokes the earth like it is a massive canvas. It reminds me of a painting I once did, years ago in a free after-school program the school offered. I create solely based on the mood that I'm feeling. Whether it be a song that ignites a feeling within me or something that triggers an emotion, like the sun, my mood sets the tone of my painting.

At my old school, I was enrolled in an art history class. We didn't get the chance to paint or much less create anything of our own due to budget cuts, but I learned a lot about art. From Leonardo da Vinci to Vincent van Gogh's *Starry Night* to the Italian sculptor, Michelangelo. The history of art is inspiring and motivating. It encourages me to seek out what makes me want to create. Painting has been the only constant I've ever had. It's a release when I feel like breaking. I admire the Greenwell's art on the walls as I walk down the steps and into their kitchen, the smell of coffee lingering in the air. My mouth waters as I near the large island.

"Good morning, Rory. Here ya go," Bea offers me a cup of coffee. "Russell has already left for his shift, and believe it or not, Lonnie is still sleeping."

My eyebrows rise in surprise. "He didn't make a peep all night." I admit, flabbergasted, before taking a sip.

"Does he usually?" She pulls out a bar stool next to her, and I take another sip of my coffee before taking a seat beside her.

"Yeah. He has horrible night terrors."

"Russell told me about the night he got the call to your foster home. I cannot fathom what you and Lonnie went through that night before help arrived. I'm sorry that you both had to endure that treatment for so long without anyone taking action."

That's the grim reality of foster care. No one wants to believe the horror stories, so they just pretend they don't exist. Unless it's your reality, then you fight like hell to change your circumstances. Which is exactly what I did when I woke up to Lonnie screaming. Moving at lightning speed I yanked open Lonnie's door to find Lloyd standing over him, his pants lowered to his ankles. I pounced on his back and saw red before I tasted it.

The rest is history.

Our foster mother, Jean, should have known to never leave us alone with Lloyd. I admitted to her once that he creeped me out. She brushed my confession off like I was just a whiny kid. All that Jean wanted, besides her monthly check to gamble away was her next fix. She never even came back. Not even when I called her from the emergency room with a gashed lip that needed stitches and Lonnie with a broken arm. Not when Miranda attempted to reach her, and not when we left the apartment for the last time. She vanished along with any ounce of respect I had for her as a woman. I always thought it was a woman's basic nature to want to be a mother, a protector. But I guess I was wrong.

"Didn't you grow up in the system?" I ask.

A minute passes and we drink in a heavy silence.

"I did. I was very lucky to have been fostered and then adopted by my parents at such a young age. I never had to go to a group home or live somewhere that...that wasn't safe." Her words come out carefully.

"You're one of the lucky ones," I say. My heart ticks like an over-wound clock. A success story. I take another sip, the warm caramel flavor glides over my taste buds. Creamer is a novelty I'm not used to.

"Russell and I would love nothing more than to see you and Lonnie succeed." Her smile is almost as enthusiastic as her wishes for us. "Anyway, we only have a couple days before school starts, so I took some time off work to see that you and Lonnie get situated."

"He's no bother. I can watch him. We don't want to cause any trouble; much less be the reason you miss work. I can tell your work is important to you." I touch the stitches on my lip. She said she was so good at them they wouldn't have to consult plastics. I hope her words hold some truth and my small cut doesn't scar too badly.

"Your health and wellbeing are literally in our hands. We

want you to be the exception to the system, just like I was." Bea's words don't scare me. It's the affection in her tone that makes me feel uneasy. I'm not used to the kindness she keeps tossing my way.

I tense, waiting for the other shoe to drop at any moment.

"I know you're used to fending off the world on your own. But this can be your home if you allow it to be. Let the adults ward off the evil from here." She places a warm hand on my forearm. It's a small gesture. She hops off her stool and goes to the sink, rinsing her cup. She's still in her pajamas—a matching lavender set—and her feet are bare. There's something so strange to me about bare feet; it's almost intimate. Bare feet exude confidence. I've never had a real pedicure like the girls at school, so I guess I've always been self-conscious of my feet. I'm thankful there were socks in my stocked dresser.

"We wanted to give you and Lonnie a night to get settled, but our good friends Mina and Shawn Jordan, who live behind us, are very excited to meet you both. They want to host a welcome dinner." She gestures out the window above the kitchen sink. "That gate connects our properties."

I cringe a little at the realization that cigarette boy must live there. He wasn't lying, or following me, after all.

"It won't be as formal as I just made it sound. The Jordans are our best friends. They have two sons around your age, and one who is just about Lonnie's age so he will have a built-in-friend." She takes my empty cup out of my hand. "Go on and get ready. I'll wake Lonnie and feed him. Then we can go school shopping to give us something to do today. A little exploring is good for the soul." Bea winks.

There are three Jordan boys, and I'm certain I already met one of them.

Pulling into the parking lot of the outlet mall, my eyes widen at the monstrosity. Cars are lined up in parking spaces as far as the eye can see. Shoppers with more bags than their two arms can carry, scurry by us as we pull into one of the only vacant spots within an eye's distance. Shopping for me has only ever consisted of going to a flea market, or secondhand store, and that's pushing it. A lot of my clothes came from the lost and found at my old high school. Worn, forgotten items became my wardrobe, as well as my identity.

"You really don't have to do this." I say as I unbuckle my seat belt. The thought of her taking us shopping and spending money on us makes me feel like a charity case. I don't like to feel indebted to anyone. We're already leeching off them, while staying in a home that looks like it could be on television. "You said that the school we're going to has uniforms, right?"

"Did I say that?" Bea smiles while turning off the ignition. "I know this may seem foreign to you. It did to me, too, when my adoptive parents took me shopping for the first time. I remember my mom kept handing my dad items on hangers. I physically felt faint and undeserving of their kindness."

"Then why all this? If you know how uncomfortable it is already." I wave to our surroundings while seated in the passenger seat.

"Because no child should have to want for necessities like clothing. I was very fortunate that my parents could provide a loving home for me."

"You're providing a home already. The clothes aren't a necessity."

"A new wardrobe is a perk. I'm asking you to please allow Russell and I to do this for you both. We'd like to make you comfortable during your time with us."

"I want new clothes," Lonnie chimes in from the back seat. "These jeans have more holes in them than Swiss cheese." He giggles.

"Then it's settled. We're going shopping." Bea winks, knowing she's won this round.

A couple of hours later, all three of us are carrying more bags than are essential. My comfort level was pushed to the brink at her persistent petition and reassurance to get anything we wanted. Lonnie was like a kid in a candy store. He got a new pair of shoes for school, but also a pair equally as expensive for playing outside. The glee in his eyes could be seen from outer space. I, on the other hand, am obliged by her generosity but feel numb by her act of hospitality.

It was hard to hide the delight in Bea's eyes as she watched us filter through racks of clothing. A time or two, I even saw her wipe a tear from them. Undoubtedly remembering her torrid past. I still don't like the thought of relying on anyone other than myself, and I certainly don't want her to get the wrong impression of me going along with her little shopping spree. My goal is still to turn eighteen, adopt Lonnie, and build a life that we have control over. Name-brand clothes and a designer crossbody purse won't change my mind.

I'm not a total brat and do acknowledge that she didn't have to spend the day doting on us and buying everything we glanced at. As much as I hate to admit it our new clothes do feel like a fresh start. A reluctant smile spans my face. I have a heap of new clothes to choose from for our dinner with their good friends, the Jordans.

I spend a little extra time curling my hair and picking out a brand-new outfit to wear. Settling on a sundress with a new pair of sandals, I'm filled with a strange surge of excitement to see *cigarette boy* again. I struggle to catch my composure and chalk my anticipation up to the loneliness and bewilderment melding together. I'm in a foreign place, and he's the only guy I've met around my age. Or maybe it's because I'm a glutton for punishment and his dark, tortured eyes still have me reeling from our two encounters. I have a feeling that he's trouble, and yet my pulse still quickens at the thought of seeing him again.

Baffled by my own confession, I study myself in the mirror. My hair is naturally golden, like it's been sun-kissed, and lays at the midline of my spine. I'm of average height, luckily, since short and tall jeans are a rare commodity at the consignment stores where I shopped. I can usually find my size and length perfectly. Faded jeans are my go-to since the brand name designers usually look tattered. No one would know that I got them for under five dollars unless I admitted it. I've never given much thought to my appearance unless it was to show off my assets to get something I needed to survive. I'm not proud of that fact.

Life isn't fair and I've had to play dirty a time or two.

I finger comb my hair, twirling the ends around my index finger. The color pairs nicely with my ivory skin. Considering I've never seen a picture of my biological parents, I envision I get my blonde hair from my mom's side of the family, and that it's sun-streaked from days spent at the beach. A place I've never even seen in person before. I picture my pouty lips come from her, as well, along with my love of the sky. Maybe we are both avid daydreamers and it was something we did together, staring up aimlessly at the clouds, daydreaming about a life where she didn't have to leave me. I don't know if that's what happened, but I like to think that it wasn't her fault. That she was forced into giving me up. That my evil grandparents made her do it despite her pleas and tears because she was just a child herself. The hope of having something we share helps lessen the ache in my chest from her absence.

I pretend that my dad was a runner, tall and lean with a tinge of pink under his tawny skin. I imagine that he was devoted to my mom, but at the age of sixteen, when I was conceived, love wasn't enough. It rarely ever is.

My imagination helps fill in the gaps where the state of

Kentucky can't. Having some sort of story, even a fake one, is better than knowing nothing about your identity or what makes you who you are.

I'm a Jane Doe in many ways.

Wanting to make a good first impression with Mr. and Mrs. Jordan, I plaster on a wide, counterfeit smile and take a deep breath, ready to get this show on the road. I can tell how much Bea and Russell admire them both by the few things Bea told me about their friendship during our shopping excursion.

A good first impression is like a camera flash when the bright light assaults you and captures you in high definition. It's what people remember you by. Your eccentricities and all. Restlessly, I make my way downstairs. Lonnie is sitting in a kitchen chair. Russell in front of him tying his shoes.

Russell decides to drive us on their golf cart to the next street so no one's shoes get dirty in the evening dew. I notice on our short trip that everyone in their subdivision must own a golf cart. There's a golf-cart gang in the suburbs. I wonder if they have T-shirts like bikers do. No, in a neighborhood as nice as this one, I bet they have denim vests.

We arrive minutes later, and Russell knocks on the front door. A tall, slender man answers it like he was waiting there for our arrival. He has a glass of what looks like whiskey or apple juice in his hand. Given the town we're in, I assume that everyone here must adore whiskey. I've done my fair share of underage drinking, but I never favored whiskey or bourbon. Although, the thought of it poured over ice seems very sophisticated. I'm more of a beer girl. Most of my foster families had that easily available. None of them were ever classy enough to drink aged bourbon. I give him a slight nod and smile.

"Welcome folks," he says, waving us in. I notice that Mr. Jordan's hair is blonde, almost iridescent, while cigarette boy's hair is a deep, tawny brown. I'm eager to see what Mrs. Jordan looks like and which parent he favors.

Lonnie pipes up, a hopeful gleam in his eye. "I heard you like to fish."

"You heard right, little captain." Mr. Jordan rubs Lonnie on the top of his head. "I bet Russell and I could get one more boat ride in before the summer is over if you're interested."

Lonnie sneaks a peak at Bea as Russell adds, "Only if you promise not to catch more fish than us." Hoots ensue from everyone before we walk into the house from the foyer.

A little boy with icy white hair, matching his father's, comes barreling into the room. "Hi. I'm Aiden. I love hot rods and basketball. Wanna play?" Lonnie nods and takes off with Aiden without a glance back at us.

I feel like I'm in an alternate universe and I've been transplanted into this life only I'm an outsider looking in. I think about what Miranda said about being lucky. I don't care to admit it, but I can't help feeling shocked that only days ago Lonnie and I were living a much different lifestyle than the one where we get to play dress up and attend dinner parties. It's surreal to say the least.

Mr. Jordan guides us past the living room, and I take in a stray basketball on the floor in front of the sofa. A strange waft, that doesn't pair well with the home, hits my nose. The smell of adolescent boys lingers thickly in the air. Both delectable and a little putrid.

Their house has a lived-in look that Russell and Bea's doesn't. Despite its size, there is a comfortable feeling about being here. My shoulders lower. A soda can sits on the table and a pair of men's slides rest on the floor. I wonder who they belong to.

We turn the corner into the kitchen and a foreign pair of dainty arms encircle me taking me off guard. "Bea, you and your modesty! She is gorgeous." Hugging strangers is something southerners regularly do. My frigid posture slackens, not wanting to give off the wrong impression. Plus, she called me gorgeous. *Bonus points.* Mrs. Jordan, I assume, is wearing red lipstick and a sleek, low bun. She chuckles under her breath. "I don't know which of my sons will be smitten first. Even little Aiden might have a crush on her before the night's over."

"Cut her some slack, Mina. You know *our* boys are wild and we wouldn't want to bestow any of them on sweet, Rory." Bea waves her friend away from me. "She's got the grades to go far and doesn't need a boyfriend tying her down during her senior year. Not to mention how inappropriate that statement is. You're a therapist. She's been through a deep trauma recently. Don't be insensitive."

Our?

I glance around. No one else seems to notice her strange verbiage. I park that thought for now not wanting to make a scene and prove to Miranda that I'm the delinquent she thinks I am already.

"Kids, this is Mina Jordan. She is our town's best therapist and worst matchmaker. She also doesn't think before she speaks. Which is odd considering her profession." Bea swats at Mrs. Jordan in a playful manner. Their connection and friendship is apparent from the looks they share. They give off that whole talking-with-your-eyes vibe.

Mrs. Jordan smiles humbly and says, "There's no shame in being blunt, friend. You're forgetting that Miles, down at the market, and Peggy, the dog groomer, just celebrated their tenth wedding anniversary, and as I recall, I introduced them." She wiggles her groomed brows. "I will, however, accept your compliment about being good at my job. I own the counseling center in town. None of that matters right now. What my dear friend here means to say is that we've been best friends for thirty years and we're fortunate enough to be neighbors." Mrs. Jordan grabs a wineglass from the tabletop and holds it up. "To a long history of friendship and brilliant bitches!"

A hint of a smile flickers across Bea's face. I suppress a laugh. Russell and Shawn engage in conversation, ignoring the antics going on between us, while Lonnie and Aiden have already climbed onto chairs and are too enthralled in a hand-held gaming device to have heard the vulgarity.

Mina Jordan is my new idol. Both beautiful and smart. I want to be her when I grow up.

I hadn't noticed anyone else in the dining room before I hear a familiar laugh. I turn to face *cigarette boy*. My cheeks grow warmer at his presence. His dark, riveting eyes capture mine and hold them. Mrs. Jordan waves him to her side. Instead, he plops down in an open chair at the end of the table ignoring her request.

Why am I always attracted to the uncouth ones? Taylor Swift's, *Cruel Summer* taunts my heart with its melody, reminding me that nothing good has ever come from falling for the bad-boy.

"This is Crew. He's our eldest and a sophomore in college," Mrs. Jordan nods in his direction. "Don't let him claim that he's my favorite child though. He has a way with persuading people, and there's a longstanding joke that I admitted that to him one night after one too many glasses of cabernet."

Crew feigns offense. "Your omission is an admission from my side, Mom." He leans back in his chair and drapes his hand over the back of the empty chair next to him, almost challenging me to take a seat. His thick, bristly brows rise, and his cool, aloof manner irks me to my core for some unknown reason. "We meet again, *Foster*."

The insensitivity of his nickname ignites a flame within me like a match and not in a good way. A way that wants to burn down buildings. Why does he get under my skin so much, and why do I keep allowing it?

"Don't be rude to our guest. It's Rory," Mrs. Jordan cautions him. I get the impression it's something she does often.

"I wouldn't dare be rude to someone as beautiful as her."

Bea intercedes quickly, confusion laced in her tenor. "I hadn't realized you had met anyone in town yet."

"I went swimming last night and ran into Crew outside by the gate. He said he lived next door," I admit hastily, excluding our first real encounter where he caught me shoplifting.

"I'm glad your swimsuit fit." Bea smiles demurely and then settles into a chair at the far side of the rectangular table, joining Russell's and Mr. Jordan's conversation.

I move to the chair next to Crew and sit.

"You dropped this last night," he says as his long fingers slide my cell phone in front of me. Keeping track of this device is going to be a chore, I can already tell.

"Thanks," I say. My eyes find Lonnie's small frame in the dining room, and I exhale seeing how calm he seems in this situation. He's normally glued to my side, but within a short time, he's taken a liking to Bea. It's not in his nature to trust adults. Last night's dinner prep and today's shopping spree must have gained her some points, while it took me every bit of the last year to win his tiny heart. It's not surprising though. She seems very kindhearted and to a kid that has been abused and discarded by every adult he's ever lived with, anyone showing him the slightest affection and respect is understandably trustworthy. With Lonnie occupied, it gives me the opportunity to turn my attention back to cigarette boy, who now has a first name.

Crew.

His name rolls around on my tongue and leaves a bitter taste due to him calling me *Foster.*

Zero points for creativity.

I've been called much worse. I manage a discourteous

reply to his previous comment as I settle in my seat and smooth my sundress. I honestly can't recall the last time I even wore one. I'm not used to being so dressed up. "Foster isn't very original, ya know?" I tell Crew. "I've been called worse, so don't hold back."

He should know that I don't back down easily.

Crew props his arm over the back of my chair. His arm brushes against my back gently. The touch is quick and innocent. I don't even know why I notice it. I inhale sharply and straighten my back against the smooth chair behind me. He diverts his eyes to my mouth. "Nice gash."

With his swift change of subject, I'm instantly reminded of the cut on my lip that has two small stitches keeping it secured. A goodbye present from Lloyd. "You should see what I did to the man who did it," I say as my mouth twist wryly.

"I hear you're going to be a senior."

"And you're obviously still stalking me." I shoot him a cold look.

"You could throw a dog a bone. You don't even have social media. What's up with that?" His brows furrow.

"Wow, you really don't let up do you?" Peering at him, I wait for a sign of objection.

"Not when someone catches my attention like you have." The amber in his eyes flick like the light from a torch.

"Lay it to rest already. You and me..." I motion between us eager to shut down any notion he has about me. "...are nothing more than neighbors. We will never be anything more than neighbors. Aren't there any girls in this town who can stand you and your cigarette breath long enough to date you?"

"There's plenty."

Crew Jordan represents everything I loathe in a person. He's cocky, a smoker, a thief (read: I only steal to survive. He did it for fun) and from the sounds of it, a womanizer. "I suggest you go stalk one of them then."

"I'm good. You caught my attention, Foster. I don't sway easily once I want something. I'm goal-oriented like that," he says in a low tone that is meant to be seductive. Rather, it makes me laugh. The sound rises from my throat and bubbles out.

I brace myself as my fit of laughter quiets, and he catches me watching him intently. I feel a sudden rush like one of the horses escaped from a neighboring farm and is stampeding through my veins. His copper eyes stun me, and no refute to his comment comes out. Just hot, unsteady breath as his admission leaves me feeling *seen*.

It doesn't sit well with me, and I stop short of countering back and instead adjust the cotton material of my napkin. I drape it over my lap and catch a whiff of a clean, subtle scent. It reminds me of bergamot. My napkin slides down my exposed leg. I bend to grab it before it hits the ground only to catch the gape of another pair of radiant eyes boring into mine on my way up.

Crew's snarl cuts through the silence. "Oops, I found your nose. It was in my business again, *brother*." He speaks eagerly and at first, I'm confused until he adds, "Don't just gawk at her. Say something or move along."

Inhaling deeply, I'm assaulted by two very different scents. I don't know which belongs to what brother. It sends my senses into overdrive, and suddenly I'm famished for something other than food.

Trust me boys, that ship has sailed.

"I'm Trice," he breathes in my ear, causing a riot of butterflies to take flight in my stomach. I silently curse myself for admiring, even for a split second, how attractive both brothers are. "You are far too cute to be subjected to sitting by my idiot brother all night. He's rude, and frankly, not as handsome as I am. Let's move?"

If I wasn't already intrigued by Mina's coy comment earlier, I would be now. I, too, am wondering which brother will be smitten first. Right now, my money is on the clean-shaven one with sandy blonde hair speaking in my ear. All rational thoughts go out the window because Trice extends his hand to me and without hesitation, I take it. Which is something else that is totally out of my character.

What is this town doing to me?

Trice pulls out my chair and I stand following him as he ushers us toward the other side of the table. I take a quick glance back at Crew, who doesn't seem bothered in the slightest. He has a reservedness about him, like he's observing the lay of the land before he interacts. I notice him scrolling on his cell phone aimlessly. There's zero need for me to feel guilty about leaving him at the table. Still, a feeling of remorse lingers, collecting the butterflies that Crew had awoken and reeling them back into their cocoons.

My meter must have been off before. Nothing about Crew, other than his physical appearance, is attractive in the slightest.

The sound of a text message and a slight vibration pressed against my thigh has me sliding my cell phone out of my pocket. Everyone who has this number is sitting at this table. Unless it's Miranda. I debate on checking my phone before my attention is stolen by Trice leaning toward his mother and planting a kiss on her cheek.

"I'm sorry I'm late, Mom." He slides into the seat next to me as I slyly hit the center button with the pad of my pointer finger and read the message.

Unknown: *I promise I don't bite. Unless you're into that sorta thing*

My eyes widen and then dart to the opposite side of the table. Crew seems blissfully unaware of anyone else in the room, including me. I highly doubt it was him texting me even as his fingers gracefully slide across his screen at lightning speed. I chalk the random text up to being a wrong number and slide my phone back into its place giving my full attention to our hosts. Unlike Crew, whose body language seems to be standoffish with everyone.

"Practice ran over again." Trice playfully rubs his little brother's head and then smiles bashfully in my direction. Mrs. Jordan notices and nudges Bea in the side not even trying to hide her excitement that one of her sons is making strides to win my friendship.

"It's Trice's senior year, Rory. Same as you. I bet you two will even have some classes together." It's her husband who winks at me this time. "Dinner will be ready any minute," he adds.

What I notice about Trice is that there is a single dimple on his cheek and there aren't any brash nicknames spewing from *his* mouth. Only genuine humanity as he introduced himself like a gentleman. He is handsome in a boyish way even though we're the same age. I can tell by the way he embraced his mother that a pure heart beats in his chest. Judging by his build, I'd say that he is a runner or a wrestler. I can picture him with his shirt hung over one shoulder and those short, goofy looking athletic shorts guys wear in the city running around with a bandana on his head.

There is a yearning I cannot explain that Trice's proximity stirs within me. Maybe it's because he is the most decent guy I've met so far or maybe it's that dimple that only adorns one cheek, which is simply adorable. His brother certainly doesn't fall into that category with his shameful nickname calling.

Trice makes innocent small talk and asks me if I've settled in well with Bea and Russell and if I'm excited for senior year, telling me that he's on the football team and aspires to play college ball. I'm too ashamed to admit that I don't have many goals aside from turning eighteen. I haven't thought of much past that. I nod my head, listening intently to his plans with a sincere smile on my face.

"Do you play any sports?"

"Nope. That whole scene isn't really my thing." I admit, trying not to sound lame. "I really like art and reading."

"I'm sure you'll love living with Bea then. She has more art than anyone I know—that and horse sculptures."

A real laugh slips by my lips. "What is it with all the horse stuff? I've lived in Kentucky my entire life, and I've never seen so much horse memorabilia before."

"She used to ride a lot when she was younger. Since sports aren't your thing, maybe horse riding might be." He nudges my side playfully and oddly, I don't cringe at his lack of boundary in my personal space.

"I'll stick with something I know I'm good at. What's the vibe at school like?"

"Senior year is a waste of time, in my opinion. We've already done all the hard work, ya know? Most of us already know what college we're attending, so I'll say the vibe is going to be extra lame. Maybe a little less with a fresh face there." He says, and I assume he's referring to me.

I admit this dinner is going much differently than I expected. We were welcomed with open arms and not once has anyone asked about our sordid histories in the system or made us feel like charity cases. Trice's sincerity calms my nerves, and by the time our salad is served, we're already acquaintances. Sitting casually together for dinner seems like the most natural thing in the world.

Mr. Jordan's voice pulls me from my thoughts. He rubs the hair of his youngest son, Aiden, with one hand, and with the other he holds up his glass. "It's been far too long since we've shared a meal together. I am so happy to be here tonight with everyone I care about. Almost everyone," he pauses, his voice resigned.

I notice Bea take a sharp breath, but she hides it quickly by clearing her throat.

The room suddenly feels alive, buzzing with energy,

almost as if the walls have seen and heard things at this table that they dare not repeat. From the corner of my eye, I see the shadow of a figure. I turn to see the back of Crew's shirt as he rushes from the dining room.

"Is that Mina's famous lasagna I smell?" Russell growls and rubs his stomach, cutting off Mr. Jordan's speech and taking all eyes off Crews impromptu exit.

"Apparently cops like that *more* than donuts." Mr. Jordan pinches his lips together in a tight smile and then continues. "It is a pleasure to meet you Rory and Lonnie. I hope you know you're welcome at our house anytime. Let's dig in."

This is the exact moment I wanted to avoid when Bea told me we were having dinner with her friends. I nod, a silent thank you and shift in my seat uncomfortably. Who invites a total stranger into their home and practically calls them family? Country folk are a different breed of people. Although, the Greenwells and the Jordans with their large homes and fancy artwork are more like swanky country people like Paula Dean.

Imitation country I'll call it.

Like imitation crab.

Trice turns to face me, a cold glass of water in hand and takes a sip, never losing eye contact with me. What I notice is the contrast of his eyes. They're deep blue like the ocean and filled with surprise and wonder. I could get lost in the sea of their Caribbean blue. Much like his older brother's, they're alluring, but in a completely different way.

One brother is fire.

The other ice.

I can't decide which one is going to burn me first.

CHAPTER
SEVEN

CREW

Apparently, rock bottom has a basement.

It never fails that someone brings up *his* absence. This is precisely why I avoid family dinners at all costs. In hindsight, I should have known when mom said Russell and Bea were coming over with their foster kids that this evening would be a spectacle.

I had to see her again, the girl with apricot-colored skin and fiery jade eyes that glowed under the moonlight. Which is why I agreed to stay for dinner in the first place instead of heading back to campus for the week. Thoughts of her sitting nestled next to Trice's side plagued me and that's precisely what ended up happening despite my best efforts. Aurora seems indifferent to me for some reason. Trice is the golden brother. It wouldn't surprise me if she gravitated toward him too.

Every time I glance over at her and see the dusty rose of her cheeks as she laughs at something my brother says enrages me. My fingers slide across my screen before my brain had time to register any rational thought. I don't know what my goal was sending that text message. Did I truly think she'd get up, strut toward me, and we'd eat together pretending the rest of my family was nonexistent at the other end of the table? One can hope. I sure as hell didn't think that dinner would be ruined before the main course was served.

It's a new record.

Bile rushes up my throat burning every inch on its way until I'm forced to sprint out of the dining room like a wild animal. As the anniversary of the accident approaches, so do these spontaneous waves of nausea. It's been two years, and yet it feels like we lost him yesterday. The voice of my therapist, Rebecca, rings in my head. *"When you feel like you're going to explode, go outside, find a safe place and scream. There is no shame in exploding in a safe environment."*

I fist my hands and roll my neck after I empty my stomach and spew today's lunch into the toilet. Screw this dinner and screw the pretense that both of our families live perfect, polished lives. That idea went out the window when Matt died, and his absence left a rift in our families. One that's been brushed under the rug, yet I know is felt by almost everyone sitting in our dining room hidden by wide, fake ass smiles.

I wipe my mouth with my hand and then slide my phone out of my pocket. Sending a quick text to Dean, my tattoo artist, I tell him that I have three hundred in cash. He can shade as far as that takes him. The needle always numbs the pain raging inside me. Nothing against Rebecca, she's a licensed clinical therapist, but the only therapy that helps take the edge off is the one where a gun with a hundred sharp needles penetrates my skin repeatedly.

Maybe I do have masochistic tendencies after all.

Damnit, Rebecca, for being right.

I tread down the basement stairs to my old bedroom, the sounds coming from the dining room echo off the walls, adding fuel to the fire in the pit of my stomach. Add it to the list of disappointments that I bring my parents.

I grab my keys off the table and slip out the basement door.

A shrill voice blares through the sound system in my car. Its deafening sound drowns out my thoughts before my tires screech on the pavement. I gun the engine desperate to flee, all the while cursing myself for leaving Aurora with Trice.

He's the competitive brother.

I'm just the degenerate asshole who ruined our family.

CHAPTER
EIGHT

RORY

Going to church doesn't make you any more Christian than swimming in a pool makes you a lifeguard. I'm especially not fond of the early wake-up call. We're packed like sardines in solid wooden pews waiting for the service to start. I inhale the stale scent of potpourri and silently ask forgiveness for the no less than fifty-times I've said the Lord's name in vain this month alone.

My fingers fidget with the hem of the dress Bea insisted I wear. I'm thankful my bare shoulders are draped with a loose cardigan because it is chilly in here. I definitely look the part of a church goer, although fraud should be tattooed on my forehead in bold letters. I wonder if they keep churches this cold to keep people awake.

The room is so full, people are standing near the back entrance. There are four open seats next to us that Bea is apparently saving. I'm thinking it's for her parents or something until the seat creaks next to me, and Trice drapes his arm behind my seat. His forearm brushes against my hair.

"You look nice," he says softly for only me to hear.

I swallow harder than usual. One should not be having the thoughts that his warm breath on my neck give me whilst sitting in church.

Before we left the Jordan's last night, Mrs. Jordan insisted I call her Mina and then programmed her cell phone number, as well as both of her sons in case of emergencies she said. I wouldn't dare call Crew in an emergency. He doesn't seem like the type of person who goes out of his way to help anyone. What she did, however, confirmed that he was the one who'd texted me last night. I didn't give him the satisfaction of responding. Although, after he stormed out, I'd contemplated reaching out to him. If anything, just to see if he was okay or not.

Why am I drawn to the troubled ones?

I can't fix my life, so I try to fix others.

Trice, on the other hand, with his perfectly white smile and pressed chinos seems like the type to serve lunch at a soup kitchen and not for extra credit. From the respectful tone and manner that he spoke with his parents to how he interacted with Lonnie last night made my heart swell, which is an odd sensation considering the calloused stone that it's incased in. Virtuousness practically seeps from his pores, which is probably why I feel so relaxed around him.

I take note of that.

Having only seen him in basketball shorts and a cut off T-shirt at our dinner last night, I gently nudge his side with my elbow. "You clean up nicely yourself, Jordan."

"Have you been to a Southern church service before?" Trice asks.

I offer him a side eye. "Should I be worried?"

"I'm just kidding with you. The pastor is actually really good. We've been coming here since we were kids."

I'm thankful for Trice's company because Bea leans over to tell me that Lonnie's number is being paged from the kid's ministry. She informed me before we arrived that all kids are assigned a number that only the parents are aware of. If it flashes on the screen, it means the child needs a parent to come to the kids ministry. Her and Russell excuse themselves. It's odd how quickly Lonnie's taken to them. I almost follow them to check on him myself, but I decide against it.

I'm not used to not being needed by Lonnie. Before I give it a second thought, the lights dim, and the church musicians settle into their places. The room grows silent. And then the gentle strum of a guitar echoes throughout the crowded space. I'm surprised when I look up and see that one of the musicians looks very familiar, with deep russet hair and even darker eyes looking out into the crowd.

"Is that Crew?" My shocked expression amuses Trice. Seeing Crew on stage has my head spinning like an EF5 tornado.

"The *only* thing my brother has on me is he's got one hell of a voice. It's a shame he's only here because he's forced to be. He's got such raw talent for music and just lets it go to waste."

I barely register whatever Trice is saying as my eyes widen. I swear I don't blink for forty-five seconds.

At least.

My mouth dries like the Sahara Desert, and I choke a little.

Crew grips the black microphone possessively. His long fingers a stark contrast to the charcoal mic. He's in his element. I can tell by the confident way he stands, his eyes soaking in the considerable sized crowd. A perfect balance of gruff and huskiness comes bellowing from his lungs. Crew's baritone strikes a chord within me. I'm convinced that all the hair follicles on my entire body stand at attention and, for the first time in forever, a genuine smile takes residence on my face.

I would never have pegged him as being the lead singer in the church choir considering our first encounter was him stealing cigarettes from the corner store. The second was making crude comments about me lying underneath him, and the third was skipping out on dinner without as much as an adios. None of those encounters peg him as a choirboy.

The song's chorus swells and most of the congregation hold their hands up in praise. The sentiment is palpable around the room.

For the lamb has overcome

Everlasting love has won

Eternal Grace, we will lift Him up for the lamb has overcome the world

I'm panting. Desperate for a full breath of air. My shock isn't solely from Crew's intoxicating voice, but how totally enthralled he is in the song. He's lost in the music, and I'm lost in him.

His hips sway effortlessly as he hums to the sweet melody being played. Cemented to his performance, I watch as he lifts his palm up with praise. I'm captivated in this moment and contemplate raising my own hands, although I'm sure everyone would stare a scarlet letter sized hole into the back of my head.

He eludes confidence.

I don't have a close relationship with God, and I haven't given as much thought to my salvation as I have to my survival in this broken world, but boy does Crew make it easy to see why all the girls around us are entranced and foaming at the mouth.

Clean up on pews one, two, and three please.

Next Sunday, Bea won't have to pound on my door to wake me up at seven in the morning. I can promise you that.

Crew opens his eyes, scanning the crowd as the next song starts.

He sings.

I swoon.

I find myself swaying to the melody, my head bobbing slightly and then our eyes connect, and the rest of the jampacked room evaporates into thin air. Momentarily, I believe he's singing only to me. I bow my head letting my hair screen my face.

Crew and the choir play two more songs before he ends in prayer. "Let us pray…" Everyone locks hands as a united front. Trice slowly thumbs my hand, while his mom reaches over Bea's empty spot and grabs my other hand, giving it a comforting squeeze.

My mind is reeling. I don't even hear the prayer Crew recites because my heart is constricting, making it hard to breathe. There is something incredibly sexy about watching him perform. Despite not knowing anything about the words he sang, the raw emotion etched onto his typically jaded face tells me he felt something deep, and that makes my heart flutter.

What is it about a musician clad in jeans and a smirk that makes women go bonkers?

I wasn't big into boy bands in my early teens and Jesus Jams certainly aren't my favorite genre but sign me up as Crew Jordan's biggest fan. I want a T-shirt too.

A battle rages inside me as one Jordan brother keeps bumping my hand and the other takes a chisel to my shield. I silently pray Crew turns into Thor and breaks through my barrier, turning my walls to ash. Can you blame me after his performance? A girl can be attracted to someone and still loathe them. I'm sure of it.

I'm lost in my own thoughts and miss the musicians exiting the chancel and the preacher taking the podium. Nor do I notice that Trice's hand and mine stay intertwined after the prayer has ended, and we sit down until a small rush of air pulls me from my stupor.

"Foster." Crew's eyes drop to my hand, now intertwined with his brother's. I unlink my hand with Trice's as Crew nestles into the empty spot next to me. A mere second later, Crew jostles my other hand with his own brushing it innocently. I'm not fond of being touched without consent. I don't jerk it away. My brain and heart are clearly on different paths. His light touch sets my skin ablaze and a shiver the size of Texas rushes down my spine.

"You didn't text me back." His eyes stay glued on the preacher standing at the podium in front of us like a good little parishioner as he speaks.

Briefly, I forget that we're in church. Knowing darn well I should not be lusting after either Jordan brother bracketing me. I push the shameless thoughts from the forefront of my mind as I tear both of my hands away from their clutches and rest them in my lap far away from either of their grabby little hands.

My inner feminist growls.

"I thought someone had the wrong number." I plead the fifth.

"I don't like being ignored." The honesty in his tone irritates me as if I'm being doused with a bucket of water. My short lapse in judgment toward him implodes with annoyance.

"And I don't have the energy to pretend to like you today." How can someone with a voice so soothing and riveting just praise God and then become so disrespectful within a nanosecond? Maybe he should have said something along the lines of, *"Hey, this is Crew. I'm sorry I'm an asshat. I'd really like if you came back and sit beside me. I'm sure you don't have many friends in town yet, and I'd like to be one."*

"You don't have to pretend. You didn't even blink when I was on stage. You were glued on my performance, and you know it."

"I was dumbfounded, not impressed. There's a difference."

"Go ahead and tell yourself that. Just don't forget we're in a sacred building. You shouldn't lie."

My voice is hollow and the wall that I've built around my

heart reinforces itself, adding extra mortar to solidify it. "Your performance *was* great. It tricked me into thinking you were a decent human for a second, singing about redemption and crap. That's all. Don't read too much into it."

"Shh," Mina hushes us from her seat.

Crew tilts his head and leans close to my ear. The fresh scent of wintergreen gum assails me. In a hushed tone he utters, "I never claimed to be a decent guy. Even the devil has weaknesses, Foster. You just might be mine." He rises and walks away before I can respond.

My brain is in the midst of wanting to know more about this guy and punch him square in his jaw. All at the same time.

The truth is I don't know anything about Trice or Crew.

Except that maybe I should steer clear of both of them.

CHAPTER
NINE

CREW

The strange fluttering sensation Aurora's presence brings me grips my chest and other places further south. I don't exactly know what I did to earn such zealous disaffection from her. Her distaste only encourages me more.

Infuriatingly, my younger brother was holding her hand when I walked up to the pew they're sitting at. Rage surged through my veins like molten lava. I don't even know how I kept my composure while singing on the verge of exploding like a volcano from their closeness. I was so attuned to her as her eyes never wavered from mine. I don't think she knows the effect she has on people. She's stunning. A mix between the girl-next-door with innocence radiating off her and a temptress with secret desires burning in her orbs. Judge Samuels was staring so long, I think he may have gained another row of crow's feet around his eyes.

Yesterday, she looked more relaxed in a casual outfit that hugged her curves perfectly. Strong will exuded from her pores like gasoline. This morning she looked lost in the sea of sinners surrounding her. Helpless, without a raft in sight, until she shooed me away like a stray dog making her dislike for me crystal clear.

She may have been spellbound by my impeccably executed performance, but she doesn't know me and once she learns about my sordid past, she'll steer clear of me. I'm sure of it. Redemption and forgiveness can fuck themselves in this town. Because everyone nestled in the pews other than Aurora doesn't give a damn about the guy singing. All they see when they look at me is the kid who killed their quarterback, not the guy trying to atone for his sins.

My guilt devours me from the inside out. Matt's muffled screams and the urgency in his voice as he went under never stop playing on repeat in my mind like a living nightmare.

We lived and he died.

They say time heals all wounds. Mine are flayed open without a suture kit in sight, and there isn't enough forgiveness in the world to absolve how I feel knowing that I could have saved him if only I'd tried harder.

I draw on my cigarette as August's sticky air hits me in the face. I've fulfilled my court-appointed duty, and I decide to skip the next service and slide into my car having already asked for enough penance for the day. Just as I slam the door, rain begins to pelt against my windshield. With knuckles taut against the wheel, I race out of the church parking lot, deluding myself into thinking that my soul is still salvageable. The reality is, I wasn't strong enough to save him. I wasn't brave enough.

The only acquittal I've had is inflicting my own pain. Numbing myself with ink. My parents would kill me if they knew that my back was covered with art. As much as an enthusiast my mom is of expressing one's feelings, I have no doubt she'd have my hide if she knew how much money and how many hours, I've spent in the tattoo studio.

Grief is a bitch that I cannot escape. I've had no reprieve

from it until my eyes locked with Aurora's. Something in the universe shifted and when it aligned again, the noise clouding my mind diminished. For a passing moment, I felt a sense of calm that I haven't felt in a long time, and I'm going to chase that solace, even if it means going to war with my own brother.

Being a dick has become so routine that even I don't know when to rein it in and it seems to rear its ugly head whenever she is near. My attitude isn't helping me win her over. That's for damn sure.

Inhaling a deep breath, the image of Trice holding hands with her without an ounce of guilt for his indiscretions and participation in the events that occurred two years ago etched onto his face cause my knuckles to whiten on the steering wheel. He met her all of five minutes ago, and he's already trying to stake his claim. Little does he know, this thing he thinks he has with her is a lost cause because she's already *mine*. It doesn't matter that I don't know her either or that she's not eighteen *yet*. I just have to convince her that I'm worthy of her, which may be harder than I anticipated since she thinks I'm Lucifer reincarnated. Something that I no doubt can change.

I won't settle until the chill between her, and I, thaws. I'll take anything she tosses my way, because for some reason, even her disdain toward me seems to have caused a riot of emotion to stir inside the otherwise bleak landscape that exists within my chest. It's seeped into my bones, this yearning to feel something. It wants to spring to life in her presence. I'll fight for the feelings that she has ignited because the last time that I wanted something so bad, I was too weak and didn't fight hard enough for it.

And it cost me my best friend's life.

The engine purrs as my car comes alive. I punch the pedal, ready to put some space between me and everyone.

CHAPTER
TEN

Nothing can prepare someone for the first day of senior year in a new school.

Thankfully, Bea removed my stitches last night, so they won't create any unwanted stares or gossip. I'm sure being the new girl will cause enough of that. Luckily, I don't have to worry about an outfit because Russell and Bea enrolled me and Lonnie into the town's prestigious private elementary and high school. The state-of-the-art facilities and over-the-top veneer they droned on about doesn't really impress me. Girls like me don't belong in schools that require a payment to learn. Russell and Bea encourage it, though, saying it's the best education in town, and they're both thrilled for us. Bea more so than Russell.

Even though she's very chill, I can tell that her social status matters to her. Which is odd, considering she just took in two foster kids with jaded backgrounds and trust issues.

Maybe it's not the money she's after but the clout that she'll get from her circle of friends for attempting to save

America's damaged youth. I climb into her SUV, dressed in a plaid skirt that oddly resembles a tablecloth.

My phone chimes in my hand, causing my nose to scrunch as I see the name of the most infuriating person on this planet appear on the screen. I debate on stuffing the device in my pocket, or better yet, blocking the scoundrel. Inquisitiveness wins, and I slide my pointer finger across the screen.

Crew: *Don't let the wolves eat you alive today. I'd prefer to have that privilege*

"Look at you, already making friends."

If she only knew. "Crew Jordan is not my friend. Trust me. I'd like to unalive him." The mere thought of his name causes my stomach to clench with hostility.

She scoffs as she checks the rearview mirror and starts to back up, overlooking my comment to commit homicide. I'm thankful she doesn't glance over and notice my cheeks are painted a deep crimson. "He was always a cheeky kid that one. He will grow on you. Give it time."

"Like mold." I hiss.

"What if I don't make any friends?" Lonnie blurts from the backseat, his small finger in his mouth.

Bea should really talk to him about biting his nails, as a physician and all. It's a dirty habit. "Friends are overrated." I buckle my seatbelt as we reach the street. "You have me. Aren't I good enough?"

An exaggerated breath leaves Bea's mouth. "Aiden Jordan is a nice boy. I think you guys might even become best friends *and* neighbors. How cool would that be?"

I turn in the front seat, reaching for his hand, adding to Bea's encouragement. "You're going to make *so* many new friends. You might even make one before me! I bet you five dollars you will."

His face widens in a generous grin. "You're on."

The silence is comforting as we listen to the radio the rest of the way to school. It allows me to think and mentally prepare myself for the first day of senior year in a new place. I like that Bea doesn't have the need to make small talk all the time. We're used to foster parents who don't care. She's different. I'm not sure how to explain it other than her quiet presence is enough. I debate on texting something snarky back to Crew, and then decide against it. My silence should speak volumes.

Leave. Me. Alone.

Bea drops Lonnie off first at his building and then pulls around to the bigger building and parks. She opens her mouth, but no words come out for several seconds. "Your first day of senior year is a monumental time. I know this may be terrifying starting in a new place and only knowing one person on campus, so I asked Trice to watch out for you today. I'm not sure if you'll have any classes together or not, but he's the quarterback of the football team and has lots of friends here. If you need anything just shoot me a text."

Just what I wanted, a pity friend to start the year off with. I open the door and bark, "Thanks."

"Wait," she reaches for her purse. "Here's five dollars for Lonnie." She shoves the money in my palm. I smile at her gesture and grab the cash before I usher myself inside along with a group of other students packing into the school's main hallway.

Other than the school being a maze, the morning has been uneventful. Aside from the numerous times I've had to stand and introduce myself. I should have just worn a T-shirt over my uniform.

I'm Rory.

I'm an artist.

I dislike pumpkin pie and eggs.

How much easier would that make these pointless introductions?

I'm thankful that the stares and whispers about the *new girl* in town have died down by lunchtime. This is the moment I've been dreading all day. The defining moment in high school is who you sit with at lunch.

At my old school, it was irrelevant. Most of the kids enrolled either left before our lunch period or were truant. School in the inner city was pointless to most. Not to me. My grades might be the only thing that sets me free from a promised life of poverty. I take my academics seriously and study, putting in the effort to get good grades. In the few hours I've spent inside these walls, I can already tell that our education has been vastly different. These kids started advanced placement classes in middle school, maybe even before that. That means I'll have to apply myself twice as hard as before. Which won't be too hard. I love learning and have been told by several teachers that I'm well read and wise beyond my years. We just didn't have a lot of options for advancement at my old school. It was always blamed on lack of resources. I think it was lack of people giving a shit about inner-city kids getting a quality education if you ask me.

A cacophony of laughter fills the large cafeteria as I enter. Hoping to eat in peace, I glide toward the assembly line of food and place a few items on my plate and then bustle to the check-out counter and type in my pin. The chatter softens as I peer into the teeming room, contemplating where to sit. Spying an empty table, I take one step forward before I feel the soft caress of a hand wrapping around my elbow. My initial reaction is to tug away. With so many eyes glued on me, watching my every move like a mouse in a cage with a snake at feeding time, I keep my composure and turn. Relief washes over me as I'm greeted with Trice's crystal blue eyes.

"Sit with me?" He gestures toward a table of his peers with a nod of his head.

This morning's news of him being asked to watch me lingers. "I don't need a babysitter."

"Who said anything about babysitting? I want the prettiest girl I've seen all day to have lunch with me." He guides me over to the table and pats the seat next to him. My cold exterior melts a little at his charisma and my resistance to his lure waivers.

"Would it make you more comfortable to sit with *just* me?" He picks up his tray and starts to stand. His question startles me. Would he move to another table and bail on his friends just to make me more comfortable?

"Are you kidding me? If she doesn't want to sit, don't beg her. It's not a good look, even on you." A girl's voice cuts through the air with a strident tone.

His blue eyes turn to ice in a fragment of a second. "Neither is being a slut, Della, but we put up with you."

The venomous girl I now know as Della, bunches her fists before she lifts her tray and storms off. I figure she must be queen of the mean girl club. To my surprise, no one follows her.

Trice may be more like his brother than I initially thought.

"Please, sit," he says.

I can't deny his request after he just clowned someone on my behalf. I plop down beside him and notice everyone at the table has their eyes glued on me. Their stares are more uncomfortable than walking out of the bathroom with toilet paper on your shoe. I glance at my shoe under the table. I'd rather be safe than sorry.

All clear.

"Everyone." Trice addresses the table like he's the alpha and the rest of the nameless faces are his pack. "This is my new neighbor, Rory."

Neighbor?

I'm almost positive I heard whispers about me being a foster kid in the hallway earlier. News travels almost as fast in small towns as the whiff of horse manure does in the country. At least no one has ridiculed me to my face so far. I appreciate that he doesn't spread my business about the Greenwells being my foster family. He has more tact than his brother.

"This is Wade," Trice says, introducing me. "He's more country than cornbread and is our running back. Geoff over there…" He motions to a dude twice the size of Trice who's eating two slices of pizza stacked on top of one another. "As if you couldn't tell, there isn't much our center loves more than food."

"Other than football and hitting people, not so much. Nice to meet ya," Geoff mumbles with a mouthful of pizza. Red sauce slides down his chin like lava.

"Ignore Astor," a girl with a delicately carved face says.

"Who?"

"Della Astor." The girl's dark choppy hair rests at her shoulder blades. Even sitting down, I can tell that she is tall. "She's on her period thirty days out of the month." Her spunk and repartee make me snort, and the rest of Trice's crew erupts in laughter at Della's expense. "I'm Andrea."

"I haven't had a period in seventeen years. Do you think I should see a doctor?" A guy to Trice's right, who he seemed to have skipped on our introduction asks, and the table awakens with laughter. "I'm Sebastian, but everyone calls me Seb."

He finishes the introductions with the rest of the group, and much to my surprise, Trice's friends are easy to get along with. Well, everyone, except Della. She seems unbearable.

Trice's popularity is solidified as I dig into my lunch and look around the room. Everyone seems to be looking our way from across the packed cafeteria. One would think it's because I'm the new girl, but by the grin on Trice's face as people walk by and shake his hand or pat him on the back, I know it's his presence that has everyone's interest heightened. He's dubbed as Mr. Popularity, and everyone here is pining for his attention.

There is an unspoken hierarchy in high school, and Trice seems to be at the top. I should be intimidated, but I'm just thankful he's taken me under his wing with Bea's threat or without it. I notice that there isn't an ounce of studiousness that comes off him, even has his peers fawn over his presence. At least I'm off the chopping block during this period.

Taking a bite of my turkey-bacon-ranch wrap, I hear a low hum of laughter coming from where Trice is sitting. My eyes dart toward him moments before, I feel the pad of his thumb brush against my bottom lip. My spine goes rigid. The surprise of his touch and gentleness of his caress causes a wedge to form in my throat.

Did I swallow a strip of bacon without chewing it first?

I swallow past the lump and pray I don't aspirate. No, I definitely chewed it. *Did he just brush crumbs off my lip?* My eyes dash around the table to see if anyone witnessed our exchange. I don't want anyone to get the wrong impression of me on my first day and start calling me Whorey-Rory. Wouldn't Bea love that?

"Thanks," my voice raises an octave. Out of the corner of my eye, I see him nod in response and he continues his conversation like my lip wasn't just scorched by the warmth of his touch.

The next twenty minutes fly by. I forget everyone's name but Andrea's, seeing as she's the only female aside from the demon I now know as Della that I was introduced to. Grabbing the edge of my tray, I'm ready to tackle the second half of day when it's removed from my grip.

"Let me." Trice's eyes sweep over my face asking for my approval before he slides my empty tray on top of his.

His act of kindness sends waves of praise to my heart. I can't help but brace myself and wait for the other shoe to drop; for old insecurities to come back for one last jab. He seems as genuine as a human can be, but I'm still uncertain. I've never met a decent person in the city in my life. It's been a long seventeen years. Pushing past his small acts of kindness, I swallow down my trepidation and smile, chalking up my first lunch as a senior a success.

After enduring three more classes, my palms itch at the anticipation of the clock striking two-fifty-five. I'm happy to report I survived. No one called me a bitch, at least not to my face, or scribbled on my locker, so there's that. It could have been because the most popular guy in our senior class walked me to my classes the entire afternoon like my own personal excursion guide. I don't know how he arranged that. It's probably because he's the football team's star player. Being the quarterback carries a certain level of authority. He might even have keys to the school.

Checking my phone, I notice a new text from Bea asking me if I want to walk home or if I need her to pick me up. She mentions that she's staying after school with Lonnie to see if he's interested in joining any sports or clubs the elementary school has to offer for his age. I'm eager to get home and claw my way out of this itchy uniform and get into a pair of shorts, so I tell her that I need some fresh air and I'll walk. I'm not sure if she's always so laid back with new foster kids or what her deal is. I gladly accept the unearned trust and appreciate that she's not breathing down my neck.

Shrubs and boxwoods flank a straight path that leads to what looks like the towns cemetery. I trudge forward curiously and glance over my shoulder to see my school in the distance. Exploring my surroundings has always been a hobby of mine. You never know when you're going to have to escape a situation.

Plodding forward, I enter the cemetery. A combination of different flowers attacks my senses at once. Thank goodness for my looted allergy meds. I'm overcome as I walk by a grave decorated with the most beautiful fresh flowers I've ever seen. An assortment of different colors tied together with a delicate clasp holds the bouquet together. *Cameron Cannon* must be one missed mother as her headstone reads.

My heart thrums as I continue forward and take in the

floral masterpieces that dot almost every gravesite. People in this town must still be adored by many, even after death.

As I near the back of the cemetery, several plots are barren. No flowers, trinkets or anything laid atop these graves. Just stones and a few leaves. It's like their memory has been forgotten completely. No visitors have knelt beside their grave with a tear-soaked T-shirt and pleas spewing from their lips.

Emptiness consumes me.

Is that how *my* gravesite will look?

Here lies Aurora Elyse Bradshaw. The orphan whose heart was so cold it turned to stone.

Deciding to right society's wrongs, I hastily grab a couple flowers from neighboring gravesites and make my own bouquet. I lay it at the head of the barren grave and gently pat the stone.

"Even if the world has forgotten about you, I won't."

"What are you doing?" A voice cuts through the quietude.

My heartbeat accelerates and my hands grab ahold of my backpack in a defensive gesture. I turn around to find Trice nonchalantly leaning against a headstone behind me, arms crossed, curiosity written on his face. "You scared the Bejeezus out of me!" I try to catch my breath. "What are you doing here?"

"Visiting a friend." Trice's eyes twinkle in the sunlight. A cloud of sadness comes over me. What do I say to someone who lost someone? Grief is like an elephant in a room that no one wants to acknowledge.

A moment passes before he asks, "Would you like to meet him?"

"Sure."

"I saw what you did back there." He says as I follow his lead.

"Yeah, about that…" I want to protest that I'm not a thief,

but that would be a lie, and I really don't want to get off on the wrong foot with my only friend in this town.

"You don't have to explain," he says, matter-of-factly. "I think it is sort of noble of you. I'm not a big believer in the whole life after death scenario anyway."

"Says the guy hanging out in a graveyard."

"Fair enough." He ducks his head. "I guess I'd like to think that this place just holds our bodies and nothing more."

"I think that you can feel however you want, and it can change daily."

"I find it cute that you feel bad for the neglected head-stones. A lot of what makes us who we are is what we do when no one is watching." Intensity twists in his words.

There's a tidal wave of emotions I want to share. Which is unexpected since my feelings are locked in the pit of my stomach under five bolts and an electric fence. Sharing has never been my thing, and as comfortable as Trice makes me feel, I refuse to let my guard down and tell him that in foster care you can be a ghost and under scrutiny at the same time. "It's just sad," I explain. Anything more gets lodged in my throat.

"I used to think we were all invincible," he murmurs, melancholy laced in his tone. "My dad always says there are two things we're promised in this world."

"Death and taxes."

"Exactly." Trice quips. His voice is warm. It blankets me, and I feel so at ease conversing with him that I forget we're standing in a cemetery.

"What happened to your friend?" The crystal blue of his eyes freezes with torment. "It's none of my business. I was…I was just wondering. I'm so sorry I asked. Sometimes when I'm nervous, I ramble."

His hands, soft, yet strong, brush a piece of hair from my face. "Do I make you nervous, Rory?"

I swallow down a small gulp that threatens to escape my lips. "Not *you*, necessarily."

He laughs. The sound is rich, and its pureness is infectious. "Well, it's certainly not the graveyard I found you wandering aimlessly."

"Well said." I almost run into the side of Trice's broad stance as he stops abruptly. I plant my heels and am suddenly acutely aware how close he is. The Jordan brothers share a commonality of stopping me in my tracks.

"Rory, meet Matt." His voice is hardly above a whisper. "Greenwell."

My stomach roils as his words sink in and settle in my gut. "Greenwell as in…" My mouth closes in disbelief. A twitchy feeling overcomes me and my eyes dart to the headstone. I register the year of his passing. He was seventeen when he died. "They *had* a son?" My brain scrambles.

"Indeed, they did. Matt is…" He clears his throat. "Was… the same age as Crew. We were best friends. The three amigos." His mouth curves into a sad smile, undoubtedly reminiscing.

My mind reels wondering why Bea and Russell never mentioned the death of their son considering it happened not that long ago. Almost two years, based on the date on the headstone. It dawns on me that it must be their clubhouse in the backyard. Trice, Crew, and Matt were the three kids in the picture I saw. A wave of emotion rolls over me, and my knees feel frail. My trembling hand moves to my neck. I clear my throat. "I'm so sorry for your loss. I had no idea that they even had a son. Much less that you three were friends."

"I wouldn't expect you to know. Bea and Russell have been in my life since I was born. But they don't talk about Matt. Like ever. It's like he didn't even exist. I know they come here, though, because there are fresh flowers every time I stop by."

"Do you come here often?" I ask.

"It depends if I have anything I want to keep Matt in the loop with."

"What drew you here today?"

"I met the most gorgeous girl I've ever seen. I wanted to brag, knowing that *he* couldn't woo her before me." Eyes blue as a robin's egg lock onto mine. His answer is like a cannonball of confetti being set off in my chest.

A long, brittle silence passes between us. I test the waters. "What if I've already been wooed by someone else?"

Trice nudges my shoulder. "That would be a shame. Who is it, so I know if I have any real competition?"

I'm vaguely aware of how close his hand is to mine as his broad shoulders and Viking legs become immobile. I stop my hand from sliding down my side, too afraid that my skin will accidentally brush against his. As much as I want it to, because let's be honest, I'm not blind nor am I a nun on a venture to my deliverance. Trice is attractive, and there is a kindness in him that's palpable.

The reality is that my heart isn't available to give. I have one goal, and that's to reach my eighteenth birthday, adopt Lonnie, and flee the northwestern area of the state. I want to move somewhere where no one knows my history and start fresh without any bias. I want Lonnie to live in a home filled with laughter and provide us both with a security that we've never had. I have no time to get involved with anyone in this small town. Sealing my fate and planting roots is something that just isn't in the cards for me.

Deflecting, I add, "I'm kidding. I barely know anyone here. I certainly haven't had time to be wooed yet." My finger fiddles with the hem of my skirt anxiously as our eyes lock in an unspoken understanding.

"Are you done aiding the flowerless? I can give you a ride home."

"That'd be cool. Thanks."

"I can pick you up and take you home, too, when I don't have practices. We're neighbors after all."

"I can see that Mina and Shawn raised you right."

"Crew was the firstborn. Mom and dad knew they had to try again." A smug smile crosses his golden face.

"What's with the bad blood between you guys?"

"That, my friend, is a story for another day. Come on." He says, his tone chilly. He leans down and pats the top of Matt's headstone a couple times. He doesn't say anything before spinning and guiding me toward the paved walkway.

Other than the beat of rap blaring through his speakers, the ride is quiet. I should have pegged him for a rap fan. It allows my mind to wander to Matt and the events of today. What a whirlwind of information I stumbled upon. I can barely keep my questions at bay.

How did he die?

Why did Bea and Russell not tell me?

Does Miranda know she placed Lonnie and me in a home where their own child had died?

"I can see the wheels spinning." Trice interrupts the loop of questions running through my mind like a speaker dialed to ten. "It wasn't my intention to bring up his death. You were just there, and it sort of happened." He takes a right turn into the subdivision.

"I'm just surprised. I didn't realize they had any children. Much less one that died. It's a little unnerving."

"Don't think of it as a secret." *Is he clairvoyant?* "The entire town knows about the accident. I honestly don't think they're keeping it from you. It was just a dark time for all of us." He shifts the car into park, and I stare up at the enormous house, plagued with more questions about the Greenwells than I had when I first arrived a few days ago.

Grabbing the handle, I push lightly. "I appreciate the ride. See you tomorrow."

The usual shine in Trice's eyes is dimmer, and I can tell

how much Matt meant to him. He gives me a curt nod and then drives off, leaving me with my unanswered questions.

The house is silent when I walk inside. Which leads me to believe that no one is home yet. The clock on the stovetop says it's just after four o'clock. After grabbing a soda from the refrigerator, I sit at the peninsula and stare out the window at the clubhouse. Curiosity killed the cat, but my sudden need for answers has me shaking my foot like a fiend in need of a fix. Needing answers and chasing a high.

I take a quick sip of my drink and hop off the stool and head into the living room. With Bea and Russell both gone, this is an opportunity to do some snooping. I notice a couple of family pictures on the mantle. I hadn't really paid much attention on the tour Bea gave us when we arrived. It was too much to take in all at once. Now I'm focused like a laser on a mission. There's no dust on the pictures, which doesn't surprise me. The guy I assume is Matt is positioned between Bea and Russell. He's wearing tailored jeans with a sports jersey.

There is a den across from the foyer that Bea uses as a home office. Her degrees and medical awards hang on the walls over the large desk. What piques my interest is the large wooden frame resting against the closet door. I turn it around to see a large image of Matt. He's in a suit. I assume it's his senior photo. Probably the same one used at his memorial.

He is handsome. The wide smile on his face looks identical to Bea's.

Feeling like a trespasser, I decide to abort my efforts and elect to give Bea and Russell the benefit of the doubt. When they're ready to tell me about their son's death they will. My quest for answers will have to stew for a while because who am I to petition the truth when I don't even know what honesty is myself.

CHAPTER
ELEVEN

CREW

My dormmate's incessant snoring is driving me over the edge. I contemplate leaping off the balcony just to end my misery. Pocketing my twitchy fingers to keep from smothering him with his own pillow, I decide to go home early rather than stay on campus for another weekend.

It's been an agonizing couple of weeks since my mom's dinner party went south, and I stormed out. The image of Aurora's face twisted with disdain and her words toward me that Sunday at church have hounded even my dreams. I don't know what I did to deserve her wrath, other than showcasing my charming personality, but even angry, she is easily the cutest woman I've ever seen.

The way her natural blonde hair hangs over her shoulders and the way that her bathing suit clung to her waist, defining her smooth stomach, has been the reason for the many cold showers I've taken on campus. Not to mention those hunter-green eyes that drink you in when they look at you. I'm hypnotized by their masterful seduction. Even though her mouth says one thing, her eyes tell another story. They spark whenever I'm near and lure me into a web that I don't think she knows she has the ability to weave yet.

I've put forth a solid effort to distance myself from the constant thoughts of her that have plagued my mind since our first encounter. It hasn't done much good and has only upped my stalker skills. Sadly, she doesn't have any form of social media. I find it a little odd, but her evasiveness just adds to her allure.

Keeping my distance seems to have only encouraged my brother where Aurora is concerned. My mom has been gushing nonstop about Trice being enamored—her words, not mine—with our new neighbor. The thought of them growing closer means I've been staying in the city on campus far too much. Sure, they go to the same school and are both seniors, but something about him already crushing on her sends my thoughts into a stampede.

"Later man," I wave to a sleeping Pete. Dude's one documentary away from doing something reckless, which is why I try to stay in his good graces even when he's sleeping.

When dad mentioned the Labor Day parade this weekend, I didn't give it much thought until he revealed that Aurora and Lonnie would be joining us Saturday evening for the bonfire. It's something we do annually, our family and the Greenwells. For years, we'd all sit around the fire pit and watch college football on the flat screen with hot cocoa. The weather is cool enough to enjoy the fire pit, yet warm enough to stay outside for hours in the evening. When Aiden was small, mom would mash up marshmallows and melt a tiny amount of chocolate for his graham crackers.

Nostalgia is fickle.

Being home used to pain me. With the presence of our new neighbor, it summons me. Not the thought of being home so much. Just the thought of seeing her. The girl next door who left a lasting impression that's haunted my dreams in the best way.

Even with a plethora of tight leggings, high cheekbones, and bright smiles prancing around campus, I haven't been tempted by many women other than Della Astor. She's been a constant in my life. It might be the familiarity or the fact that she was friends-*without*-benefits with Matt first, which made her my friend by proximity. She is self-righteous and thinks just because of her last name and what it means to the horse industry that she's more important than anyone else. Maybe to some in our town it means something. Not to me. I don't care about her money or the fact that her family owns thoroughbreds. Status doesn't mean jack to me.

We've had this on-and-off fling going on for a while. She is, *was*, my safety girl. The one you keep on the line, stringing along.

Dick move.

Except I no longer want a safety girl.

There's only one person who I *want*, and she doesn't know my history. She's a fresh start. A breath of fresh air. Della never crosses my mind the way Aurora has in the short time I've known her. We've only been around one another three times and each encounter has been brief. And painful. Yet here I am, foolishly white-knuckling my steering wheel on my way home to try and catch a glimpse of her and to make her yearn for me the same way I've been for her.

Boy, Della is going to go off the rails.

That girl has never heard the word no. Surely not from daddy dearest and ordinarily not from me.

The realization that I have it bad for a girl I hardly know has me punching the accelerator and speeding toward my hometown like I'm competing in the Daytona 500. The thought of seeing Aurora tonight has me on edge, but in a good way.

CHAPTER
TWELVE

A slew of miniature American flags line the sidewalk as Lonnie and I make our way on foot to Main Street. I really wish I had my driver's license. In the city, I never longed for it since everything I needed was within walking distance. Luckily, our new subdivision is close to town, but having a car and more independence would be nice.

I file the thought in the back of my mind under "things to obtain." It's something I'll have to acquire when I turn eighteen and petition for adoption of Lonnie. No judge in their right mind would grant me parental rights without a vehicle to get a kid to and from doctors' appointments and school.

It's endearing how Russell and Bea show they care and are present, but still give me enough space so I don't feel smothered. I'm used to steering clear of adults at all costs and forging my own path. Curfews, dinner times, and family game nights are as foreign to me as speaking in Swedish. The constant need to prepare for danger has slowly faded with the Greenwells over the past couple of weeks. I don't want to get too comfortable in their lap of luxury. I'm keeping my goals in sight despite how welcoming they've been to Lonnie and me.

The small trees lining the buildings prepare to change colors welcoming fall's quick approach with open arms. Summer's last hurrah is celebrated with Labor Day festivities, including a parade.

Parades in the city were dangerous. There was always the threat of the unknown. I'd preferred to climb onto the apartment's balcony and watch from the safety of above. There was always something about being surrounded with people pushing against me that didn't sit right. I'd seen the news and the trouble that can happen when too many people are gathered together. It left my nerves unsettled, and even now, in the safety of our new town, has me glancing over my shoulder apprehensively.

To be honest, our walk here was uneventful aside from an accidental bump from someone on the sidewalk. It's much different than in the city. The woman stopped and apologized with a smile. Who knew humanity could be kind to one another? Guess I just had to get out of the city limits to find out. This rural town continues to blow my mind.

Everyone is huddled on the street waiting for the parade to start. Lonnie's small fingers intertwine with mine as we weave in and out of the crowd attempting to find a good viewing spot. I notice a small crowd of kids from school as we near the street line. Della and her cadre give me the side-eye as Lonnie and I approach them. Sadly, the proximity to them gives Lonnie the best view. There are far worse things than high school bullies. I don't give Della or her blonde-bimbo friends a second glance as we slide in beside them.

"I wish Bea and Russell didn't have to work. They would love this!" Lonnie exclaims.

"I'm sure they would, buddy. Look," I point across the street. There is a small table perched on the sidewalk where a lady is painting kids' faces. "Want to get your face painted after the parade?"

"Do we have money to do that?"

"Bea left some cash for us. If you want to get your face painted, we can make that happen." I've never felt loved or cared about like I have from Russell and Bea in such a short amount of time. Another crack forms in my heart. Pretty soon it's going to crumble and turn to dust. I can't let that happen. I can't allow myself to get used to this lifestyle.

I won't allow myself to rely on anyone.

Even if it breaks me.

The parade commences with a procession of people walking down the street. Some pass by on foot, holding banners and flags while others drive by on tractors decorated by various themes. Country folk are endearing.

"Well, if it isn't *Foster* and her little foster brother." Della's voice grates against my eardrum threatening to bust it. Another syllable from her painted pink lips and, I'll go deaf. Maybe being hard of hearing wouldn't be a bad thing. I wouldn't have to hear her schmoozing with our peers and trying to spread gossip about me like I give a chicken-fried-fuck about her opinion of me.

I'm not sure who spilled the beans about me being in the foster care system. Word travels fast in small towns, and one could assume the only other twerp who calls me Foster is who informed Della of my history. Apparently, Crew and Della are a *thing*.

"If I catch you flirting with my boyfriend," she nears my side. "We're going to have trouble. The other Jordan brother is up for grabs. I'm sure he'd lower his standards for you." She glances over her shoulder at her small crowd of varmints. I silently thank my lucky stars that Andrea isn't with her. Being friends with Della would be enough to warn me away from her entirely.

"Fuck off," I huff, turning my attention back to the street lined with people.

"I just thought of what you remind me of. A hot dog." Her voice raises an interval, and she snickers like she's a comedian and just made a joke so comical she all but slaps her own knee cap.

A compulsion to slap her silly has me counting to ten. Physically assaulting her in public won't do me any good, and I swear to God if karma doesn't hit her, I will succumb and do it just to right the universe. "Excuse me?"

"You're like the scraps and parts people don't want. Like a hot dog. Trice would be foolish to date someone with your background anyway. Even your own parents didn't want you."

One. Two. Three... I'm about to give her a reason to use her daddy's money and get a nose job. I inhale, deeply and try to push down a boatload of hatred toward her. Because in this moment I don't want to be levelheaded. I want to unalive her and dispose of her ridiculously tanned body. I compose myself and swallow my anger, but like a beast it roars against my ribcage and begs to be set loose.

"You're delusional. I'm not interested in either. But if I were," I square my shoulders. "You'd have to watch your back. Because trust me, I'd have both eating out of the palm of my hands. You'd be forgotten about in a split second," I say with edge in my voice and avert my attention.

"Screw you." She tosses her hair.

"Right back at ya," I spew as she stalks away with her little minions hot on her heels.

This is why I avoid social activities whenever possible. If it wasn't for Lonnie, I'd be in my room painting or reading a good book. Instead, I'm here being insulted by Haley Bieber's doppelgänger. Della and Crew seem to have more in common than I initially thought.

There are plenty of things more enjoyable than being

around either of them: root canals, stepping in a pile of fresh dog poop, chapped lips, cold showers, not having a driver's license, popcorn kernels getting stuck in your teeth.

Rolling my eyes, I turn my attention back to the parade in front of me. There's a guy on stilts dressed like Abraham Lincoln. He's blowing up balloons and twisting them into funny shapes. He passes by and hands Lonnie a blue balloon sword. Pretty impressive.

"Thank you." Lonnie's small voice gets lost in the commotion.

Chanting and roars fill the air around us as the ground nearly vibrates from the sound of loud drums and the school's marching band as they near. I flinch, unsure of what's going on and consider ushering Lonnie away from the crowd mere seconds before I see an army of gold and navy jerseys come into sight. The football team is marching in unison like toy soldiers. Their expressions stoic. The closer they come, the louder the crowd gets. Booming shouts ring out and reverberate in my chest. It's too much. The noise, the crowd. I'm on sensory overload and ready to find reprieve anywhere but here.

"We need to beat the crowd. Let's go." I give Lonnie's hand a tug. Only a second later he drops his hold on my hand causing sudden panic to take flight in my stomach.

"Where are you running off to?" Trice's smooth voice summons my attention. I glance up to see him giving Lonnie a high five. His team meanders around his sudden stop in the middle of the parade. They keep walking onward without their quarterback.

"I was trying to escape the pandemonium."

He's close enough that I can see the sun glimmering from his irises. Even its rays are jealous of the light shown on his face. Warmth radiates from his pores. "Don't leave so soon. I was thinking of getting my face painted."

"You were? Rory said I could get my face painted. Didn't

you, Rory? Can we do it together? Please!" Lonnie shouts enthusiastically.

"I would love nothing more than to hang out with you both. Will you wait for me after the parade ends?" he asks Lonnie, knowing there's no way he will turn him down.

I give him a sharp nod as he salutes us and then turns to catch up with his team.

After the parade we meander around searching the crowd for Trice. He shouldn't be too hard to spot with his tall stature, wealth of blonde, wind-swept hair, and a football jersey with the letter "C" on the left chest. I didn't peg him as a football player. That night at dinner I recall him saying he was late due to practice running over. He doesn't act like a jock. At least not in the ways I would assume of a meat-head football player.

His buddy Geoff is as kind as a teddy bear and is the picture-perfect description of a jock. He's big and brawny. Whereas Trice is all the above but exudes gentleness. I haven't seen an ounce of cockiness in him yet, and he doesn't act like he's better than anyone. At least I haven't seen him shove anyone into a locker. He has that going for him, although my bias of jocks may be slightly skewed.

Sorry, jocks of the world. I kindly ask for your forgiveness.

"Rory!" I hear him before I see him. Trice waves us toward a booth with a tent. It looks like he's already secured a spot in line with the face painter. Gripping Lonnie's hand, we push through the crowd and make our way closer to the booth.

I freeze.

Why must the universe find ways to torment me at every turn?

Standing directly beside Trice is his unpleasant brother with his holier-than-thou swagger. Even from a few feet away, I am trapped like quicksand by his arrogance. It seeps from his pores like thick honey. The more we're around one another the more I sink.

Right now, as his hands drape over his little brother

Aiden's shoulders in a protective stance, smiling from ear to ear, I want to hurl myself into oncoming traffic. Because as much as I hate to admit it, his bad-boy persona with dark clothes and lashes for days sends my heart beating into overdrive. My desire for him is getting harder to compress and I swear for the life of me I've tried.

I've fought the urge to look him up on social media using the account I just made for myself last night.

I've fought the urge to ask Bea about the stark difference between the golden Jordan brother and the precarious one, and why they're in what seems to be a lifelong feud.

I've fought the urge to ask Trice when his brother normally visits just so I can make up an excuse and be at their house to casually run into him.

All I seem to do is argue with myself about Crew. Someone I barely even know, should not have such a strong foothold on me already.

He's done nothing but irritate me, but the heart wants what it wants. And what it wants is the guy with the blue-jean clad legs, maroon Henley shirt, and dark tendrils of hair loosely tucked behind his ears, looking like a model slash tortured artist.

The irritation I feel in this moment at myself for my wishy-washy feelings burns somewhere on my body I'd rather not admit to. That should be a red flag in itself.

A wicked grin masks his face and I'm melting into a pool of longing, knowing good and well that I should avoid him at all costs. Nothing good can come from giving in to my desire, just because Crew has a pretty face. I cannot afford to lose sight of my goal.

Turn eighteen.

Adopt Lonnie.

Start living.

Lonnie spots Aiden and takes off running in the direction

of the Jordan trio. I trot forward cautiously, half-expecting Della to pounce on me from behind a shrub.

"Foster," Crew purrs when I'm within an arm's length.

Hurt and anger have festered in me long enough. His name-calling, coupled with Della's ignorant comment from earlier, pushes me over the edge. No matter how good looking I find Crew, his nickname unhinges me. I forget that we're surrounded by people. "My name is Rory." I shout. "Not *Foster*. I don't appreciate your digs and stop saying it like foster care is such a derogatory term. It's nothing to be ashamed of."

I steal a glance at Lonnie, who thankfully, is lost in conversation with Aiden. He's too young for his heart to have had time to harden like mine while being in the system. He still wonders why his birth parents didn't love him enough to keep him, not understanding that sometimes love isn't enough. His birth parents did the most selfless thing in this world by placing him in the care of someone else. Someone who could properly take care of him. It's the system that failed us. Ushering him into different homes. Not getting placed or chosen for adoption as an infant or at any age is the real curse.

This world has been hard on him and sure as hell has me mixed up with someone else if I let Crew's off-the-cuff nickname for me bring anymore hurt or shame to his sweet little heart.

"You wonder why I never text you back," I demand. "Isn't it obvious? I don't like you, and I don't want to hear Foster ever leave your lips again or so help me."

My index finger meets his chest. For someone who usually doesn't like to draw attention to herself, I sure do a number on Crew. Despite the loud crowd still milling around from the parade, several onlookers side-eye my sudden outburst as they pass us by. "I honestly can't stand you and your stupid-ass smirk. You're like a fungus. It grows and spreads until it's ruined everything within its reach."

Trice interrupts, startled by my outburst. "He's been texting you?"

I don't have time to respond before Crew seizes my hand with his, holding it captive. "If I've had enough time to fester into a deplorable mold, that must mean that you've been thinking about me. A man will take what he can get."

I almost gag at his arrogance. His subtle wit makes me want to slap him and knock him down a peg or two or give in and kiss him relentlessly. I take a deep breath before acting on impulse and slapping him to knock some sense into him. It's apparent by the smirk etched on it; he thinks I'm the kind of chick who sits back and takes someone's harassment.

I'm appalled by his expression before he curses under his breath. "Shit." Crew usually seems to be resigned. But the look that dances across his dark features makes me feel culpable, and I didn't even hit the guy. "Foster will not leave my lips again, *Aurora*."

I tug my hand from his and place it on my chest, protecting my maltreated heart. He angers me to my core. But the sultry way my name sounds rolling off his tongue makes it thrum and the yo-yo of emotions that Crew stirs within me is giving me a massive headache from the back and forth of my emotions.

"Bones," he grinds the word between his clenched teeth. In a swift motion I wasn't ready for, Crew grabs my hand stealthily and feathers his lips across my knuckles.

I'm torn between wanting to deck him in his flawless face for touching me so intimately without a warning and wanting to lower my guard and sink into his embrace. No one has ever looked at me the way that he has. Even at the corner store where we first met. His intense glare wordlessly spoke to my soul. That's something not even the best social workers in the city have been able to do. I draw in a quick breath as the final smack of his lips reverberates in my core.

He repeats the word bones like a promise. I give him a sidelong glance, downright confused and hot. Bewilderment adds to my crimson cheeks that already burn from Crew's proximity and him still holding onto my hand.

Our eyes lock.

My thoughts are too erratic to form a single sentence. Trice clears his throat next to me. I glance over to see him watching our exchange. He takes the opportunity to slide in front of me, breaking our moment. I had forgotten about his presence. For a flash, it was just Crew and me on the sidewalk.

Stupid, stupid girl.

I had my mind made up. I had decided to despise Crew and ignore any thumping of my heart in my chest at his proximity, and then he shows up and plows through my wall with expert precision that no one has ever been able to do before. What is it about him?

Pull it together, Aurora Elyse Bradshaw.

"If you declare bones, it means you take something to the grave," Trice explains. "It's our version of pinky swearing or forcing the truth out of you. A long time ago, Matt wanted Crew to admit he cheated off him on a test and he asserted bones. It sorta stuck, and since then when we want to get the truth from someone or make a promise that we'll take to the grave we declare bones and it's *final.*" Trice clarifies the phrase and clears any remaining confusion.

Crew arches a brow and his attitude changes from scorching to icy in a nanosecond. "What does she know about Matt?"

"We visited his grave together." Trice answers and I don't like that he leads his brother to believe that we had a planned outing, but I don't correct him either.

Crew covers Aiden's ears, his hands like mittens. I don't know what he's going to say so I mimic his movement and cover Lonnie's ears too in preparation. The last thing I want is either of them to report back to Bea or Mina that we were all cursing like sailors around either of them.

"She has no fucking business being at his gravesite. Neither do you. You shouldn't have brought her there, man."

"Me?" Trice's shoulders widen. I'm acutely aware of his towering physique. "He was my best friend, too. I can visit him whenever the hell I want." He inches forward toward his brother's face. His mouth is pulled into a grim, straight line; his jaw set like stone. "When was the last time you visited him?"

A muscle flicks angrily in Crew's jaw. He doesn't respond, and his eyes go vacant. This is the version of him I remember from the store the night we met. He looked void of emotion then too. I'm relatively sure of one thing; whatever the reason for the strain in their relationship has to do with their mutual friend. I still don't know how he died, but I get the feeling that the budding tension is going to spill over, and I'll have answers sooner rather than later.

When Crew's eyes flick to mine, there is a sorrow that seems to gnaw at them.

It's as if he's become a shell of himself in a single blink of an eye.

I'm half-tempted to raise my hand from Lonnie's ear and brush it against Crew's tormented face. Sadly, I get the feeling he's more hurt by Matt's death than what Trice believes. His rough exterior is beginning to look like a disguise.

Every fiber in my body warns me to not feel sorry for him. I'm all too familiar with being utterly alone in this world. I know I don't owe him anything, especially my empathy. Yet, I can't help the tiny seed that flourishes inside my ribcage from being planted. It takes root and pretty soon, if I'm not careful, flowers will flourish from the inside out and then I'll really be screwed.

"Aiden, I forgot I told mom I'd get a couple things for her

for dinner tonight. Stay with Trice, and he'll be sure you get your face painted. I'll meet you at home. Okay?" The deep timbre of Crew's voice cuts the silence.

Too afraid to admit that a garden may soon blossom in my chest, I bury the thoughts for the broken boy in front of me and give his back a weary smile as he walks away.

CHAPTER
THIRTEEN

Spots flash in my vision as I storm through town, irritated as hell.

My jackoff of a little brother got under my skin.

He's never been as vocal as he was about his disdain for me not visiting Matt's grave. Sure, he's been a dick and told me Matt would be hurt on several occasions. But this outburst takes the cake. It was different. Raw. He had the courage to come toe-to-toe with me. *That's new.* I guess we can thank Aurora for that. She's bringing things out in both of us that I don't care to admit to.

I saw red, and it wasn't the flags waving from every storefront and patio. Storming off was the only way to protect Trice from the wrath that's threatened to surface since the accident. I've wanted to rock his world for ruining mine every day since it happened.

The truth is, I visit Matt's grave regularly when I'm in town and bring flowers every time. I miss my best friend more than anything. I choose not to share those details with Trice because it's none of his business. Frankly, if he wants to loathe me so he doesn't hate himself for what he did, he can have at it. I'll be his scapegoat for however long he needs me to be.

I'm rattled. Usually, I'm numb to his insults. With tense muscles and fury radiating through me, I dip down an alleyway, heading away from town, needing to distance myself before I explode and pummel my brother in the face. He'd deserve it. Trust me.

Being devoid of emotion is what has gotten me through the nearly two years since Matt's passing. The truth is, I'd rather be numb than be forced to feel his loss, and at every corner, there's Trice throwing it in my face like the rest of the town.

He should know better than anyone.

Bea and my mom were childhood friends. It only made sense that Matt and I would be too. I remember my mom and Bea showing us pictures at each other's birthday parties when we were in grade school. How many friends can honestly say they've known one another since they were small children? Matt and I were thick as thieves and then along came Trice. He threw our balance out of whack.

Matt was a rare breed and tolerated my little brother. We all fell into a routine and eventually a circle of trust. He had a good head on his shoulders and was talented on the football field. We won our first championship in years because of his ability on the field. Everyone gravitated to him. He was going places. Now Trice is living in Matt's shadow as quarterback. It pisses me off how easily he stepped up in the wake of his predecessor. He got off the hook and came out on top.

I never aspired to do much during high school. My looks got me by; everyone wanted to tutor Matt's best friend and if I wanted something, all I had to do was ask and it was given to me.

Even when Matt was helping me cram for the ACT that night and Trice came up with the stupid idea to take our dad's boat out. We knew Trice was wasted, and we still caved to his incessant pleas, needing to take a break. Trice was three sheets to the wind, and Matt and I let him drive anyway.

That's what haunts me the most. After years of Matt saving me on the football field and with my grades, when the tables were turned and he really needed me, I couldn't save him.

My feet cross the threshold of the graveyard, and I register where I am. After walking aimlessly, it seems I ended up here. I take a step forward, still on autopilot, and find his gravesite. Its location engraved in my mind. The town held a vigil when he passed, but I'm not one of those people who commiserate and grow closer over tragedies that bind people together. I needed to be alone with my grief. I shut out the sorrow with an iron gate, so I don't have to deal with it.

After the accident, I was only permitted to attend the actual funeral. I didn't even get to attend my best friend's wake. It was a closed casket, my parents had said. I'm thankful for that. No one wants the last image of them to be ingrained in their family and friends' minds while lying in a coffin.

The rumor mill went wild.

My name, my parents' names, all went to hell in a handbasket.

I clutch my arms to my chest and sink to my knees. My hand finds the top of his gravestone. The hard edge almost cuts into the flesh of my hand. I push harder, begging for the agony to make me feel something. Anything.

Words stick in my throat. I shift on my knees uncomfortably and stare at the flowers resting at the head of his grave. They're fresh and aren't the ones I left here last time I visited. It's no surprise that he still has friends who come and see him often. Wishing I were anywhere else on this planet except here, I close my eyes, conjuring up the image of my cell at the county jail. At least when I was there, it felt like I was atoning for his death.

The sound of a leaf crunching under a shoe pulls me from my thoughts.

"Crew." The sudden familiarity of Aurora's voice, etched with concern, surrounds me like a big hug. Just the sound of her voice brings me a moment of peace.

"Aurora, don't," I plead. Holding up my hand, I try to stop her from coming further. Her abdomen hits the palm of my hand as she ignores my request. I'm afraid of her being disgusted with me for not visiting my best friend's grave, even though it's clearly not true. Trice laid it on thick and I don't think I can stand any more hatred today. I'm sure she believed every word that came out of my dear brother's mouth.

If she did believe him, she wouldn't be standing here. Right?

I'm stunned by her boldness. I glance up through heavy lids and unshed tears. She takes another step toward me, towering above. Usually this position would make me feel inferior; not having the upper hand is something that doesn't sit well with me. After the night Matt died, I've made sure to hold onto control at all costs.

Aurora's eyes bore into mine begging for answers. She's curious. I can almost hear her voice asking what happened. But the words never come. She just offers a sorrowful look. I can feel it penetrating my soul. The world around us ceases to exist. I don't know how she knew I was here, or if she just stumbled upon me and thought I looked pathetic on my knees. Hell, I don't even know where my brothers and Lonnie are right now. All I care about is the tranquility that her presence brings me.

I've been clinging to it since our chance meeting when she ran into me in the store. I've tried to fight it. To push away the feeling of needing her to center me. I've failed miserably because I crave it. Desire it. The harmony that she makes me feel is addictive when you've been used to feeling nothing at all. Which blows, because I'm absolutely screwed since she detests me like I have a bad case of chlamydia. I'll own up to the shitty way I've teased her and called her Foster.

Shit. I'd hate me, too.

Glutton for punishment, I hop over the imaginary line between us and stretch my arm out into an unknown territory and catch her by the elbow. My arms wrap around her midriff tightly, folding her in my embrace and I bury my face in her shirt as I smother a sob.

"I got you. Let it out, Crew." Her voice is as soft as rain in the summer.

It's then, for the first time in many, many months, the tears I've kept at bay break and the dam crumbles. I half expect her body to stiffen when sobs erupt from deep within my chest. We're practically strangers. We certainly don't know one another enough to share this…moment. I lay my burdens at her feet, and she picks them up as if they're her own, tossing them on her back and carrying them.

Aurora's strength surprises me as she holds her ground and comforts me like we've known one another our entire lives. Wave after wave of emotion leaves my body. I've never been as vulnerable in front of someone as I am now. Not even in front of my parents, the town's judge, or jury when I was sentenced.

I cry for Matt. My best friend who died too soon.

I cry for myself. For the years of torment this town rained down on me after he died.

I cry because I hate what Trice did that put me in this predicament, and how his actions robbed me of *my* hopes and dreams.

My body shakes violently, and the cradle of her arms tightens. Aurora doesn't say a word as her fingers run across my shoulders. My wall of self-loathing disintegrates under her touch. She draws the pain from me, and for the first time in two years, I don't have to be strong. She's doing it for me, and I know that what we have hasn't even scratched the surface of what we could be together.

I just don't know how I'll be able to convince her of that.

"Aurora," I rasp, her name a plea on my lips. Her hand rises and plunges into my hair, and she tugs, pulling my head back so I can look up at her. I study her face. Each delicate feature is etched with concern for me.

Through the roaring noise in my head, I hear her exhale. "Bones?"

Standing up, I knock a loose leaf off the leg of my jeans and clutch her small frame. Color me shocked that she even lets me hug her again now that my tears have stopped. I want to confide in her more than I want my next breath. She wants the truth, but it's not mine to share. I don't have the words in me to tell her about that night or that I'd rather take the blame than see this town disown my brother like it did me.

"The truth isn't mine to share." I roll my lips to keep any secrets from slipping.

I look down and get lost in the emerald lights of her eyes. A look of sadness passes across her delicate features before she leans forward and shocks me to my core.

Aurora places a tender kiss on the side of my mouth. Surprise siphons all the blood from my face. I don't have time to register what just happened, much less reach out and grab hold of her before she spins and leaves me standing with my mouth ajar.

The innocent brush of her lips sears my soul in a way that only an angel could, and a part of me revels with her display of affection.

There may be hope for me after all.

CHAPTER
FOURTEEN

Torn by conflicting emotions, I hurried to the one place I hoped Crew would be. I couldn't have prepared myself for finding him on his knees, holding on by a tether. Ceaseless questions peaked at the surface of my mind. I wanted to pry into the past and beg for answers as to what took Matt's life. I don't feel comfortable asking Bea or Russell yet. But the story of what took Matt's life keeps me turning at night.

Especially living in his house with shadows dancing all around me. No one has brought him up other than Trice. Secrets hang heavy in the air regarding his passing. It isn't the time or place to demand answers. Not when grief and despair are etched onto the pallor of Crew's face as I near him.

No one in this town owes me anything.

Even answers.

Offering Crew whatever comfort I can, I hold him. In those moments, it felt as if there were a gravitational chain, invisible to our eyes, pulling our souls together. My stomach flutters, and all rational inhibition strays with the wind. I lean forward and place a soft kiss on the corner of his mouth with the brush of my lips.

My heart demanded I do something to sooth his pain. Paired with the bolt of attraction I feel for him, I give into his torment-filled eyes and selfishly choose to be the reason that the anguish there fades. Because as much as I hate to admit it, if even to myself, Crew makes me feel…something.

Wanted.

Desired.

I just feel compelled to help him in his time of need.

Our fading embrace only raises more questions. What do I want from Crew? When was the last time I truly enjoyed kissing a boy?

"I'm sorry. I have to go." I choke on my words as I look into his wide eyes and find myself flushed as I exit the cemetery.

Things have shifted between Crew and me. He was a stranger a couple weeks ago. Someone who rubbed me the wrong way with his annoyingly good looks and smart mouth. Seeing him so…exposed seems to have stirred something deep within the depths of my emotionless heart. A need to fix him and remedy his aching is like an invitation to a challenge. I walk away, my heart thumping like a piston, wondering if his heart is also beating erratically, mirroring mine.

We're two strangers with fragmented hearts, calling out in agony, and linked together by tarnished metal.

Like calls to like.

Guilt clamors in my chest knowing that I fled from Trice and our brothers to go find Crew as my cell phone chimes in my pocket bringing me back down from my kiss-induced bewilderment.

Trice: Did you get lost trying to find the restroom?

Trice: Meet us at the ice-cream store. I'm getting bonus points with the boys ;)

I hurry back to the center of town before typing a reply.

My throat tightens as I try to think of an excuse as to where I've been for so long. I can't possibly admit to Trice that I chased after his brother only to find him, barely holding on by a thread in the cemetery.

Me: Sorry. There was a long line

I hate to bring Trice into this mess. Whatever is going on with his brother is only going to get worse if I drive a wedge further between them. I had asked him to keep an eye on Lonnie while I went to the restroom knowing I didn't have to pee. I fidget with my phone before sliding it into my pocket and approach the ice cream parlor. A wave of unease washes over me at the sight of Trice's infectious smile.

I've never been a girl that guys pine after. Who covets the girl with no money, designer clothes, or even a nice home to hang out at? Here I am, in this peculiar situation with two guys, brothers at that, both throwing grins my way that make my skin sizzle. Truth be told, both Jordan brothers are growing on me, and I know nothing good can come out of that.

I. Am. So. Screwed.

"Lonnie said you liked cookies-and-cream milkshakes so that's what we ordered for you." Trice hands me a cup, looking down at me through Nordic blue eyes.

I swallow my anxiety along with a generous gulp of my shake. "Thank you."

The boys sit at a small, metal table and enjoy their cones while Trice and I lean against the wall behind him. "Lonnie mentioned something that I want to talk to you about." Seriousness paints his face and I shoot Lonnie a side-eye. He's oblivious to anything but the sugary cone he's demolishing. "He said Della called you a hot dog."

"Did he now?"

"Care to elaborate?"

"Not really."

"Do it anyway." His tongue darts out of his mouth as he licks slowly around his cone.

Where did coy Trice go, and who replaced him with a dominant devourer of ice cream? Either my brain is short-circuiting or I'm about to start my period because the amount of hormones racing through my body right now should be illegal.

"She's a bitch," I say. "Her comment isn't even worth repeating."

"Humor me."

My attention focuses on his mouth a moment too long. "Fine. It was something along the lines of, 'I'm like hot dog meat all the parts people don't want' or something. Trust me. Her words hold no value to me. Lonnie shouldn't have brought it up."

"Do you trust me?"

Like any good actress, I draw in a deep breath and answer. "Yes," slips out of my mouth as I hold his eyes with my own.

The truth is, I don't trust anyone.

"She's going to have a conniption fit I. Cannot. Wait." I squeal as Trice places two-hundred dollars' worth of hot dogs in his trunk. Normally I'd be appalled by someone spending money on something so ridiculous, but not today.

Moral compass be damned.

The night sky dances with a blanket of stars shining brightly as Trice gestures me toward the passenger's door. "Get in. We're going to drive to the park and get the skewers in the dogs and then we'll be ready to roll."

Being weak isn't a luxury I've been afforded in my life. The impulse to put Della in her place runs deep. I turn all the feelings of humiliation that she's caused me into rage. At my old school in the city, kids were from all walks of life. No one gave two shits about name-brand clothing or whose house had the biggest television hanging on the wall. Most kids were like Lonnie and I. Barely holding on and forced into adulthood long before nature intended.

As the new girl, I'll admit some of my self-confidence has faltered. With Della's perpetual reminder that I'm an outsider, I got my feelings hurt. I'm big enough to admit it to myself. Not to Trice though. Although he obviously can read between the lines which is why he developed this whole ploy in the first place.

"Thanks for this—" Words lodge in my throat and my eyes widen like a deer in headlights. Crew stalks toward the driver's side door and pounds on Trice's window. We haven't even made it down the driveway.

How is it that I cannot escape him?

Not ready to face him after our kiss, I turn and look out my window. But his steady pounding draws my attention. Crew leans down. His voice is loud enough to penetrate the thick glass. "You do know that mom will kill you for missing the bonfire, right?" He crosses his arms over his puffed-out chest in a visual standoff with his brother. Trice rolls down the window. "This is her favorite part of ending summer and welcoming autumn. She will literally withhold doing your laundry for a month if you ditch her tonight."

A tinge of worry pricks at me. I don't want Mina to have a reason not to like me or to think that the troubled foster kid in the neighborhood is influencing her children in a negative manner. The thought makes me second-guess our excursion. "It's fine, Trice. Just forget it. It's childish anyway." I start to unbuckle my seatbelt.

"What's childish?" Crew raises a thick brow. "Wait, what are y'all doing?" The southern drawl makes me want to laugh out loud. It contradicts his hard veneer and bad boy persona. Hearing his small-town southern twang slip out makes me titter. It's like a different light shines on him and an alternate personality peeks out from behind a curtain. His slip of the tongue may have shown a softer side to him that he's buried with his fondness for heavy metal and lewd comments.

"Nothing. Just go tell mom we had an errand to run. We'll be back before dinner is ready." Annoyance laces Trice's tone. A warning to his brother to piss off.

"An errand, my ass. I want in." Crew opens the rear door and jumps in just as Trice starts to back up.

"You'll be an accomplice, and that will piss off your girlfriend."

Even in the evening's dimming light, I can see a wide grin cross Crew's face. His specialty is pissing people off. I should have known better. White teeth on display, he affirms, "I assume you're referring to Della, who you know damn well isn't my girlfriend."

"My bad. Your fuck buddy."

"Quit being a dick and fill me in on this little caper." Rubbing his hands together feverishly, his dark eyes narrow on me. "I'm always down to ruin someone's day."

"Wouldn't I know it." Trice rolls his eyes and scrubs a hand over his face before we hit the main road. We both reach for the volume button at the same time to turn up the radio.

"Sorry," my hand retreats. He gives me one of his panty-dropping smiles and I'm once again ambushed by a passing feeling, confusion. I glance up, looking heavenward, pleading for lightening to strike and put me out of my misery.

Mina and Shawn must have super DNA or something to have made not one, but two guys who make my heart do that stupid pitter-patter thing. Even Aiden is so stinking adorable. I know in a few short years he'll be breaking hearts and walking in his big brothers' footsteps.

There's an uneven rhythm to my breathing when I look up into the rearview mirror and find Crew staring at me. Our eyes connect and I wish I could read the meaning behind his pointed gaze. Their murky depths, as they look fixedly at me, have yet to be explored. I'm fearful I might get lost in them and forget which way is up if I gaze at him any longer. My eyes drop downward, breaking the spell. The next time I glance in the mirror, Crew is busy on his phone. It's a brief relief.

A short distance later, we find a spot and park on the side of the road in another subdivision. The night's air is breezy and a reminder that autumn is near. "Do you want a sweatshirt?" Trice asks as we move toward his trunk.

"I'm good. Thanks, though." I do something out of character for me and playfully nudge Trice, which causes a groan of unease to come from Crew who is staring at us. I ignore him.

Trice quickly fills his brother in on our plan and then we find a comfortable silence as we race to put the hot dogs on the skewers.

"She's going to be pissed." Crew exhales forcefully.

"She deserves it for what she said to Rory. Trust me dude." Trice nudges me with his shoulder as we stand at his trunk with our arsenal in front of us.

"What happened?"

I huff. I'm already mortified that Crew chose to embark on this prank with us. "I'm not rehashing it again. *CliffsNotes* version is she's a terrible human being and deserves to be put in her place. Everyone in this town either worships the ground she walks on or is too afraid to stand up to her." The authority in my voice is invigorating. "She deserves to be knocked down a few notches or twenty."

He pats the trunk of the car. "Okay."

"Okay. That's all you have to say. You agree with all that?"

"I said okay, didn't I?"

"Don't punk out on us just because you know shit will go viral when she sees her yard. Her dad will put out a bounty on our heads if we get caught." Trice's stooped posture has me second guessing our prank. I cannot get in trouble. A mark on my record won't bode well for my attempt to adopt Lonnie after my birthday.

Crew chuckles. "Oh, I'm not punking out. I'm just thinking about how she does this thing with her tongue and how I'll miss that little party trick if she learns that I helped you two with this prank."

Instant regret that I kissed him washes over me. I don't give in to his gloating, though, and act like his remark doesn't bother me. "Let's get back on track, fellas. You can go down memory lane with your little minx later." I shove a black piece of fabric at Crew's chest.

"And we're not going to get caught, Trice." I mumble with false bravado. "Let's go. I'm ready to teach her a lesson."

Showing us just how much of a team player he is, Crew shoots Della a text message to see if she's home. His cell phone buzzes almost an instant after he texts her.

Desperate much.

"She's at a friend's house. She said her parents are out of town. So that gives us about an hour if I'm guessing."

If I thought that Bea and Russell's house was massive, Della's could eat it twice over and still have room for dessert. Seriously. No wonder she's a bitch. She probably has a butler.

We quickly go about with our little prank, and before I know it, we're erupting with laughter as we climb back into Trice's car and speed away from Della's house. The three of us had worked in unison silently placing hundreds of skewered hot dogs all throughout Della's front yard. I feel an odd satisfaction. Not only did both Jordan brothers go out on a limb for me, but they also did it voluntarily. Being part of a team is a feeling I'm not used to. Or the mere fact that both brothers offered to defend my honor so easily is swoonworthy. Despite warning bells banging loudly in my head, my heart swells.

We pull back into the Jordan's driveway, and we all exhale

in unison. Littering hundreds of hot dogs in someone's yard was hard work. My stomach growls.

"Boiled or grilled hotdogs?" I look over my shoulder to see Crew waiting for my answer. Both of his hands are folded behind his head. He looks relaxed which is something I'm not used to from him.

"I don't know. Boiled, I guess."

He gags. "You were a solid ten. That knocked you down at least two points. Boiled hot dog water is the grossest thing in the world. Trice, do you remember when mom used to volunteer at the concession stands for my games. I remember she had to fill up the Crockpot several times to prevent the dogs from sticking to the bottom. I want to hurl just thinking about that nasty water."

"She still does that, idiot. Just because you went to college doesn't mean the rest of us aren't still here. Together. Mourning." There goes our happy little trio from this evening. Trice opens his door first. "I'm going to let mom know we're back."

The hot and cold between them is enough to cause a tornado. Whatever damage was done to their relationship runs deep. I know beyond a shadow of a doubt that I cannot get in the middle of their drama. Trice and I are friends. He's the first person who has made me feel like this town may not be so bad for the next several months. He's made being the new girl tolerable. I wouldn't consider Crew a friend. He's more like an acquaintance, that I kissed and as much as I tell myself he's trouble, I find myself longing to be around him.

"Aurora." Crew took my threat seriously about no longer calling me Foster. I swivel in order to face him in the back seat. "This is strange."

"What is? The fact that you two could get along long enough for us to spread dozens of hot dogs on your girlfriend's lawn because she's a raging bitch?" I ask, confused.

"I could keep correcting you both, but why waste my breath." He flings the door open with a flick of his wrist. The way he glares causes my palms to twitch. "I'm not the boyfriend type. Della is well aware of that fact, but if I were, I'd be a damn good one."

I stiffen, frozen by his outpouring of thoughts.

"You could give me the benefit of the doubt. I'm not a complete douche bag. Contrary to whatever nonsense I'm sure Trice has told you, I'm a decent guy and a good friend. You'd know that if you didn't keep pushing me away." He goes to climb out of the backseat.

"Wait." I chew on my bottom lip as he halts his movement. "Look, I don't really know you other than things I've heard, and I can admit to that being shitty. I shouldn't have allowed others' opinions to paint an image of you. What I can judge is someone willingly dating, *not-dating,* whatever you and Della are. She's awful, and if that's the type of girls you're into, then—"

"Then what?" There is a ravenous hunger in his eyes as he speaks. "Haven't you ever found solace in someone just because being with anyone, even if they weren't a good fit for you, was better than being alone? Sometimes the loneliness is too hard to bear. Finding any reprieve is better than the solitude I've endured. I'll admit to being a dick and using someone—Della—if you admit that we're not mortal enemies and more alike than you want to admit." His hand stakes a claim on the back of my headrest.

I dare not move and lean into its warmth. Although my body relished his touch when he held me and sobbed into my shirt at the cemetery, I can't keep lowering my guard with him. Letting someone in fully would be detrimental. That much I know in the depth of my soul.

"Trice isn't your enemy either. I'm not sure what the bad blood is about. But you're his brother. You both should be better role models for Aiden."

"This isn't about Trice. He's a big boy and can deal with his feelings however he sees fit. This is about you and me. I'm sorry for calling you Foster. I was a jerk. For what it's worth, I've learned my lesson. I'm not your nemesis either, and you should know that I don't back down easily."

"What do you want me to say right now?" I hold in a shaky breath as I wait for his response.

"I just want you to let me get to know you. I don't think that's asking too much." His gaze and honesty make me squirm. Under his scrutiny, I feel naked and exposed. I don't like the feeling of being out of control, and I certainly don't like that Crew makes me feel that way. Trice has told me countless stories of his brothers' debauchery that left me feeling dirty and my skin crawling. Not to mention his admission about him and Della hooking up.

In my mind, I didn't believe Crew had any redeeming qualities until we shared that moment in the cemetery. Tonight, he gained a couple points in my book when he helped us put his 'non-girlfriend' in her place by planting hot dogs in her yard.

I don't trust myself to speak as his walnut eyes watch me with a critical squint. My mouth might slip up and say something along the lines of "Kiss me stupid." The thought of thawing toward him has me putting up my defenses tenfold.

I do the only sensible thing I can muster up the strength to do. I fling open my door and step out into the night's cool air offering a small truth before I walk away from him again. "It's asking more than I'm able to offer. I'm sorry."

My exit is almost as hasty as pouring a bucket of water over my head like a baptism of common sense.

CHAPTER
FIFTEEN

CREW

Rejection isn't something I'm used to. Before the accident, I never gave a shit about what people thought of me. After the accident, the town's opinion sent me into a deep spiral and almost buried me whole. My only goal was to do my time and leave for college. Putting distance between myself and those who wished me to be prosecuted was the best solution I could think of at the time.

Then Aurora ran into me and jump-started my heart. Her low opinion of me matters more than it should. It's disturbing and addicting. I want to show her that I'm not the scumbag she believes me to be. I don't need to prove my worth to anyone, but she makes me want to.

The town's judgment of me is nothing but a distant memory. The truth will one day be revealed and the whole story will come out. Isn't that how life works? I don't need to plead my case. I no longer have the need to justify the events of that night. Now, I just want this defiant girl to see *me*. The real Crew. The guy who laughed and joked, played football, enjoyed making music, and relished life before the death of his best friend. Not the unfeeling version that I've hidden behind or the miscreant the town has labeled me as.

I want to breathe her in like she's the air I desperately need to expand my lungs. I'm drowning in her existence, and I'd rather die from lack of oxygen or being stampeded by a thousand horses than to be stuck in the friend zone with her.

My phone chimes in my hand while I'm still in the back-seat of Trice's car.

Della: WTF!! (Picture of her front yard)

Me: Who did you piss off?

A shit-eating grin spreads across my face. I debate taking a screenshot of Della's text and forwarding it to Aurora.

Della: The Foster bitch! It had to have been her. I'm going to make her wish she never moved here.

I step out of the car and shove my phone into my pocket. Della has another thing coming if she thinks there will be any retaliation against Aurora.

I'll see to it myself.

A month passes in a blur, and I'm bummed to admit that I haven't seen Aurora as much as I'd like to. Usually, our paths cross at church on Sundays when I come back to town, or when I visit my parents and Aiden and she's there, hanging out with Trice. I feel like we made a step in the right direction, only to take ten steps backward. She's so hard to read. Except, on the rare occasion when she lets her guard down and does talk to me, it's usually laced with sarcasm. It's like our own secret language. She might be trying to snub me, but her sharp tongue and comebacks let me know that she enjoys our teasing just as much as I do.

Our banter knows no bounds, and that gives me hope that

one day I'll be able to hold a relatively civil conversation with her.

Luck is on my side this week because I happened to be in town for a dentist appointment that's scheduled for late afternoon. When I opened the door and saw mom in the kitchen making a snack tray, she announced that Trice had tested positive for strep throat and can't go to school all week. Knowing that this is a perfect opportunity to see Aurora, I ask her to contact Bea and tell her that I'll pick Aurora up for school today, so she doesn't have to worry about her getting there since Trice isn't going and beg my mom to ask Bea not to tell Aurora about the change in driver. I can tell by her smirk that my mom sees through my sudden friendliness and knows my real intentions. I'm not ashamed to admit that Trice's ailment might just be the best thing that's happened to me all month.

Snatching Trice's car keys off the table in the foyer, I decide to drive his car instead of mine, so Aurora doesn't refuse to come outside altogether when she realizes it's me playing chauffeur. His engine rumbles as I slide the gear into drive and glance up to his window just as the outline of Trice's body and the sight of his fist pounding on the window makes me smile wider than I have in a while. Pissing him off is by far my favorite pastime.

With a quick toot of the horn, I lower my body in the driver's seat. Aurora walks out the front door in her school uniform and I instantly regret my decision to pick her up. Just the sight of her in the school's skirt has me chastising myself for my unadulterated thoughts. The door swings open and she climbs in without a glance in my direction. As soon as the door shuts, I hit the lock button. "Good morning, beautiful."

Aurora's head spins my way like it's on a swivel. "Is this a joke or something? Where's Trice?"

"He's indisposed. I'm the superior Jordan anyway. By age,

looks, and sense of humor. Trust me, you're leveling up by getting me to play chauffeur."

"More like bothersome." She says as her hair blows about.

I let off the pedal in the middle of the street, Trice's car coming to an abrupt stop. "I guess you could walk to school from here."

"My tolerance for bullshit is extremely low today. Just go. I don't feel like walking."

I can't help but notice her profile as she stares out the front window and the way her thick crop of golden hair covers her shoulders. Add that to the tantalizing scent that wafts off her, and I may need to readjust myself before we even get out of the subdivision. "Seriously, if you want to walk and free yourself from my company, I'll gladly pull over."

As she turns in her seat, her plaid skirt rides up, exposing the softness of her thigh. "I don't want to walk. Sorry, I'm not a morning person. I didn't have time to get a cup of coffee because I hit snooze too many times, and well, that should say enough right there."

"Fair enough." I nod and turn in the opposite direction of her high school.

"You didn't graduate that long ago to have forgotten that the school is that way, did you?"

I chuckle. "I'm getting you some coffee first. I don't want the next person who tries to open a door for you, or let you cut the line in the ladies' room at school to get their heads chewed off for trying to do something polite. If I don't get you caffeinated, I could be at fault."

Aurora's features become more animated at the mention of coffee, and I can see her trying to suppress a giggle. "For what it's worth, I truly am sorry for being a bitch just now. I hate that Trice is sick, but I am thankful for the ride. I can't wait to get my driver's license."

"Why haven't you at least gotten your permit? You're old enough for that." A shadow of discontent crosses her face, and I want to swallow my words after I've said them. We pull into the drive-thru at the coffee shop and I glance at Aurora asking for her order. Thank goodness she isn't one of those girls whose coffee order is a mile long. She's simple and requests a mocha. Nothing extra and nothing special like pasture-free soy milk or whatever those highfalutin coffee snobs say.

We sit in a peaceful silence other than the low hum of the radio providing some background noise until we get to the window, and she reaches for her bag. "My treat." I slide my wallet out of my back pocket.

"Why are you being so kind to me?" her tone is rueful.

"Thank you," I acknowledge the barista in the window and then place my drink in the cup holder before offering Aurora hers and driving off. I tilt my head to the side, just as she takes a sip of her hot beverage. "I'm a nice guy. You just haven't given me the opportunity to show you."

"If you show up with coffee every time I see you, you'll have my undivided attention. Coffee is my love language."

I store the information for the way to her heart in a file under "Things that make her happy."

"Noted," I say.

The drive back to her school is filled with music satisfying the gaps in our conversation. She confesses that this is only the second time she's had coffee that wasn't from a pot in the kitchen and tells me that Bea bought her first-ever mocha when they went school shopping. I guess stopping for coffee isn't something you do when you're a foster kid. My mom has told me horror stories from some of her clients who have deep-rooted trauma from their foster care experiences. Looking at Aurora, you'd never guess she's in the system. She's so beautiful, it's almost painful. I can't imagine her having to fend for herself. It makes me want to hunt down anyone who has ever wronged her just thinking about the hardships she's faced before moving in with Russell and Bea.

"Thank you for the ride and for the coffee," she says as I pull into the drop-off line.

"Same time tomorrow."

"I'll find another ride. Thanks though."

Exasperation bunches my brows. She doesn't make things easy. "I said, same time tomorrow, Aurora. It wasn't a question. I'll come prepared with coffee now that I know how you like it."

"Deal." She offers a tentative smile before climbing out of the car and shutting the door behind her without as much as a goodbye.

***

I've been sleeping at my parents at night, so I'll already be in town and able to drive Aurora to school. The week flies by and our time together comes to an end on Friday. This week has been the best I've had in a long while. Her presence is comforting. Even though we don't talk much during our short rides together, I can feel her warming toward me as the days pass. Trice is feeling better, sadly, and is no longer contagious and is up and out the door before I even finish brushing my teeth.

I find my mom standing in the kitchen. "He beat you to it today."

"I'm keeping him on his toes by giving him the impression that I can't always win." I wink in her direction as she hovers over the stove cracking an egg.

"You know she asked Bea and I if she could clean up the clubhouse for the boys." My mom tells me that they agreed without hesitation and that they're both thankful that the younger kids will get some use out of the space.

"That's cool."

It pained me to think about someone distorting the space as we left it. As Matt did. It should have been Trice and I cleaning it up. Neither of us should have neglected the space, and we're both too proud and stubborn to admit it. Aurora's gesture is sweet and shows that there is more to her than her hard exterior leads people to believe. She said she wanted a space for Lonnie and Aiden to hang out and explore, my mom adds.

Aurora's adoration for her foster brother is obvious. It's endearing, and it reminds me that I've been a flake with my own little brother since the accident. Mom said Aiden was hesitant to go into the clubhouse because he knows what it meant to Trice and me. It pains me to think about how our decisions have affected him.

<hr>

Time seems to fly, and before I know it, it's the end of October.

Halloween used to be the holiday that Trice, Matt, and I looked forward to every year. Our costumes were always in sync, and we'd win the coveted "Most Original" award year after year. This year is different. Trice and I aren't on speaking terms since he's trying to woo my girl. And my girl doesn't even care that I exist.

This year's Halloween festivities might be a wash.

Della's parents always allow her to host a big bash at their house, and this year is no different. She hasn't slandered Aurora's name anymore, to me at least. Not that I've been around her much either. Trying to distance myself from her and nip in the bud the public claim she thinks she has on me has been part of my big scheme to get Aurora to notice me. She thinks there's something more between Della and me even though I admitted it was just sexual. There were no feelings involved. Believing there was more was probably instilled in her by my dickhead of a brother. If I'm going to be honest and show her I'm not some scumbag who lets his hormones think for him, I need to stop the occasional hookup between Della and me. For real. Which makes tonight's event that much more awkward since it's in Della's lair.

I climb in my car leaving Dean's tattoo studio, Ink's Pawn. His wife, Belle, is a professional makeup artist and graciously brought my idea to life. Black and white paint curves over my skin in expert strokes, etched like velvet tight against a cushion. Belle created a masterpiece of evil and deceit. I look the part with black pants, a long black sleeve T-shirt and Doc Martens. If Aurora thinks I'm a hellion, at least I resemble one now too.

Coming to terms with having to play dirty against my brother settled in my gut the moment I saw Trice slide his football jersey over Aurora's blonde head the other day. Jealousy surged through my veins, like a drug being injected into my bloodstream. Tonight, I will make my intentions for her clear.

CHAPTER
SIXTEEN

RORY

grit my teeth and glare at Andrea in the bathroom mirror. She lets out a laugh that's deep and cunning, and I regret letting her talk me into going to this stupid party.

Her fingers sweep my hair out of my face and pin it to the side. She examines my bare face before going to town, plucking and priming like she's a licensed esthetician.

Bea has been encouraging Lonnie and me to branch out and make friends. She thinks Trice shouldn't be my only comrade here. Trust doesn't come easy for me, but when Andrea texted me and asked to hang out, I decided to embrace her offer after declining her several times previously.

She's persistent, I'll give her that. I am wary, though, since she runs in the same circle as Della. The last thing I want to do is get blindsided and look like a fool. We met for coffee one Saturday afternoon, and she seemed sincere about wanting to be friends.

Our second "friend date" consisted of going to the mall. Russell gave me money after helping him rearrange the living room furniture to accommodate Lonnie's soccer net since it's getting too cold for him to play outside. I suggested we set it up in their three-car garage, but he claimed it was still too cold out there and he didn't mind having Bea's aesthetic compromised to accommodate the next David Beckham.

While we were shopping, Andrea confessed that she isn't a huge fan of Della and only hung out with her because she'd had a crush on Matt since elementary school. She even admitted to a secret kiss they shared weeks before he passed as we shared a pretzel in the food court. "He started something we didn't get the chance to finish," she'd said as her lips trembled.

"I'm really sorry for your loss," I'd told her. "I can't imagine going through something like that. Matt would have been lucky to call you his."

While we sat in the food court that day, she talked about the town, filling me in on the local gossip and school drama until I pressed her for information about Matt's death. Her lips sealed quicker than a vault during a robbery. It seems that the Greenwells and Jordans aren't the only ones in this town that have a secret under lock and key.

I stare at the wall above my bathroom mirror while Andrea works her magic. The anticipation of tonight claws at my stomach. I'm not a fan of huge crowds, and I'm certainly not a fan of Della Astor. Being coerced into attending her Halloween party makes me want to turn my head and hurl into the toilet beside me. The only thing that keeps me from spilling my guts is the death grip Andrea has on my chin as she dabs at my face with a little pink sponge.

"You look amazing! Trice is going to blow his load when he sees you!"

"We're *just* friends, for the last time," I scoff before taking in the person staring back at me in the mirror. My reflection jars me. The soft palette she used on my skin makes it appear flawless, like a magic potion was applied to my cheeks and eliminated any hint of imperfections. My eyes are hooded and smokey. I feel a sense of power and fearlessness. "Wow," spills over my lips. My hair is slicked back and styled into a high ponytail with strands woven around the tie. Who knew Andrea was a ponytail sorcerer?

She claps enthusiastically. "Wow is right. Move over and let me work some magic on myself. You can't be the only one leaving men with hard-ons tonight."

Less than an hour later, Bea joins our glam session and not so subtly reminds us that we're not of age to drink legally, but if that were to happen, we should never take an open container from anyone. She also prattles on about sex before marriage. No one has ever cared about my well-being before, so her talk is both exasperating and endearing. We agree to be responsible, and I give Lonnie a short hug on my way out the door.

"What are you supposed to be dressed up as?" He frowns.

"Honestly, buddy, I'm not sure." I'm wearing cut-off shorts with rips on each side, fishnet leggings we picked up at the mall, and Trice's football jersey. It's not really a costume, but Andrea reminded me that Halloween was the one time of year that girls could look like hookers without being one, so I went with this strange get-up.

"You look weird." I wince at his brutal honesty. "But your face looks pretty. I've never seen you look so…spicy."

"Thank you. I will take your compliment and hold it all night." I pinch his cheek. "Now, go get yourself ready. I saw some Trick-or-Treaters already down the street from my bedroom window. You're going to make an incredible Captain Hook, and I expect you to get tons of candy for me to look through tonight."

We head toward Andrea's Jeep with only my phone tucked in my back pocket and courage on my sleeve. Too bad the liquid kind was deemed prohibited by Bea, although what she doesn't know won't hurt her.

A short drive later and Andrea parks her vehicle on the

side of the road. Cars already line the sides of the road and fill the driveway. From what Andrea has told me, Della's parents are horse racing people, and in this area that means they're practically royalty. Hence why her family is probably richer than Jeff Bezos. I grab my phone and shoot a message to Trice letting him know that we've arrived. He wanted to bring us, but I told him no, since I wanted some of my own independence.

People already have the wrong idea about us and there has been constant buzz at school that we're dating. That could be why Della has been so lax toward me. She probably thinks I chose a Jordan brother after all, eliminating any competition that stood in her way from getting what she wanted—Crew Jordan.

His name stirs a feeling deep within my gut that I've tried to fight. He's like a bad dream that you can't wake up from. The type of dream where throughout the day you keep trying to piece it back together like a puzzle to make sense of all of it. Then you dread going back to sleep the next night, afraid you'll dream the same dream. He's my own version of Freddy Krueger, except his face is anything but frightening, and I'm not running from him in my dreams. I'm running toward him.

He leaves me frightened, nonetheless, and feeling out of control.

I hope he's not here. He made it clear he and Della weren't dating the last time I really talked to him. I'm not sure what would have changed, unless he was a big, fat liar. Which is most likely the case.

Why would he even want to hang out with a bunch of high schoolers? Certainly, the college he attends has better parties than what we're about to walk into, where the alcohol doesn't have to be snuck in.

Andrea hands me a red solo cup and I take it hesitantly. She doesn't know about my plan to adopt Lonnie and I don't want underage drinking on my record when a judge reviews my case. "Don't worry, Della's parents basically have the town in their pockets. When you're as filthy rich as her dad, you're pretty much untouchable. No one is busting up this party tonight."

The contents are questionable, but after she reassures me, I decided to live a little on edge and dare I say, act like a normal teenager. I take a gulp and scan the crowded living room taking in the array of costumes. From vampires, playboy bunnies, and serial killers to those ridiculous blow-up dinosaur suits the room is jampacked with our classmates. I don't immediately see Trice which causes a ball of anxiety to form in my stomach. Other than his friends that have embraced me and started to become my friends, I don't know a soul here.

"The doorman is evidently letting in anyone who knocks." Della snarls.

She's already taunting me, and we haven't even been here five minutes. I half expected her to be wearing a witch costume. "Apparently so," I say. "After all, it's Halloween. I'm dressed up as someone who can stand to be around you. Can't you tell?"

Andrea clears her throat next to us suppressing a laugh.

"I'll have to remove you from the premises if you piss me off," Della responds. "I suggest you steer clear of me the rest of the night."

"Don't threaten me with a good time." Sarcasm laces my tone as I take a slow sip from my drink. An arm slings over the back of my neck and shoulder.

"Can we pretend to get along for one night, ladies?" Trice saves the day. We stand in unison as Della storms away. "We should have worn hot dog costumes."

"You're so, so wrong for that! I love it." I squeal as he

spins me around and does a once over of my ensemble. It's not like me to entertain going to parties, much less mold into the role of a normal high school student. Nothing about my life or living situation is ordinary. Somehow, Trice's friendship has helped me loosen up a little to the idea of acting my age and letting the adults in our lives do the worrying for once.

Lonnie and I are in the most stable home either of us have ever lived in. The refrigerator is always stocked, we have clean clothes, and we haven't taken a cold shower since we arrived at the Greenwells. Things could always be worse. They have been worse. I think back on our social worker's words when she dropped us off. Miranda was right, although I hate to admit it.

Russell and Bea *are* decent people.

"Let's go find a seat downstairs." Trice ushers Andrea and I down into the basement.

As we near the bottom landing, my eyes rake over tables of food and beverages. "This is crazy. I've been to a couple parties in the city. None like this I can assure you. Is that a Chick-Fil-A buffet?"

"Wait until you see the sorbet station." Trice replies.

"You know when men have small man syndrome?" Andrea asks. "I think Della has the female version. God should have made her flat-chested as punishment."

"Cheers to that." I smile and we all clink the rim of our cups in unison.

"Sit down, ladies. I think I heard someone say we're getting ready to play spin the bottle." Trice pats the empty seat next to him.

"What are we twelve?" The thought of sitting around in a circle at our age is embarrassing.

Andrea cuts in. "It's not like normal spin the bottle. One person starts the spin. The caveat is that the spinner is blindfolded. So, whoever the bottle lands on has to kiss the spinner, and then the spinner rates his or her kissing abilities in front of everyone. It's completely anonymous."

"A couple years ago it got a little heated when Mallory rated her boyfriend a three. He was so pissed. I think he broke a lamp and then left." Trice winces at the memory. "I'm a solid eight. I think," he jokes.

"Do you ever reveal who kissed you?" I ask my attention focused on the cup in my hand. "Like when the game is over? Do we just spin and kiss in silence?"

"Calm down, I got you." Trice says. His promise doesn't help as a wave of dread sweeps over me.

"If I wanted to kiss anyone at this party, I would. No one needs a game to do that unless they don't have balls. Plus, I don't just go around kissing people for fun." I admit and steal a glance at Trice. He opens them like he wants to say something. Perhaps to defend himself. Before he can, I continue. "You apparently do though. How many years have you guys been playing this petty game?"

"Too many to count," Andrea tips her cup back. "I'm empty. Save my seat."

A couple minutes pass, and Andrea hasn't returned. My palms start to sweat when Della announces we're getting ready to play. "Everyone spread apart and give people some space to move around. You know how wild this game can get," she announces.

I want to get up and go back upstairs. It didn't look like any childish games were going on up there. The small circle Trice is making on my forearm keeps me held in place. His touch is harmless, friendly even. Nothing remotely flirtatious.

Pulling out my phone from my back pocket, I shoot a text to Andrea pleading for her to hurry up. I debate on going to find her myself and glance over my shoulder only to find a guy with a skeleton painted on his face watching me intently. At first, I don't recognize who it is. But when our eyes lock, his maple-colored irises send a memo straight to my brain.

Crew stalks toward the couch. The swagger with each step is intoxicating and it's not due to the contents of my drink. The familiar shiver of awareness of his proximity engulfs me. I'm so lost in my own world that I don't even hear my phone chime in my hand. I bite the inside of my cheek and glance away from the hold his eyes have on me and try to play it cool, although my insides are boiling.

The cushion next to me dips down. "Is this seat taken?"

"If it were, would you care?" My eyes dart to his. "Don't answer that."

Crew lets out a laugh that catches me off guard. Even with the intensity of his gaze, his laugh seems genuine in a way that I haven't noticed before.

"Honestly, though, Andrea was sitting there."

"How about I just save it for her then?"

"That's very chivalrous of you."

"That I am." His voice is deep and low, and the admission sends a shiver down my backbone.

"Nice of you to join us, Crew. To what do we owe this pleasure?" Della's lips smack, exasperation seeping from her tone.

"I haven't missed a Halloween party yet. Why would I start now?"

"I didn't think you were coming. You never texted me back." She reaches forward from her seat on the coffee table to touch his arm, but he jerks it away. No one else seems to notice, but I do as I watch their exchange out of the corner of my eye. She shakes his dismissal off and begins gathering people around while explaining the gist of the game. I'm thankful that Trice already filled me in.

"I'll spin first since it's my party." Della's pearly white teeth hide behind a sneer before she slides a black eye mask over her face. I wait and see how this little game will play out.

Whistles and amusement erupt from the small crowd gathered in a circle as the bottle comes to a halt on Geoff. He's a gentle giant from what I've observed at lunch. He's also in my English Lit class which is also amusing considering I wouldn't peg him for a literature lover. Everyone around me grows silent. Not even Della makes a peep. Chewing my bottom lip, I look to my left to find Crew, his thumb sliding on his phone, not caring that his ex-lover is going to be kissed by someone else right in front of him.

I guess he wasn't lying when he said he and Della were no longer a thing.

Geoff looks reluctant, stealing his own glimpse at Crew who looks up just in time to offer a shrug of his shoulders. That's all it takes for Geoff to get off his seat on the recliner and make his way to where Della is sitting nestled between two of her friends. The kiss isn't passionate, but also isn't hurried. It lingers before a smacking sound fills the silence and everyone cheers. Before Della removes her mask, she announces, "seven" to the room. Geoff seems okay with her rating and sits down, while the girl next to Della puts on the mask and takes her spin.

What an odd game.

The faint buzz of my phone reminds me to check on Andrea. I scroll to my messages and see she texted minutes ago saying that she's upstairs chatting with someone and to play without her. I want to protest and whine that she left me down here, sandwiched between the Jordan brothers, but for the life of me, I can't. I'm too eager to know if my spin will land on either of them.

When it's Trice's turn to spin, I feel his hand land on my knee cap. He gives it a gentle squeeze and then slides the mask over his cobalt eyes. The blonde spikes of hair on his head are matted down on the sides from the strings of the mask. He looks silly and carefree. Nerves inch up my spine with the flip of his wrist. The bottle does a three-sixty and then lands on the devils' daughter.

Della.

Half in dread, half in anxiety, I turn to look away. I don't want to see her prance over to him with her long, slender legs and lay her lips on his. There isn't a single ember of anything romantic happening between us, but I can't mask the feeling of her lips having kissed not only Crew's devious mouth but also Trice's. It sends my thoughts into a frenzy for some reason. I settle back into the deep, tawny cushions while my fingers rub at the holes in my tights.

I don't see the kiss, but I know it's happened when people start cheering.

I want to punch Della once she opens her mouth. "Eight," she rates Trice. "Now I know what both brothers taste like."

"It's supposed to be anonymous," someone declares.

"Since it's my party, I guess I make the rules." She glares at me. "Your turn, Foster."

"That's enough, Della." I turn to find Crew seething. "It's not cute to belittle someone," he adds. I go to stand as a firm hand clamps around my wrist and pulls me back down.

"That's rich coming from you," she fails to heed his warning.

"Ignore her. I am. Sit and spin." Crew gives me a level look. "You can punch her lights out sometime when there aren't as many witnesses as there are right now."

Trice chimes in. "It's just a game." He nudges my shoulder, trying to convince me not to let her get to me.

Just what I need. Two cheerleaders from the same family.

I blow out a breath and then take the blindfold from Trice's hand and slide it on my head. I don't immediately spin the bottle. The darkness hasn't always been a friendly place for me. Shaking off my nerves, I muster all the courage I can and reach forward to spin the bottle. The guys are right. I won't allow Della to get in my head more than she already is. Hearing a few snickers, my stomach drops to my feet like that ride where people sit around in a circle, and it lifts you into the sky and without warning, drops with record speed.

That's how I feel. Disoriented and afraid to freefall into the abyss.

I place both of my hands under each leg and wait for a stranger's mouth to claim mine. The sound of commotion ensuing followed by the racket of hoots and hollers bouncing off the basement walls as what I assume is a quarrel erupting has me regretting playing this game. I grip the mask and give it a gently tug to see what is going on. A warm pair of lips meet mine. My hand becomes frozen on the string of the mask, and I'm taken off guard for a split second by the warmth that radiates from my lips down my spine. A hand snakes around my head and holds me in place, pushing my face closer to his.

At least I assume it's a guy kissing me.

Fuck.

No one mentioned what would happen if a girl spun, and the bottle landed on another female. Thoughts abandon me in a swirl of sensations as a tongue explores the recesses of my mouth with urgency laced with every sweep. The kiss is hard as if my kisser is searching for an answer to an unspoken question. His lips pull away, their absence leaves my mouth burning with fire that only he can extinguish.

"You broke the rules, Crew. You need to leave." A familiar voice cuts through the moment my mystery kisser and I are sharing. "Just get out!"

I quiver as a tender grip tilts my head upward and a pair of lips dust my forehead with a chaste kiss as if it's a goodbye without words. I'm left sitting wondering what the hell just happened. With hesitation, I remove my mask, not wanting to learn what just transpired. "Wha—what happened?"

"Don't play dumb. It's not a good look," Della stands and stalks away.

Andrea appears standing at the end of the couch confusion written on her face. "What did I miss?"

I feel like I've been knocked on my ass. My body jolts as I

look to each side of me only to find both Trice's and Crew's seats vacant. "Geoff, what happened?" I plead.

"Well, it looks like you're in a pickle, my friend. Even Della never messed with both of their hearts." He states with heavy irony laced in his tone. "You see, the bottle landed on Trice, but that's not who ended up kissing ya."

Swallowing, I know exactly who kissed me, but I need to hear him say it. "Who was it?"

Geoff grunts. "I think you know who it was by that look on your face." He takes a swig from his cup. "You're playing with fire, new girl. Those boys already lost enough. Don't be taking something from one of them you can't give back."

Misunderstanding clouds my features as I ask, "What would I take from one of them?"

"It looks like you already stole both their hearts considering the way they looked like they were about to kill each other. You need to give one back, if you ask me."

"Let me drive you home." Andrea hooks her arm through mine. "I'll even stop and get you something greasy to soothe your sorrows, because you are in a predicament that even I don't envy."

CHAPTER
SEVENTEEN

CREW

Jitters claim my body as I peel out of Della's driveway. The glum face Trice held when I lifted off the cushion and cut in front of him stealing his turn to kiss Aurora will forever be ingrained in my mind.

It was a dick move.

I'll admit it.

I can also admit that it was so, so worth it.

Aurora tastes like raspberries, and I will relish the way her lips nipped so eagerly at mine and invited me in until I take my last breath.

Almost like it's on autopilot, my car pulls into the cemetery's parking lot. I know I should head back to campus. I can probably even make it to another party if I hurry. I'd like nothing more than to drink away the problems I started tonight before the truth surfaces on the horizon tomorrow. Too bad drinking isn't my coping mechanism anymore and the tattoo studio is closed. That leaves me in the one place in town that is always open. I'm wearing all black clothing and creeping around in a cemetery on Halloween night.

What a cliché.

Truth be told, the only place I want to be in this town is close to the one person who makes me feel anything. After our lips parted, I could feel how desperate Aurora's mouth was to find mine again. Her pleasure radiated outward and if we weren't in a room full of her classmates, I would have devoured her. I don't even care that she's a senior and not eighteen yet. I'd never pressure her into doing anything she was uncomfortable with anyway. I would, however, like to know what she'd rate our kiss.

After exiting my car, I trudge through the graveyard toward the only real friend I've ever had. He's an expert listener, even in his afterlife.

"Hey man." I stoop down and rest my hand on top of his headstone. "Halloween isn't the same without you. What an evening tonight ended up being. Trice probably despises me."

I fill Matt in on the evening and although he's no longer here on earth, I swear I can hear him chastising me for pulling such a juvenile stunt. *"Who aids and abets the obliteration of their own brothers love life?"* Guilt spoils my decent mood. I nod as I pretend to hear him scolding me when I'm not actively listening.

The truth is, Aurora and I had our meet-cute when the end of summer brought her to town, and we collided quite literally. Yeah, I know what a damn meet-cute is. Della used to gush about them in all those rom-com books that fill her reading app. It just so happens that it doesn't only happen in novels. It happened in real life.

To me.

Someone who doesn't deserve happiness but is hanging onto a thread of hope and optimism that Aurora will be mine one day.

I'm not even home an hour before Trice staggers in through our walkout basement door. Silence stretches between us as vast as an ocean. I've been so numb since the accident that we drifted apart. Matt was our common ground. Without him, there isn't a relationship between Trice and me to salvage.

We've always been opposites. In looks and demeanor. His hair is icy and mine is dark. He's the life of the party and a people-person to his core. Hell, he'd strike up a conversation with a homeless man on the street corner and probably invite him to a bonfire or something. Trice is the spitting image of our mom. Put a blonde wig on him and paint his lips red, and he would be Mina Jordan.

Honestly, I don't really resemble anyone in my family. Aside from following in my dad's glory days of playing football, I feel like an outcast most of the time. I used to joke when Trice was younger and tell him that he was the milkman's baby and mom had cheated on dad. That didn't land well, and my parents grounded me for an entire summer.

I feel like I fit in more with the Greenwells. Russell's hair is coal black as was Matt's. In all honesty, Matt always felt more like a brother than my own flesh and blood. Trice and I have always just tolerated one another. One-upping is more like it. Trusting people has never come easy to me. Even at a young age, outside of my friendship with Matt, I wasn't a talkative kid. Sure, I played football and went through the motions, but when Matt died, a part of me died too.

It's probably why I've never had a real relationship. No one has ever cared enough to put up with my antics and had it in her to break through my barriers. It's easy to play the town's bad boy when they all think I killed their quarterback. Eventually, I just settled into the persona they created. As a senior in high school, it was a seamless transition, since I was a loner outside of the football team and Matt's friendship. Most of my team shied away from me after that. Music had always been my salvation. My own form of therapy before I turned eighteen and could legally start getting tattooed. Even that didn't feel right after Matt's passing. That is until the judge made singing in the church choir part of my sentencing.

Trice stepped into the role of the golden-boy his senior year as flawlessly as one could. He became the town's hero as their new quarterback, and I slipped into the shadows.

There's a loud clang as Trice teeters into a lamp near the door.

"Did you not learn your lesson last time?" I demand. "You could have called me, and I'd come get you." I rub my hand vigorously over my face. My palm comes away smeared with black paint residue.

"You're the last person I'd call for a ride."

"Are people's lives that much of a joke to you? I've given you everything. A chance to do anything in this world and you're just going to throw it away with your stupidity."

"You're a coward. You know that?"

"Really, I'm the coward between the two of us?"

"Her spin landed on me. If you weren't brave enough to kiss her outside of a high school game, then you shouldn't have stolen my chance to."

Based on his level of intoxication, I know nothing good will come from trying to reason with him tonight. My jaw clenches and my eyes narrow as he makes his way to the couch, barely, and then plops down on the opposite end. His head is bowed, and his body slumped. I want to lay into him about driving drunk, but it's pointless when he won't even remember in the morning. I'm just glad he made it home in one piece. I'm not burying another brother.

"Matt wouldn't have fought me for her."

"Not tonight, baby brother. Come on, I'll help you upstairs."

We shuffle up the basement steps and into his room on the first floor. I all but carry him and lay him on his bed. Sliding off his sneakers, I toss them on the floor and then drape his comforter on top of him. He's going to regret drinking so much in the morning. Especially if our parents find out.

The hallway is quiet. I softly shut his bedroom door and head back to the basement as my dad's raspy voice cuts through the silence. "You're a good brother, Crew. I want you to know that."

I turn to find him standing behind me, wearing his robe. He places a firm grip on my shoulder and squeezes. "Thank you for getting him home safely on multiple occasions."

I nod, not trusting myself to speak, and then head back downstairs.

CHAPTER
EIGHTEEN

RORY

Andrea is a lumberjack. Between her snoring and blanket hogging, I didn't get much sleep. I'm thankful that last night's festivities are behind us. When I wake and finally roll out of bed, I'm rather embarrassed at my inability to quiet the nerves that Crew left swirling in my gut after our kiss. I make my way downstairs in a dire attempt to caffeinate my brain and stop the pounding in my skull thanks to the remnants of alcohol and my roommate's sawing logs.

"You're up earlier than we expected," Bea holds out a ceramic cup.

"I feel like I could sleep for a week. Andrea's snoring sounds like a pig being brutally murdered and drowning in mud. No one could sleep through that."

"Why do you think we're up so early?" Russell adds with a smug look and then takes his newspaper and coffee into the sunroom where Lonnie is playing on the floor with a set of magnetic tiles.

"How was the party?"

I groan. "It was eventful."

We sip our steam-brewed drinks in silence for a moment before I dredge up the energy to vent to Bea. "We played this stupid game," I say, filling her in on the details of spin the bottle. I don't know why I speak to her as if she's my confidant, but I need to get it off my chest. "Apparently, it was Trice's spin, but Crew was the one who kissed me. I had the blindfold on. I couldn't see what happened. But I know it was Crew." My body warms thinking about his lips against mine.

"How do you feel about him kissing you? Would you rather it had been Trice?"

"No. Not at all. I mean, I like Trice. He's adorable and he's been good to me. But I don't get butterflies in my stomach when he's near like I do with Crew."

"Sounds like you've caught the eyes of both Jordan brothers. I should have known that would happen. You're stunning. Mina called this one. She's going to be happy to be right. Although not so much when she has two bickering men under her roof."

I butter a piece of toast and take a bite. With my mouth full, I ask, "What do you mean? I know at our dinner she teased about them, but I thought she was just being playful."

"The thing about Mina is she doesn't sugarcoat anything. I think she gets that from being a therapist. What she says is what she means. She knew that they'd both be drooling over you. When I called and told her we were opening our house to you and Lonnie, even I knew that you'd attract at least one of the neighborhood boys. How could you not? You're smart, beautiful, and if I'm being honest, you have this mysterious allure. Befriending one of them and not the other was sure to put them in a squabble. You know that beauty is in the eye of the beholder. Art is like that in a sense. It's subjective to the viewer. And you, Rory, are a work of art."

I slide down in my chair. She's comparing me to art like I'm not a piece of trash that's been discarded over and over by society. The paper-thin façade that I've wrapped around me like a cloak of armor starts to unwind by her pep talk. I'm not some heroine who can weather a storm. I became the storm to survive. Now I'm a tornado of emotions. There's nothing remotely beautiful about this feeling of being torn between a friendship and a situationship.

"The last thing I want is to cause a division between brothers."

Bea reaches over and squeezes my shoulder with her hand in a simple gesture. "That division was there long before you arrived on our doorstep."

Her assertion sends my mind reeling. I know that whatever caused their tension had to do with Matt's death. I can feel it in my gut and my gut has never failed me. Here goes nothing, "Will you tell me about the accident?"

This isn't light breakfast conversation, and it may not be appropriate to bombard someone with a question like this before they've finished their first cup of coffee, but I can't go on believing that I'm the reason Trice and Crew are in a feud. I want to know what happened.

The light in Bea's eyes falters a tad, and I can't help but feel responsible.

"Why don't we push pause and wait until your friend upstairs heads home?" she says. "I think that story is long overdue. It deserves not to be rushed or interrupted."

The morning passes so agonizingly slow, it physically causes me torment. My stomach clenches at the conversation I know will be had when my friend leaves. I try to wake Andrea by all but rolling her off the side of the bed, but to no avail. This girl would be better suited to sleeping in a crypt.

After countless attempts, she finally woke and headed home. Bea must've noticed her leaving, because she called

Mina and asked if Lonnie could have a playdate with Aiden this afternoon. Lonnie loves going over there because they have all sorts of fun things to do, from a pool table in the basement to a trampoline. My heart swells knowing that he's made a real friend in such a short time.

I walk into the living room to see Bea and Russell already sitting on the couch. There's a book in her hand. This must be hard for them, being willing to share the worst day in their lives with me, so I put away my intrusive questions, and I sit across from them and wait.

"Matt was your age when the accident happened," Bea says. "He only had seventeen short years with us." Russell grabs her hand and holds it tightly, silently sharing his strength. "For a long time, it was just Crew and Matt. We did everything with the Jordans. Russell and I knew we only wanted to have one child. With both of our professions it was hard enough finding balance. So, when Mina and Shawn decided to start trying to grow their family again, we were elated for them. When Trice was born, he was so little. He was in the NICU for a couple weeks."

"Eventually, the boys got a little older. I remember we had to scold them a few times for excluding Trice. He was younger by two years, and sometimes the other two forgot about that. Around middle school, Trice hit a growth spurt and was just as tall and strong as the other two. It was always us adults and our kids. Between birthday parties and swimming lessons, they were thick as thieves."

I can tell by the throaty sounds Bea makes as she speaks, her attempt to keep control of her emotions is wavering. The anguish on her face is enough to send me into a tailspin. I want to apologize for asking about Matt, reclaim my curiosity, and hide it behind locked doors. I don't get to do any of those things, because as I shift uncomfortably in my spot she continues.

"Trice and Crew were very competitive with each other

and always vying for Matt's attention. But still, our houses were filled with so much laughter when they were younger. I think that's why the silence eats away at me now." A single tear slides down Bea's cheek. It's endearing to watch as Russell raises his calloused finger and brushes it away.

"One night Crew and Matt were studying for the ACT's. I don't even recall Trice coming over, but Russell said he knew that he had been drinking. They all left and said they were going to play basketball. Only they didn't. They went to the dock in town and took Shawn's boat out on the lake without permission." Momentary panic sets in when Bea gasps and buries her face in her hands as a deep, guttural sob shakes her body.

Russell intercedes, "We don't really know what happened out on the lake."

"You don't have to say anymore. I can see how hard this is. It's not my business. I'm sorry for being nosy." I can't take it any longer. Just thinking about the pain that they must be going through reliving this story shatters me and tears at my insides. Even my stone-cold heart constricts with their honesty and willingness to share the truth with me.

"You live here, under the same roof that Matt did. We should have told you the day you moved in. That's on me." Russell's voice lowers. "Crew has never openly talked about it. But there was a crash. The boys hit another boat head on. Crew and Trice made it, and Matt didn't. By the time help arrived, it was too late. Matt had drowned. It had been too long to revive him. Crew claimed that he was the one driving, so he took the fall. I know he wasn't drinking though. I vaguely remember Trice stumbling into the house and begging for them to leave with him. He was always trying to act older than he was to fit in with the other two. I have no doubt that he was the one who crashed the boat that night."

My words come out in a mumble. "How can you...how

can you be okay with seeing *Trice* all the time knowing he may have killed your son?"

Bea gathers her strength by inhaling and squaring her shoulders. "Because they were all like our sons. We were a tribe raising the three of them. We didn't just lose our son. The Jordans lost one, too, and Crew and Trice lost a best friend. Did it pain me at first? Of course. Mina got to hug her children that night, and Russell and I didn't. It took a lot of grief therapy and praying to be able to smile again and they're our best friends. We had to lean on them during our grief. Even if one of their sons caused it."

I respond in the best way that I can. "I can't fathom what losing a child must've been like. I am so sorry."

"Now that you do, nothing will change, Rory." Bea scolds me before I even say what I'm thinking. "Trice and Crew have been through hell and back. We don't have any solid evidence as to who was driving and even if we did, what would it change? Those boys lost a brother that night. No one wins in this scenario. Crew, as the eldest, took responsibility and everyone practically ran him out of town. He's still finishing up his community service. Did you know that's why he sings at church? He was given so many community service hours and the judge decided they would best be spent in the church. Not to mention he was on house arrest for a year. He lost his football scholarship and had to miss his freshman year of college. He lost so much too." She clasps her hands together. "I love those boys, and still having them in our lives has made living without Matt...bearable."

"I'm even more confused now. Why would Crew take the blame for something he didn't do that so royally messed up his life?" I pick at my fingernail feeling gutted by the truth I wanted so desperately, and now, I wish I could rewind and be oblivious to this town's sorrowful history.

Russell answers me first. "I think that's a question for Crew to answer. And, Rory, go easy on him. He's not as tough as he wants people to think he is. This town chewed him up and spit him out. Matt's death was ruled an accidental death, since Crew was sober, and no foul play was apparent. The judge made a point to teach the towns youth about consequences of our actions and sentenced Crew to house arrest for a year and community service."

His words are a torrent of information, and my head is spinning. What I'm learning causes my stomach to clench, but it seems that I'm a glutton for punishment because I still have questions.

"Why did you guys become foster parents after so much tragedy?"

"It was the first anniversary of Matt's passing. Aiden, Mina's third son was turning five and I just couldn't stomach the silence in our home anymore. We did all the necessary paperwork and visits. But we never took the plunge to be an open, awaiting foster family. I think we were both scared to welcome a child, or children back into our lives. Like we would somehow be forgetting Matt's memory by filling this house with a child's laughter again. That was until the night Russell brought you and Lonnie into the emergency room. You had a look of defeat in your eyes that I instantly recognized. Crew had that same look at his court hearing. He was broken. It was then I knew that we were ready for a placement. I called Russell and he didn't hesitate to agree."

"In our line of work, as an inner-city police officer, you have to understand that the stuff that we see is forever ingrained in our minds." Russell holds the back of his neck.

"We can't save Crew from the demons that live within him, but I knew that I could try to save you and Lonnie. I paged the social worker on call and offered to foster you and Lonnie."

My world had been drab. Emptiness had lived within me for years after I realized that I was too old to be adopted by people like Russell and Bea. The stories that are told in group homes and in counseling are like fairytales. No one was going to swoop in and rescue me from the big, bad world. Year after year, I grew more and more detached. More hollow. It was easier to feel nothing than everything. My shield became stone, and I grew to believe that I was unlovable. Unwanted.

Hearing Bea's truth, her raw display of compassion, has me holding back tears after a lifetime of feeling like my tear ducts were broken. I want to let them fall but conditioning myself for too many years to not show weakness won't allow one to break free. No matter how much I will it to in this moment.

"I'm thankful for all you've done for both me and Lonnie." My confession is the best that I can give them for now. I hope it's enough.

The hug that Bea wraps me in tells me it's enough. She understands on a level that someone who hasn't been in our position can't. As an adoptee, a mother, and a friend, she understands my hesitation and sadness, and through her tight embrace, takes it from me. It's no longer a burden I have to bear, and for the first time in my life, I breathe in a sigh of relief, and then bury my face into the crook of her neck and relish her motherly touch.

My heart, however, is filled with sorrow for Crew. The boy I ran into head-first had the most closed expression on his face. It makes sense now why he seemed like he didn't have a care in the world. He could have gotten caught stealing. Crew maybe even wanted to get caught. I can tell that he's been parading around town living up to the stigma of being a delinquent that was placed on him.

I just don't know what to do with the truth now that I have it.

CHAPTER
NINETEEN

Wednesdays usually have a bad reputation. Honestly, I don't know why. I personally love them. They're the sign that the school week is almost over and as much as I love learning, I love sleeping in on the weekends even more.

I hitch my bag over my shoulder and saunter over to the picnic table where I usually meet Trice after last period, and it dawns on me that he has practice this afternoon. Sliding out my cell phone, I start to type a message to Andrea to see if she has plans when a honk from the side of the road startles me. I look over, ready to eye roll whoever keeps laying on their horn as the window rolls down.

"Hey," Crew says casually, like showing up at my school unexpected is typical for him.

"Trice has practice today. He might still be in the locker room if you hurry."

"I'm not here to see Trice."

"I haven't seen Della around." Scarcely aware of my voice, I try to hide my mortification as my insecurities flare and trick me into thinking that he could be here to see *her.* They have history. Jealously twists in my stomach as I step onto the sidewalk and decide to just walk home. I've learned that it's a short distance if you cut through the cemetery.

"I'm not here for Della, either. I thought I made that clear, Aurora. She's. Not. You." He calls out the window as he slowly drives at the same pace as my stride. It's very *Pretty Woman* of him. "Hop in, I got you something." Curious, my head swivels. He raises his voice so I can hear him as another car speeds by. "It's the coffee you've been getting but in a Frappuccino. Try it. It'll change your life."

I'm not one to turn down an afternoon pick-me-up, so I park his *she's not you* comment and say, "okay, " while reaching forward to grab the cup.

"Get in and you can have it." His natural appeal paired with the way the veins on his forearm tighten as he holds the wheel and the coffee have me feeling a sugar high before my very first sip of blended coffee.

"One condition." I set my chin and cross my arms over my chest. "Whatever you have planned is not a date."

A smile stretches across his face wider than the equator. "I wouldn't dream of calling this a date. We're just two neighbors being neighborly. Nothing more. Now get your ass in the car before I get out and drag you in myself."

Coffee is the only reason I get in the car with Crew. It has nothing to do with the feelings for him that I'm trying to keep a tight lid on. At least, that's what I tell myself. "Care to tell me where it is you're taking me?"

"Nope. I want it to be a surprise. You'll be less likely to protest if you don't know where we're headed." His eyes stay glued to the road as I slurp my drink through its straw.

The drive is short. I'm thankful because the silence hanging between us is becoming uncomfortable. Truthfully, I'm not big on small talk and apparently Crew isn't either.

When we pull up to a large building with a giant car on the roof, my eyes widen. "You brought me to drive go-karts?"

"Dammit. I thought you'd like it." Shaking his head, Crew doesn't seem to notice the enthusiasm in my voice.

"First one to the door doesn't have to pay," I holler before opening my door and jogging across the parking lot leaving him with his signature smug smile in my wake.

We spend the next two hours playing countless arcade games and golfing eighteen holes of Putt-Putt. Saving the actual go-karting for last, we each hand over our tickets to the worker and chose our karts. Mine is painted yellow with small flakes of rust on the bumper, while Crew chooses a red one. When the light turns green, I put my foot down and push as hard as I can. Wind blows through my hair making it fly in the air behind me. It's exhilarating. I don't even notice when Crew's red kart passes by me in a rush, and he throws out a thumbs-up in the air. There's no way I can let him beat me. Taking the next turn wide, I gain some momentum and rocket past his kart. The faint sound of laughter fills the air between us, and I slide my kart in front of his and take the lead in the last lap.

I pull into the bay first and exit my kart. Hair is strewn across my face and in my mouth. "Are you going to confess?" I ask. He looks dumbfounded. "That you let me win."

"Isn't that what guys are supposed to do?"

"Maybe, if this were a date. Which it clearly isn't." The spite in my tone is unmistakable. I need to remind myself that dating is not in the cards for me. No matter how kind he is for this spontaneous afternoon of fun. I won't let myself fully open up to him. Even if my heart wants me to.

I can't.

"I was just being courteous, but you asked for it now. Let's go again and prepare to eat my dust. I've been coming here since I was a kid."

His skill is unmistakable. There must've been a camp he

attended as a child or something because he flies by me on several laps. Honestly, if his eyes were closed, I still think he could win. After my last lap, I pull into the bay to find Crew already standing against the fence, legs crossed and playing on his phone looking bored.

"Don't even," I warn with my mouth puckered. "I don't want to hear about how good you were out there. Just know that Lonnie and I will be coming here on a regular basis now just to get good enough to beat you. You'll be eating my dust next time."

He looks amused. "Is that a threat?"

"It's a promise."

Amusement flickers in his eyes as he guides me back toward his car. "I guess that means we'll be having another non-date then."

"If you're lucky, Jordan."

"Want to stop for burgers? My treat. It's the least I can do for kicking your ass." He opens the door for me which is a total date move.

Something disturbing flutters in my chest. It happens often when I'm near Crew. At first, I tried to chalk it up to heartburn or my illogical dislike of the guy. I see now that it's neither. Crew makes me want to spread my wings and explore. He pushes me out of my comfort zone and makes me want to be a normal teenager who dates.

I just don't know if I'm even capable of a relationship.

Cold heart and all.

Residents and alumni rally in the stadium in support of the last football game of the season. I've come to learn Friday nights in this town are holy. Trice is in full-on game day mode. I shot him a text this morning before school with a photo of me wearing his jersey and a good luck quote I found on the internet. His response was clipped.

I've never played a sport, much less had something so important riding on my shoulders like this game is for him. Being quarterback comes with a lot of pressure. I can understand his irritability, but I hope that he pours it all into the game and leaves his sour disposition on the field, win, or lose. Today was a drag between classes and Trice's stoic mood. I'm ready to get this game over with.

Minus the chain-link fence separating the bleachers from the field, the view is impressive. There is a sense of solidarity I've grown accustomed to in the crowd. When Miranda first dropped off Lonnie and me, I was hesitant of this quaint town. It's since grown on me, and so have its inhabitants.

One of whom arrives wearing a black hoodie with a gray beanie. I get a sublime view of his profile as Crew stands with his hands in his pockets and peers toward the field. It's not lost on me that he once played on the same field with his best friend beside him. I want to go comfort him, but it's not my place. We haven't talked since our spur-of-the-moment outing.

I don't hate the guy. It's quite the opposite. Putting distance between us is how I'm staying afloat. I know if I let myself stop and revel in how I really feel about Crew, like an anchor, I'll be stuck in the metaphorical pool of longing.

His gaze turns from the field and meets mine. His cheekbones have more structure than my life and leave me breathless as his smile spreads across his face as he recognizes me in the crowd.

I try to hide my smile that matches his, but Andrea catches me. "You two just need to hate fuck already," she nudges my shoulder. "He has it bad for you and it would honestly do a lot for our community. I mean look at all these girls drooling, wishing that it was them he is pining after."

"Sorry for eavesdropping." A girl I recognize from my

history class chimes in from beside Andrea. "It's the truth. He made my friend come without even using a finger. That's raw talent. You should just put the rest of us out of our misery and screw him. Della did and look how happy she was. I mean he's so sexy, I would cook my ramen noodles in his bath water."

It's as if the world decided to be a treacherous witch today and rain down Crew-fondness over the entire town. First with Andrea calling me out and now with this random girl.

"I call bullshit," Andrea rolls her eyes. My brow shoots up at her response. "What? It's the truth. Della is a liar. I know for a fact they've never had sex."

"Whatever," history class girl stammers. "I was just saying what a friend told me."

"I hate to tell you, your friend is a liar, and I don't think you'd like it if people were spreading gossip about your sexual endeavors now, would you?" Dynamite spews from Andrea's mouth.

The girl moves down a row and doesn't glance back.

Astonishment colors my cheeks. "They never, did *it*?"

"Honestly. I don't think so. She was always complaining that he would start something and never seal the deal. They weren't as close as she led people to believe they were."

I'm too stunned to talk. My brain is turning into mush with all this new information. I don't think I'll survive another revelation so close to the last one. I glance on the field and see Trice's number. I'm torn between cheering on my friend and being irritated at him for letting Crew take the blame for Matt's death. There is a fine line between the truth and a lie, and it seems that they've been in a constant tango since the accident occurred.

One thing is for certain, the scoundrel scaling the steps of the bleachers two-by-two with fiery determination in his eyes is doing something to my stony heart. It beats in unison with the band's drummers on the sidelines. I'm thankful we're at the top of the bleachers as he nears us. It gives me extra time to gather myself and my outlandish thoughts.

"If you're going to ignore my texts, turn off your read receipt. It's hurtful." Crew says by way of greeting as he plants himself beside me. "I guess I'll just have to show up again, unannounced, just to get your attention."

"I'm still getting used to having a cell phone. Poor girl and all. Sue me." I perfect my hard exterior once more and no sooner than the words leave my mouth his thigh brushes against mine and my heart starts to thump wildly in my chest.

"Try again. I saw your name on Trice's phone. *He's* not getting ignored."

"That sounds a lot like jealously." His magnetism is so potent, I pop a kernel of popcorn in my mouth and turn to look at the field to distract me. I can feel my heartbeat throbbing in my ears now as Trice's team makes their way onto the field and the crowd goes crazy. Cheers and chants are so long and loud, I forget that it's just a high school football game.

"I've never been a jealous guy, until I met you." He nudges my fishtail braid away from my earlobe with his nose and whispers.

I can't think straight when he's near, and my attention should be on the field watching Trice and his game. He deserves that. Even if I'm upset with him. "Is this the first game of Trice's you've been to this year?"

My attempt at small talk is squashed as Crew gives a curt reply. "Yup."

"Why is that?"

He steals a piece of popcorn from the red and white striped box in my hand. "If I tell you the truth, will you tell me why you ignored my texts?"

Reluctantly, I nod, "You first."

"The last time I was on that field was the last time I felt an ounce of worth. The town was shouting my name so loudly it was hard to concentrate. I felt alive. It seems like a lifetime ago now."

My heart refuses to believe what my heart tells me as Crew Jordan's words offer a vulnerability that I'm not prepared for. What do I do with this information? I hold my hands in a steeple motion silently praying that I don't make a fool of myself. "I'm ignoring you because I'm scared of what will happen if I don't," I say before turning my face away from him to collect myself.

"Thanks for your honesty." His index finger knuckle brushes under my chin sending my face ablaze. "I'll catch up with you later."

I stare blankly at his back as he descends the walkway before I make eye contact with Andrea and give her a look of disbelief. "What the hell just happened?" His hurried exit is as exhausting as watching Trice's team run after the football. It doesn't help that I don't have a clue how this game works.

She scoots closer to me and drapes her arm behind my neck. "I honestly don't have a clue."

History class girl chimes back in from her seat a row in front of us. "He has more game than he's letting on and you claim he's a virgin. Girl, you're blind or just plain stupid."

The game finishes with a flash of color running onto the field. Sadly, it's not our team bellowing and celebrating. I ask Bea and Russell if I can skip out on their plans so I can hang out with Trice, knowing that he may need a friend. They agree and leave me standing by the locker room waiting on him for a ride. Andrea decides to go with Geoff, Wade, and a couple other players who plan to soothe their disappointment with alcohol. It's not really my scene, so I hug her farewell and wait patiently outside the locker room for my best friend to appear.

Disappointment clings to him like a second skin when he appears. His blonde hair is damp and sticks to his forehead under a hoodie. His electric eyes are steel and don't even widen when he notices me. Teammates usher around him as I reach forward and give him a hug as if to say I'm sorry. It's pitiful, and he doesn't even squeeze me back. I haven't seen this side of his personality. He's always so happy-go-lucky. Ending the season on such a sour note warrants his grumpiness. But I don't have to like it.

"How about we go watch a movie and chill tonight? I'm not sure I feel like going out with everyone else, and I think your parents and mine are taking the boys to the trampoline park tonight."

Did I just call Russell and Bea my parents?

"My dad texted me and told me earlier. That's fine." We walk toward his car, and he tosses his helmet and pads into the trunk and then opens the passenger-side door for me. Even with his anger and disappointment so palpable, he's still a gentleman.

The ride back to his house is silent. It's a little unnerving. Knowing that he just lost a big game and is already in a piss-poor mood, I offer him a little grace and watch out my window as trees pass by my window in rows. Sliding my cell phone out of my pocket, I use the free time to check my phone and re- read the messages that I haven't replied to.

Crew Jordan: *Meet me at the clubhouse*

Crew Jordan: *Are you still up?*

Crew Jordan: *I need to talk to you*

He's persistent. I'll give him that. Stowing my phone away in my back pocket, I devote my time to my friend who needs it right now. "I think you played really well for what it's worth."

"Not well enough."

The glumness radiating from him comes off in waves. My attempts to make small talk and take his mind off the loss don't work. Putting myself in his shoes, I try to imagine how he feels to work hard toward a goal, only to have his dreams of winning the state championship ripped from his grasp. I've felt that defeat many times. Only it wasn't something as juvenile as a football game. It was life and more than a state title was at stake.

As we pull into his driveway, he continues with the cold shoulder. "I'm going to take a shower. Why don't you grab us something to eat. I need some protein. Then we can see what's streaming to watch."

"No problem." I trudge upstairs. It's a little odd being up here without anyone else home. We've hung out several times, and I've been over here a handful of times to get Lonnie when he and Aiden were playing after school, but it's never been this quiet. It's a little unnerving.

I grab two bottles of water from the refrigerator and then swing open the door to their walk-in pantry. It's enormous and almost sickening. I can't blame Mina and her husband for being wealthy when they're the most down-to-earth people I know. They give to charities and seem to be noble people. It's funny because I always thought of rich people in the suburbs as the type of people who were the ones who didn't care about their community and helping others. When in fact it's the opposite.

Still, the fact that they have a coffee bar, an industrial ice machine that looks like it belongs in a fast-food restaurant, and an island in the middle of their pantry, sends a wave of envy down my spine.

It feels odd flittering through the Jordan's kitchen like I'm a pirate on a treasure hunt for pizza rolls. I smell Crew's scent before I hear his voice. Like a dog in heat, my body goes rigid knowing he's nearby.

"Can I help you find something?"

I turn to find him leaning against a cabinet, a green apple in one hand and a knife in the other.

"Sorry. I didn't know anyone else was home. Trice sent me up here to get something for us to eat."

"Post-game fuel. He's going to need more than pizza rolls."

"You're probably right." I open the refrigerator and pull out ingredients to make him a sandwich all the while knowing that Crew is behind me. His presence is unsettling.

"I didn't realize you and Trice were a thing. You're already serving him."

"He just lost the most important game in his high school career. I'm aiding him like a friend who needs to refuel his body and rest." I snap, allowing my words to resonate. "You might not understand that concept of a guy and a girl being just friends since I'm sure you've never had a platonic friend in your life. Women are probably tossing their panties at you like Mardi Gras beads on campus." I unzip the plastic bag of turkey and pile it on two slices of bread.

"Are you trying to convince me or yourself? And you know what they say about assuming, don't you?" He asks as he cuts the apple with his knife and slides a piece into his mouth. It crunches between his teeth, and I stare a little too long at his mouth and those lips that I've tasted briefly.

Rolling my eyes, I swing open the door and shove all the contents back into their spots in the refrigerator. I can never get a good read on Crew. Either he's a major pain in my ass or he's smooth like butter and makes me want to let my guard down around him. "You're insufferable. You know that don't you?" He closes the distance between us, and I hold up a hand warding him away.

"You should hear what the ladies say about my favorite appendage. If you're going to assume things. You should assume that I have a really big—"

"Stop! I'd rather not."

"I think you would, you just don't want to admit it."

His presence is enough to make it hard for me to think. He makes me feel lust and rage all wrapped into one. Trice warms my heart too. He just doesn't set it on fire the way being near Crew does, which is why I need to leave right now. His proximity leaves me feeling jumbled, and I don't trust myself fully when he's nearby.

Pull yourself together.

After all, he's the one who bolted at the game. Now it's my turn. I swing open the door of the butler's pantry and hastily stride through the kitchen, my hands full of drinks, goodies, and Trice's sandwich. I'm headed toward the basement door with Crew hot on my heels, his incessant chewing grows louder the closer he gets.

"What are you doing?"

"I heard we were getting snacks. One can only assume if you're hanging out in the basement, you're getting ready to watch a movie."

"Your insinuated assuming makes you an ass." I toss his own words back at him.

"I've never claimed to be anything else. Now move along. I can't wait to see what we're watching."

And that is how I spent my evening crammed between both Jordan brothers on their couch in the darkness of their basement. It's not lost on me when I see the palms of both of their hands laying waywardly on the cushion inches from my body taunting me.

You couldn't pay me to tell you what the movie was about. I was too busy thinking about the back and forth between Crew and me. At one point, I had to snuggle my face into the pillow trying to hide the blush that crept into my cheeks at the thought of kissing his full lips again, only without a blindfold this time.

CHAPTER
TWENTY

"Shh, dude, she's sleeping." Trice's voice is barely above a whisper. I feel a soft material drape over my legs on the couch. My eyes are still glued shut but beg to open and steal a glimpse of who just covered me up. "I could have covered her up, dude."

"Yet you didn't," I hear Crew's voice spit out quickly.

Trice's body tenses next to mine. I can feel his weight shift on the cushion, much like the tension in the room. "What's your problem, dude? I'm the one who lost today. Not you. And I already told you, I didn't want to talk about Halloween and you stealing my chance to kiss her. Matt wouldn't have—"

"Don't," Crew warns. "Don't say his name."

Huffing, Trice moves to the edge of the couch. "Listen, I don't mean to bring him up, but you've been on level ten lately. More so than usual. I'm the one who got cheated out of kissing her and out of tonight's win. Why are you so bent out of shape? It should be me who wants to punch your lights out."

"Rory is off-limits," Crew says matter-of-factly changing the subject. The sound of my name leaving his mouth has my heart hammering in my chest.

My eyes beg to open, but I keep them shut and hope to disappear into a wormhole. This is not a conversation I want to be present for. I most certainly do not want to be a wedge driving their already damaged relationship further apart.

"The heck she is," Trice bellows and my eyes almost spring open again at his hostility. "She's my friend. You just use her as a verbal punching bag. You think I didn't see her face when you called her Foster all those times and your little girlfriend teased her at school. She's a good person and deserves happiness. You don't have an ounce of that in your body to give someone, so don't come at me. She's not Della. She doesn't deserve to be screwed and then tossed aside."

"Get the hell over the Della shit. You and I both know I didn't fuck her once. I've let her suck my dick and that's it. Shoot me. I'm a guy. You only bring it up when Aurora is around anyway. You never said a word about it before she moved in next door."

"What's with the Aurora name calling anyway?"

"That's her name," I hear Crew counter.

"Call her Rory like everyone else. It's annoying."

A threat of warning laces Crew's tone, "I'll call her Aurora if I want. It's a beautiful name for a beautiful girl and, you know what, I think you owe me that. Back. The. Hell. Off."

"I owe you. Ha-ha. You fucking embarrassed me in front of everyone when you stole my spin. You always get whatever the hell you want." Trice speaks in a tone I've never heard coming from him before.

"I get whatever the hell I want?" Molten anger pours from Crew like acid. "Did I get my way when I sat in front of a judge and an entire courtroom and get punished for a crime I didn't commit?"

A beat passes.

The silence is deafening.

I want to plug my ears, but my movement will be too noticeable, and they'll realize I've been up this whole time and privy to this moment of truth.

"I did that for you, little brother. I took the heat, so you didn't have to and now this is me cashing in the IOU. You owe me that much and we both know it. You *will* back the hell off. Do you hear me? I don't care that you're friends with her. Just know your place where she's concerned."

"Loud and clear." The tenor in Trice's voice is unsettling.

"Do not touch her. Don't even think about it. If I even see you this close to her again, everyone will know the truth."

The blood drains from my face at Crew's words.

"I don't understand. You'd out me over a girl? We declared bones."

I steal a look through hooded lashes to see Crew leaning against the wall behind the large sectional I'm settled on. His hands are curled into fists and his nostrils flare with each deep breath he takes. The shirt he's wearing clings to his body making me acutely aware of how broad and proportioned his build is. I can almost count his hard abs through the thin material and imagine that the guy standing before me is used to people heeding his warnings. Even his younger brother.

"I'd out you over *this* girl." Crew licks his lips and then runs his hand through his hair leaving wisps of dark hair resting at the nap of his neck.

"Bones doesn't mean jack if you don't take it to the grave. When did you even start to like Rory? You pester her any chance you get. She's never once given me the impression that she was interested in you."

"Why would she? You're my brother. You think she's going to gush about me to you. You're delusional." A raucous sound leaves Crew's lips. "That kiss meant something."

"Now who's delusional?" Trice's voice weighs heavily in the air. "She's my friend. I haven't had someone who made me feel so seen…important…since Matt died. Now you want to take her. You staking a claim for whatever freaking reason isn't going to stop our friendship. You know she would have a conniption fit if she were awake. She's special, Crew. Something you wouldn't understand. She's been through a lot, and she doesn't need you diminishing any light she has left in her."

The defeat in Trice's tone makes my stomach churn. I'm not willing to be claimed by anyone, much less someone who thinks he is entitled to claim me. The disdain between the two Jordan brothers is tangible. In the last few months, I've noticed this game that they play. It's like they're in a tetherball match without a winner. The game just keeps going on and on. I'm pleading for the string to break to end this imprudent match. I just don't want to be the one who breaks it.

The sound of someone leaving and the door slamming shut behind them is a relief. I sit up tongue-tied and dizzy from their heated exchange eager to see which brother remains in the basement with me.

"How much of that did you hear?" Trice sinks in next to me.

"Enough."

"He likes you."

"I know." My mouth drops open as I realize the truth of my words after I say them.

"Do you like him?"

"I'm afraid to answer that." I watch Trice out of the corner of my eye cover his face before he exhales with a loud huff.

"He's not good enough for you, Rory. He might have been before, but not now. I don't even recognize him anymore."

I speak without hesitation. "Before what, the accident that no one acknowledges?"

Trice nods wordlessly as his face hardens.

Huddling under the blanket, I feel small but courageous. "What happened that night on the boat, Trice? I'd like to hear your account of what happened." I omit that my foster parents and I had a heart-to-heart and they told me about the boating accident and that night.

"I think you've heard enough for one evening."

"I heard him say he took the heat. But I wish you would elaborate on what happened. I want to know your side of the story."

"You know why this friendship works, Rory?"

I don't say anything knowing he's not truly asking by the bite in his tone. "It works because we don't pry. You don't think I want to know about your past and how you landed with the Greenwells. Or why you flinch when I hug you sometimes. I want to know so many things. So many things about your life and childhood. Sometimes I have to physically bite my cheek to keep the questions at bay. You've had a crappy life, that much I know. But this," he scoots away creating a distance that began with my indiscreet questioning. "This is too much."

"I'm… sorry. I just—"

"I'm heading to bed. It's late. I'm pissed we lost the game, and Crew got me all riled up. I don't want to damage another relationship tonight. Just go home. We'll talk tomorrow."

This was not how I envisioned the night ending. With my tail tucked between my legs, I gather my hoodie and bag and leave. The dewy grass slides under my feet as I walk through their backyard and through the gate dividing the two properties. I really want to be alone and collect my thoughts. I eye the clubhouse and walk a couple steps to its door. Since I cleaned it up, the boys have been in there playing almost daily. I'm happy it's getting used. I think Matt would be too.

Opening the door, my breath hitches as I glimpse the outline of a body and the red dot of a cigarette burning. "What are you doing?" It's cold enough that you can see my breath as I step inside.

"I needed to take a beat."

"Same." In the shadow of the window, I can see Crew leaning against the metal frame of the bunk bed. I sneak a glance at him.

His voice fills the air. "I needed some space to think away from Trice and—."

"I'll leave you to it then." I take a step back.

His hand darts out and catches mine at my side. The grip is firm and then he tugs and urges my feet forward until I'm standing directly in front of him. Enough light shines in through the window from the luminous moon that I can see him lowering his knees, so they're flush against the floor. I've thawed toward Crew so much that when he gives me that award-winning smile, I inch closer to him.

"Sit," Crew says with a closed-lip smile.

"On your lap?"

"It's the best seat in the house."

Surprising myself, I lower myself onto his lap without hesitation. Each of my legs glide on the outer thigh of his. It's hard to remain composed when I'm straddling Crew's lap in such an intimate position. His mouth is a hair's breadth away. My body wants to lean in. It yearns to have his arms wrapped around me.

So many times, since Halloween night, I've thought of what it would be like to kiss him again. The comprehension of that is not lost on me. My mind takes over and pulls all rational thought to the forefront. As always, it's on guard, protecting itself since my heart can't when he's in the vicinity.

Lifting my chin, I meet his steady gaze and break the stillness between us. "I overheard you guys."

"I know."

"Why didn't you say anything?"

Clearing his throat, he offers a delayed response. "I wanted you to hear me. You *needed* to hear me warn him away."

"Why would you want me to hear that? I'm not into whatever game you're playing."

The tip of Crew's nose gently bumps mine. When he opens his mouth to talk, I can feel his warm breath leaving his parted lips. "Because I think the only way you'll admit to feeling something for me, is if Trice knows where we stand, and doesn't feel led on by you."

My thoughts are scrambled like eggs frying on high heat. "I have nothing to offer you here."

"I think you do. You're just so scared to admit letting someone in to allow yourself to make sense of it." He trails his fingertips up and down my arms. "It's okay to let me in, Aurora." I can't help the way his request makes my heart race. "Give me the opportunity to show you I'm not the monster you think I am. What do I have to do to get you to let your guard down for me like you have for Trice?"

"Let my guard down? I haven't let my guard down for Trice. For anyone. Not once have I ever let it down and had it benefit me. Look, what happened earlier at the football game when I let it slide for a split second?" His eyes are hard and trained on me silently pleading for more. "You asked for my honestly. I gave it to you and told you I'm scared of *this*, whatever this is between us, and you… you just fled and left me wondering what the hell happened."

"Is that what you thought, Aurora?" I can feel his arms slipping around my waist pulling me in closer; so close, you couldn't slide a sheet of paper between us the way my chest is pressed into his. "I had to leave because if I didn't, I would have pulled you in and kissed you so fiercely right then and there that even the referee would have stopped and whistled."

All the air in my body leaves at once. My heart swells with his honesty. A truth that he's been holding onto. I fiddle with the hem of my sleeve. My eyes dart in several directions, unable to meet his. If they do, I'll come unglued. I know it.

Ignoring the swarm of butterflies in my stomach I change the subject, scared of what may happen if I don't.

"I can tell how entranced you are at church when you're in your element singing and playing guitar. It would've been cool to see a different side of you and been able to watch you play football with Matt."

"You don't like this version of me? People call it artsy."

"More like tortured."

"A part of me died the night Matt did," he admits, and his honesty takes me by surprise. He's never been forthcoming with me and always seems so shut off with everyone. "All the parts of me that we shared like football, gaming, and fishing, it just doesn't seem right to do any of it without him here anymore."

"Bea told me about the accident." I say with a slight hesitation.

His eyes catch and hold mine. "And?"

Reaching forward, I cup Crew's cheek in my palm before realizing how intimate it is, and I lurch it away. My movement is halted by an iron grip. Crew gently places it back on his cheek before he leans into my touch and closes his eyes. "They know you weren't the one driving the boat. I don't understand why you'd take the heat for something you didn't do. Especially something as serious as an accidental drowning."

"I don't want to talk about the accident. I'd rather talk about you. How have you survived this long without letting anyone in?" His question is loaded. It catches me off guard.

"It's easy. The only person I rely on is myself."

"Can you make an exception?"

I smooth my hair, my voice resigned. "Give me a reason to."

Other than the sound of our breath, it's quiet. He's stealing my air and I his. We share a desperate look into each other's eyes. I lean into this moment as we allow ourselves to give into the gravitational force that keeps pulling us together. Keeping Crew at a distance took so much work. I'm tired of fighting. Both in life and with my heart over this boy.

"You're so gorgeous. I told myself tonight, I'd show you how I felt."

"Gorgeous, huh?" My eyes grow amused by his choice of description. I've been called a lot of things in my life. Gorgeous has never been one, I can assure you.

"Boys call you hot or pretty. Men call you things like gorgeous or exquisite. Things with actual fucking syllables."

"And you claim that you're a man?"

"When Matt died, I lost a lot more than a friend. I was forced to miss out on a lot. Some by choice. I'm a college student. I buy my own groceries. Even though my mom still does my laundry on the weekends," he laughs. "I'd like to think I'm not a kid anymore.

"I like that sound."

"Of what?"

I place both hands on his shoulders knowing that I'm straddling him and am in a dangerous position. It's a bold move that I blame solely on the budding feeling in my core. "Your laugh. You should do it more often."

"Noted."

"Why do you come home so often if you live on campus? Other than for clean underwear."

Crew's eyes darken. "Grief attracts grief." He slices through any reservations I have left. "I've felt a connection to you since the first day I laid eyes on you. My resolve is gone. I want you to know how I feel. What you decide to do with it is on you."

If I were standing, my knees would be weak. I try to steer the conversation in a different direction and hide my thudding pulse. "Maybe you're right about the grief thing. That's how Lonnie and I bonded so quickly. We both knew what it was like to be in a world where we've never felt love before."

My cheeks heat at my voluntarily admission. "I live in a state of emergency and you're…you're the picket-fence kid. You and both of your brothers. You guys have it so good. I'm envious of that, ya know?"

"Everyone has a sad story. Me included. It sounds like you know what I've had to sacrifice to keep people I care about safe. My truth is painful, and that pain runs deep. I can't say it out loud. You help numb it. Since I met you, I haven't been nearly as miserable." His eyes cloud. "As for my upbringing, there's nothing I can say that will change how you feel. I have amazing parents, and I've had a decent life. Trice, Aiden, and I are blessed to have been raised by two loving parents. I won't pretend to know what it was like for you before you came to live here. Hell, I don't even want to think about what you've had to endure. I was an asshole by taunting you and calling you Foster. I will beg for your forgiveness for as long as it takes you to really forgive me for being a dick."

He raises his hand and caresses my jawline thoughtfully. "You're here now and you can have a great life too. People care about you here. You just need to notice them doing it."

"I notice." My voice is barely audible. Crew has the capacity to crush me. To shatter a heart that's been broken more times than I can count. To have that kind of power over someone should be illegal. I know that this might possibly be the worst decision I've ever made, but I decide to stop fighting against my feelings for him and just let them be.

Raw and untamed.

"Then you've also noticed that I can't seem to stay away from you, and I'm sick of fighting it. You told me once not to touch you without permission."

I don't think before I answer. "Granted."

Before the last syllable is spoken, Crew's mouth crushes mine. I part my lips and allow him to take control. I'm at his mercy. All the torment we've aimed like daggers at one another for months vanishes as we surrender to a need only *we* can fill within each other.

For once where Crew is concerned, I'm not filled with irritation, but with pure lust. It ripples and courses its way through my body sending shivers of desire for him all the way to my toes. The push and pull of our mouths is maddening. Our teeth collide, each of us desperate to fill a void in one another that only we can each quench.

I. Am. Here. For. It.

Crew tests me and pushes me in the best way. Seeing this part of him, with his shield lowered has all the blood in my veins flowing to my heart with tight constrictions. I can no longer deny the way he makes me feel. I just pray that our decision to do this—to break this barrier between us—doesn't hurt my friendship with his brother.

"I want to taste every inch if you, Rory, but right now, I'm going to start with your mouth and that's going to have to be enough."

Breathlessly, I ask, "What if I want more?"

"Contrary to what you think of me, I'm not a sex fiend." His eyes lower to my mouth with a sinful gaze. "In fact...I'm a virgin." There is nothing about him that screams he has an unpunched V card.

I rock back and desperately try to hold in my potentially cavernous laugh. "I've heard all the gossip, Playboy. You don't have to lie to me."

"Believe it or not, I've never cared about anyone enough to want to have sex with them. Don't get me wrong. I'm not a saint. I'm a nineteen-year-old guy in college. There are a lot of opportunities there to learn and explore without sealing the deal."

Giving a deep, weighted sigh, I put a hand over my face. "With all of the sexual innuendos you're always dropping, you could have fooled me."

"So, you did get those texts? I was beginning to wonder.

I'm a flirt, and I wanted you to see me. Most people prefer the cavalier version anyway."

"I see *you*. You don't have to pretend to be the playboy of the town in front of me. The vulnerable one who took the blame for a horrible accident just to protect his brother and his future. I like this version much more than the unattainable bad boy." I feather a kiss on his lips. "Although, I am curious. I heard someone claim you made them get off with just your mouth." I'm thankful that it's dark as I can feel a deep blush creep its way onto my cheeks like a high tide.

His laughter echoes in the small cabin. "I'd love to show you sometime. Right now, I just want to taste your lips again and hold you." His fingers twirl in my hair. "That night at Halloween you didn't give me my score."

I suddenly remember Halloween night. That stupid game is ingrained in my mind like a core memory.

"You left before I even knew it was you that kissed me."

"You knew exactly who it was. I know you did." A hint of boastfulness is laced in his words.

"Solid nine."

I watch as his brow furrows and his lips thin. "Why not a ten?"

"Because I wish I could have seen you lean in, but I was blindfolded remember?"

Lacing his fingers behind my back, he pulls me forward and claims my mouth again. My mind drifts off to a place where this could actually work between us. I'm needy of more than his kisses. I want him, too. His time. His affection. Now that I've tasted him. I want it all. When I breathe in his woodsy, pine scent, I feel at home for the first time in my entire life. His touch grounds me in the moment and awakens every nerve in my body.

"How about that?" Crew asks, his voice sounding purposively seductive.

Breathlessly, I answer. "Ten."

Uncertainty about what tomorrow will bring dampens the moment. "What happens between us now?" My heart aches under my breastbone as I await his response.

"If you'll have me, we can face it together."

"Together, as in together-together?"

"I don't know what that means. What I do know is you're the most beautiful girl I've ever seen. You're feisty and a little infuriating at times. In the months I've known you, although they've been spent loathing each other—mostly you, not me—you showed me that there's so much more life for me to live. Losing Matt was awful, but so is living on autopilot. You, Aurora Bradshaw, are a girl without a fuck to give, and you greet life with balls of steel. You inspire me to do the same and have given me purpose to keep going because of all you've endured. I know that I can handle more than I give myself credit for now. You are my reason. Let me be yours."

"I have demons. Dark ones."

His whiskey-colored eyes drink me in. "You don't have to lead me into temptation, Aurora. I know the way. I've been living in the dark for long enough not to be frightened of it anymore."

Crew said he never cared about anyone enough to be with them intimately. In this instant, I'd willingly give him everything. My heart, my body, and my soul.

I lean toward him knowing that nothing great has ever come from being afraid.

CHAPTER
TWENTY-ONE

CREW

hold my breath waiting for those three telltale dots to appear indicating that she's responding as I stare down at my phone.

Me: *Good morning, gorgeous*

I reach above my head and stretch while lying across my queen mattress. It's plush like I imagine a cloud would feel, and my back feels incredible after a solid night's sleep. Compared to the hard-as-a-rock twin mattress in my dorm that isn't even fit for an inmate, I feel more refreshed than I have in a while. A lot of that may also have to do with the outpouring of revelations that Aurora and I shared well into the night.

When I finally walked her to the back door of the Greenwell's house, it was too late to drive back to campus. We talked and kissed for hours, making up for the lost time that we spent arguing with one another over the past couple months instead of allowing ourselves to feel an ounce of happiness together.

I think we've finally turned a corner with each other and,

as I stretch, a steadfast, serene peace, settles in my chest. I haven't felt serenity like this since before Matt's death.

Scenes from last night roll by like a photo reel. I can't believe I came clean about being a virgin to her, and she didn't laugh in my face. I've never told anyone that other than Matt and Trice. The truth is, I have no desire to just roll in the sheets with anyone who I don't feel an emotional connection with. Sex to me seems so vulnerable. I've had no issues with making out, or surrendering to cravings and doing oral with females, but the actual act of lovemaking with someone I'm not in love with is revolting. It's been hard denying Della when she's very pushy and persuasive. But I've held my ground and now I know why. It's Aurora I've been waiting for to share that moment with.

Rolling onto my stomach with my cell phone in hand, I stare at an empty conversation like a desperate boyfriend.

Boyfriend.

The title sounds legitimate. Della and I never had a label for what we were. I also never cared about Della the same way I do Aurora. Sure, I felt something toward her. I'd be an utter moron not to admit that. She's attractive and, in the beginning, she used to be one of the kindest people I'd ever known. Her ego has gotten the better of her since she became a senior and captain of the cheerleading team. Now she has people fawning for her attention. Her true colors aren't a pretty shade. Let's just leave it at that.

Truthfully, I owe her a lot though. More than I give her credit for. She was one of the only friends who stuck by my side after Matt's death. When the brothers on my football team abandoned me and Trice and I grew distant, she was a constant. If it hadn't been for her, I honestly don't know where I'd be. I can't take that from her. Even if we've drifted apart. I will always owe her respect for not flaking on me like everyone else did. For that, I will forever be grateful.

When no text comes through, I make my way to my bathroom and shower and then head downstairs. I walk into the kitchen and spot my mom in a robe, hair piled on her head with one of those strange claw contraptions. She's dancing to the beat as music blares from our Echo Dot on the counter as she flips a pancake on the stove. My stomach rumbles.

"I didn't know you were here, honey. Grab a plate. Aiden requested banana and chocolate chip pancakes this morning."

"Thanks, Mom. Is dad here or did he have to go to the office?" I need to vent, and he's also unbiased, which makes a good sounding board. Even with the distance I've put between my family and me, I'm his son and need his advice.

"Is everything okay?" She tosses a dishtowel over her shoulder and leans against the counter, a spatula in her hand and a worried expression on her face. The sun peeking in from the window above her casts a glow on top of her mane. "What's going on? Spill." Her voice has more edge in it.

I plop down on a stool at the island forfeiting my quest to find my dad as a jumble of pent-up thoughts leave my mouth. "I like her. Aurora. I really like her. She's special. I don't want to ruin what could be."

Mom flips the pancake, turns off the burner, and saunters over to the island where I'm sitting, giving me her full attention. "Obviously liking her isn't the issue, so what is?"

"Trice." I take a swig of coffee and lean back on the stool, swiping my face.

"Truth is ugly sometimes. The thing about brothers is that you're tied to one another for life. No feud will change that. Especially drama over liking the same girl. He'll find someone who makes him feel like Rory makes you feel. Even though you both are getting on my last nerve loathing one another. I'm so glad your dad and I had a third child. Now we have the perfect mix of you both. Aiden is truly my favorite." She mocks me, making light of our running argument of who she favors more between the three of us.

"He's honestly my favorite too, Mom. He doesn't talk

nearly as much shit as Trice does. Just wait until he starts dating. We'll be cursed if him and Lonnie like the same girl."

"Crew." She chastises me with just the sound of my name like only a mother can do. "Rory is breathtaking. She's smart and full of mystery. If you and Rory like one another and want to embark on seeing where things lead, then so be it. Don't let your brother steal another moment of happiness from you."

Letting her words resonate, a glint of hope stirs. And she's right. I've given up enough to protect him.

I choose Aurora.

I choose to allow myself to have a sliver of happiness.

"He's going to be pissed that I made my move. You sure you're ready to deal with the fallout."

"Not at all. That's where your dad comes in. I'm washing my hands of you and your brother's drama." She laughs and then strides back to the stovetop. "She seems like a sweet girl. I know she's been through more than any child should have to endure. Bea arranged for her to meet with me as her therapist. But if you tell a soul I just told you that, I'll have to beat you over the head with this frying pan."

"Don't you think that's a conflict of interest, Mom?"

"Why? I'm not the one dating her." She shrugs her shoulders and adds, "Bea said that Rory only feels comfortable with female therapists. But before we meet, I will reach out to her and see if that's still okay since you're clearly dating her."

A smile stretches across my face. "I'm thankful for that. Can you imagine if I had to compete with *you* and Trice? I hope she doesn't mind, Mom. You're an amazing therapist."

"You're just saying that because I'm making pancakes. Your flattery doesn't work on this cook because I already know there'd be no competition. Look at me." She twirls, and small blonde hairs swing with her movement.

Even in her robe and house slippers, my mom is a sight.

"You're stunning, Mom. Now get back to your motherly duties. I'm hungry."

My phone chimes in the pocket of my sweatpants causing me to fumble like a bee is in there as I try to pull it out. I smile wider than I thought possible as Aurora's name pops across my screen for the first time ever. Who says guys don't get giddy when a girl texts them?

Aurora: *Morning*

I exhale sharply like a football being deflated. *Morning?* Either she didn't wake up as enthusiastic as I did, or she wasn't lying about being a bad texter. With my mouth still agape, Trice strides into the kitchen fresh from the shower.

"It smells delicious in here. Dang, pancakes. Thanks." He opens the refrigerator and grabs a glass and fills it to the rim with milk. No wonder his body is stacked. I'm a bit envious. I haven't been in the gym in ages. We used to live there together. It was like a ritual since we all trained for football. I might have some competition where Aurora is concerned with him after all if he's going all bodybuilder for his senior year.

Aiden struts into the kitchen wearing only his briefs. "Mom, have you seen my leg sleeves?"

"You mean pants, honey?" She chuckles. "Look on the dryer. I just folded some this morning and didn't want to wake you by putting them up."

It dawns on me that I am a picket-fence kid. Aurora nailed that one.

"Why are you getting ready so early?" She asks Aiden who is hobbling out of the laundry room with one foot in a pair of jeans.

"Trice and Rory are taking us painting."

"Excuse me?" I chime in.

A look of satisfaction dances across Trice's face. His triumphant blow leaves me wondering what the hell is going on. Didn't Aurora and I become a couple last night? Why would she make plans with my brother and not me today? Wait, has she already been texting him this morning?

All I received was a simple, "Morning."

"Rory and I are taking the boys to *Painting with a Twist* today. You know she loves art and this way we can get her and Lonnie out of the house since Bea and Russell are both working this weekend."

"What do you mean she loves art?" I counter.

"She's always admiring art and talking about things that inspire her to paint or draw. I guess you don't know as much as you thought about our new neighbor do you, bro?"

Our new neighbor is now my *girlfriend*.

I woke up this morning with no intention of choosing violence today. Trice apparently woke up with determination to wreak havoc. Showing no signs of him relenting, I slide off my stool. "Give me ten minutes to get ready. I'd love to hang out with Aiden today too. I think we both have some time to make up for don't you, Trice?"

I know he can't deny that truth right in front of mom. He thinks he's a sly little sucker. But he's playing with fire, and I'm the one holding the matches.

CHAPTER
TWENTY-TWO

RORY

I wake to a dozen texts from Trice filled with apologies after his behavior that will undoubtedly require caffeine before they have my full attention. He doesn't need to grovel, even though I do find it sort of endearing. At least he still cares enough about our friendship to come to his senses and realize what a big scumbag he had been yesterday.

Losing the game, understandably, unraveled him. Pair that with the heated confrontation he and Crew had, and his foul mood grew larger than a tsunami sucking under everything in its path. I'm not a human punching bag and won't stand for being made into one, no matter the reason. It's not justified.

My breath catches in my lungs as I walk downstairs in need of coffee and see Crew's name on my phone nestled between texts from his brother. I make it to the last step with my bottom lip in my mouth.

Crew Jordan: *Good morning, gorgeous*

How does one respond without sounding like a lovestruck moron?

Me: *Morning*

I hit send and toss my phone onto the counter in search of the coffee pods.

"Are we going painting with Aiden and Trice today?" Lonnie scares the living heck out of me as he pops up from the living room couch adjacent to the kitchen.

"Buddy, you have to give me warning before you just pop up out of nowhere. I almost peed my pants!" Lonnie chuckles and makes his way into the kitchen with his iPad in hand. He's wearing a pair of dinosaur pajamas. "Let me get a cup of coffee and then we'll discuss whatever it is you are talking about, okay?"

I turn on the Keurig and pop in a pod. My phone chiming repeatedly from its place on the counter is grating on my nerves. I always thought I was an outcast for not owning a cell phone. Right now, I want to run it over with a car. Rubbing my tired eyes, I grab the device and answer the call trying to juggle a coffee mug from the cabinet and the creamer in one hand. "Hello?" I bark.

"Well, don't you sound like a ray of absolute sunshine this morning." Trice's greeting is heavy with sarcasm.

"Sorry, it's just early and as soon I got up my phone was chiming. Lonnie is already up and asking me about painting. Apparently, we have plans?"

"We do. Aiden was FaceTiming Lonnie this morning before the sun was even up. I made a reservation at one of those painting classes in town. You know the ones where everyone gets a canvas, and you watch the instructor and then follow the steps to make your own masterpiece?"

I vaguely know what he's referring to. I've seen them advertised on television recently. As much as I love to create, having to wait for someone to instruct me isn't really appealing. I itch to have a paintbrush in my hand, so I agree to go, and tell him I'll need no less than an hour to drink my coffee in peace and then get both Lonnie and I ready.

Trice: In my mom's SUV. Be there in five

It's a little strange that Crew never replied to my response. Maybe he went back to sleep or drove back to campus and has his phone on silent, not wanting to be another billboard statistic. I don't want to sound clingy. I'm new to this relationship stuff. I park my thoughts and swing open the door only to find a blissfully happy Crew standing on the porch.

"What are you doing here?"

I notice his smile first and the way it reaches his eyes. It's different and catches me off guard. There's a cheerfulness coming off him that's contagious. Sliding his hands into his pockets he boyishly rocks back on his heels. "Picking you up for our adventure."

"Did you plan this little outing?" A smile plastered on my face, I feel drugged by his clean scent, fresh from a shower as I guide Lonnie out of the house and lock the door behind us. Sliding my key into my back pocket. I tell Lonnie to go get in the car while handing him his booster seat.

"I wish. Honestly, I didn't figure that our first date would be a group affair. Yet, here we are. I'm down to make the best of it." He leans in and I jolt backward a step instinctively. Hurt clouds his face and gone is the golden glow in his eyes. "I won't be a secret. If we're going to be together, it's for the world to see. My brother included. I want a *real* relationship. I thought we established this last night."

A painful knot forms in my stomach. "Does he know we're *dating*? He's my friend, and I don't want to see him hurt when he obviously planned a fun day for us all to enjoy."

"You don't mind hurting me?" A tinge of pain is laced in his tone. The dejection is clear on his angular jaw.

I reach forward and cup his cheek. "I don't want anyone to be hurt. Let's just go and have fun with the boys. I'll talk to

Trice when we get back and tell him that we've decided to see where this thing between us takes you and I, and we'll see—"

"We'll see what? How he feels? His opinion doesn't matter in *our* relationship. It's fine that you're friends or whatever. Don't let him dictate what we both know is between us."

A play of emotions dance across his face. His eyes saying what his mouth doesn't. Why does he always feel inferior to Trice? It can't be just about the accident. I decide it's best to park those thoughts and focus on the one thing that I know can reel him back in.

"This thing between us is more than casual," I say. "We confided in one another last night, and you're right. I'm in."

"You can't be one foot in and one foot out the door. You need to come in and deadbolt the lock, Aurora. If you want to, that is. I can't go back to how it was before last night though. If you don't want this, tell me, and I'll stay on campus and leave you alone. It will fucking suck, especially since I've tasted your lips, but I will respect your decision."

"I want *you*. I choose you. I thought I made that clear."

He's completely right though. We can't start a relationship off on the wrong foot. The hard exterior he wears is merely a shell of the soft vulnerability that's inside. Taking a step forward, I slide my arms around his waist. A thrill dances down my spine at his nearness. Memories of last night flood me.

The confessions.

The kissing.

The promises made.

Parting my lips, I lean forward to meet his mouth and melt his worries away. With my eyes closed, I hear Crew inhale sharply in surprise. A surge of electricity ignites my body, and I pull him closer. Kissing Crew is inebriating. It's like the first page of a new book series, brimming with adventure and promise weaved into every chapter, taking your bra off at the end of a long day, the first stroke of paint against a blank canvas, and the first step into the ocean on a long-awaited vacation.

It is *that* good.

If I could weld our bodies together, I would do it in a heartbeat. *Pass me a welding hood and a torch, please.*

I can't even blame Della for throwing a fit when he ended things with her. If she was used to kisses like this. Soul shattering, knee buckling, make-out sessions that leave you questioning all previous smooches of your entire life?

Yeah. I should write her an apology letter tonight.

The shrill sound of a horn honking ends our embrace. I pull away slightly to keep my body in front of Crew's, trying to avoid eye contact with Trice, who is undeniably staring at us through the window wondering what's going on. I can feel his eyes. His glare burns a hole right to my beating heart, popping it like bubblegum. I can almost picture the steam rolling from the window before I even take a glance and give him a quick wave. He doesn't try to hide the grimace on his face. Each line of distaste for what he just witnessed is etched thickly on his frown. With furrowed brows, he honks again.

This is going to be so much fun. Not.

If you could taste my pessimism, it'd taste like charcoal.

"The cat's out of the bag," I whisper, as I lace my hand with Crew's. We walk toward the curb where the vehicle is parked, and he opens the passenger side of his mom's SUV, allowing me to slide in. The thick silence from Trice speaks volumes. I'm a bad friend. I should have texted him this morning and told him about Crew and what happened last night. The moment he called and said we had plans, I should have just blurted it out. He shouldn't have found out like this. Even if he and I were never even remotely involved romantically, I can still see the hurt on his face. Whether it be jealousy, anger, or just plain surprise, his response has my face heating up as I stare out the window. Knowing that I've caused him to be upset doesn't settle well in my gut.

Comfort, happiness, companionship. That's what friends are for. Right now, the vibe Trice is giving off doesn't feel remotely like any of those things. A parade of internal dialogue erupts in my head as I buckle my seatbelt and silently beg that our reservation is lost, and we have a reason to end our outing early today.

Rows and rows of trees pass by outside my window in a blur of oranges and luminous yellows. As the days get shorter, and the air chillier, winter is ready to make itself known. Pretty soon, we'll be confined to the house for months on end. I'll need to salvage my friendship with Trice during the gloomiest times of the year, despite dating his brother. I'm big on sunshine. My mood thrives on it.

The winter has notoriously not been my friend. Coming from foster care, it's not like I sported the warmest clothes or had access to brands that are built for this weather. Thin blankets are my nemeses and wearing extra socks is a trend I set ages ago. A smidge of hope settles with me, knowing that this winter will be different. Lonnie and I haven't wanted or needed for anything from shelter, clothes, or food. I still haven't fully embraced this new lifestyle. Trauma like ours doesn't just evaporate overnight. It's fading, though, and I find myself warming up to this town and the people in it the longer we're here.

The radio turns on and *Kidz Bop* blares through the speakers. Lonnie and Aiden sing along to the lyrics that they know by heart. Crew is right for not wanting to be my dirty little secret. I just needed time to tell Trice so he wouldn't have been taken off guard. He's shook. On the other hand, there's no way I can stomach Crew not feeling like he's enough for me. Doubt clouds my judgement. Maybe I'm not emotionally stable enough to start anything remotely romantic with anyone. I still have the same goal to turn eighteen and adopt Lonnie.

Will dating Crew be over before it really starts?

We make our way to the paint shop in record time since Trice's foot doesn't let off the gas pedal the entire ride. The shop is nestled in a row of stores that Bea would love. On her days off she likes to take us exploring. Most of the time we frequent the distilleries near town since they're a dime a dozen and rich in history and feature lots of different styles of architecture, which we found out Lonnie loves. Bea is big on trust. I guess that makes sense with her own history in the system. She's constantly trying to build a rapport with me and Lonnie. Pair that with her love language of gift giving, and she's basically a walking hug.

Lonnie loves reaping the benefits of her generosity more so than I do. I still find myself cringing a little inside every time she insists on buying me clothing or a named brand bag. I know she means well. Fancy labels don't do anything for me, so I usually decline, but she's determined to show us what it feels like to be taken care of and adored.

Today, for instance, there was a note about dinner being in the refrigerator ready to be put into the oven, along with a hundred-dollar bill for us to do something fun today. I appreciate the gesture even though Lonnie and I are accustomed to doing things like reading in the library or drawing. Stuff you can do without money. The first few times she and Russell left us cash, I pocketed it. For someone like me, you never know when you'll need it.

"I only bought four tickets, Crew, since you know, you weren't invited." Trice says coolly as he opens the door and waves the kids inside. I steal a glance at Crew from over my shoulder. He doesn't look remotely bothered by his brother's unfriendly comment.

"Good thing I didn't come to paint. I just came to spend time with my girl."

"You didn't even know she was an artist." Trice scoffs. "Aren't other creative people supposed to spy one another in a crowd or something?"

"We're not wolves. We don't just sniff each other out." Crew pads forward with his hand on my lower back.

"If an all-out pissing match ensues, I promise you both, I'll leave," I say. "We can talk things through later. This is the only warning you're getting." I give them both a stern look. Trice heeds my warning and goes to the counter to get our supplies and seating information. Crew looks annoyed, and I can feel the aggravation radiating off him.

But he's the one who pushed our new relationship status in Trice's face this morning. The tension is the consequence of that.

I can only hope this class is over sooner rather than later.

CHAPTER
TWENTY-THREE

CREW

A stab of guilt hits me. I knew barging in on the plans that Trice made would piss him off. What I didn't fully expect was seeing him fall over the edge as Aurora kissed me. If there was any doubt in her mind that he was harboring a crush on her, there isn't now.

It might be for the best. Now she'll be able to clear the air, he'll see that I got the girl, and all will be right in the world. Except, as much as I want to raise a triumphant flag declaring my victory where Aurora is concerned, I'm not a total tool. It pains me that my little brother is hurt. Even if it means that he has feelings toward the only girl who has ever made me feel an ounce of worth.

I should have let her talk to him first. Hindsight is 20/20.

Sauntering to our table, I notice that there are four easels aligned on a white table. Each with a blank canvas. I slide beside Aurora and rest my hand at the curve of her back. "I didn't know you liked art."

"There's a lot we don't know about each other."

"I know that I like your laugh and your mouth. Are there more important things than that in a relationship?"

"I really hope you're kidding." She seems dissatisfied as she sets her phone on the table and shakes her head. The ponytail holding her hair on top of her head sways, and I get a whiff of her coconut shampoo.

I reach forward to pull her chair out, only to grab hands with my brother, who also tries to pull it out at the same time. Awkward is an understatement. She's my girlfriend, and I'm determined to make that clear. "I got it, bro."

Trice's nod is swift, and he lets go of the metal chair and turns his attention toward Aiden and Lonnie settled beside him. I'm too old to play juvenile games. I know this. That doesn't stop my intrinsically competitive nature that has been buried since I gave up football and is now crawling back to the surface.

Aurora watches as Trice ties the aprons on for both Aiden and Lonnie. The hint of a smile tugs at her mouth. It's a small gesture. I won't lie and say a tinge of jealousy doesn't affect my mood. I should have taken the initiative to get them ready, since I'm not even painting anything today. I'm selfish of Aurora's time and am too hyper-focused on getting her to like me than to help the boys paint. I can control that. I can flirt and show her why I'll be a good boyfriend.

It still makes me jealous seeing how much of a natural Trice is as both boys give him high fives before they settle into their seats. He's the epitome of mannerly. Where I'm more of a talk first, think second kind of guy. He and Aiden have always had a special bond. Especially in the last couple years.

When I withdrew following the accident, they forged a union that I'm not a part of. It irked me at first. Not enough to do anything about it before now. I solemnly vow to change that and invest more time in my relationship with Aiden. Scout's honor or whatever.

I glance at Aurora and see how happy she is to be here

with everyone. She's beaming. This is her in her element that much is clear. Laying out her brushes, she sits patiently for the class to start. Even with the level of anticipation written on her face, I'd bet that she could fill her canvas without the help of today's instructor. Her smile is beautiful. I want to see it more which means I need to give her more reasons to be happy.

Every time that I'm with her, my attraction grows and intensifies. My hand aches to reach out and touch her. Instead, I settle on just looking at her. My eyes roam the creamy expanse of her neck that is bare since her hair is pulled up high on her head. I notice the way an artery pulses, and I wonder what she's thinking. If we weren't in a room full of people, I'd lean forward and place a kiss on the spot that's beckoning me like the crook of her finger.

The instructor starts the class and I zone out. My body is attuned to our proximity, but my mind is elsewhere. Letting out a long audible breath, I can't help but wonder if Trice is the better choice for her. Hell, he knew she liked to paint. Who knows what else she's confided in him. I don't know her favorite color or song. Or if she plans to attend prom as a senior this year. More importantly, I want to know her soul. What makes her feel pride and accomplishment. Does she plan to go to college or where does she see herself in five years? They've been friends for months. She and I spent that time bickering and fighting our feelings for one another. That time could have been better served. I make a mental note to get to know Aurora in ways that don't involve kissing her senseless, although I plan to do plenty of that as well.

As the instructor drones on about which colors to paint on what area of the canvas, I watch Aurora. She chews on her bottom lip with each stroke of her brush. The delicate way her hand dips her brush into the paint and then mixes it with another color, knowing exactly what blends best, has me watching her in awe.

She's an artist who has honed her craft. That much is evident. It's in the casual way that her hand holds her tools to the way that she's already ten steps ahead of the instructor. I'm thoroughly fascinated admiring her in her element and silently kicking myself for not knowing how much art meant to her sooner.

Thirty minutes later, a sense of pride spreads across Aurora's face as she finishes with one final stroke of her brush and lays it down. She glances over and catches me watching her intently. My gaze is intense and appreciative. I want to photograph her with my eyes. She is the epitome of beauty with her hands covered in paint; a small, dried flake of white on her cheekbone; and the light shining in her eyes.

This is definitely her happy place. Not here in this studio, specifically, but rather with a brush in her hand and a canvas in front of her. I store not only this memory of her in my brain's filing cabinet, but also how thoroughly pleased and satisfied she is with her masterpiece.

I want to be the reason she smiles this big too.

"You're amazing."

"You mean my painting?"

"It's nice. You're what is amazing, though. You should have told me how much you loved to create stuff."

"When was the most opportune time? When you caught me shoplifting allergy meds or when we were avoiding each other after Halloween for weeks or what about when we kissed for hours last night? Should I have stopped you and gave you a list of my hobbies then?" She ducks to hide her face.

"I wondered what you were stealing that day." I touch her cheek and turn her face toward me. "We jumped into this thing headfirst. It's not lost on me. I want to know everything about you. The luxury of the holidays coming up is that we have time. We'll both be on winter break, and I want to fill it with getting to know you the right way."

Her body slides forward on her chair. "I'd like that." I take the hint that she wants to be closer to me, and I inch forward and place a soft kiss on her temple. "First things first. I need to talk to Trice and hash out some things."

Swallowing my pride, I grumble, not caring in the slightest that I sound like a scorned lover. "Don't go switching teams on me."

I can't help but wonder why she feels the need to explain our newly forged relationship to him in the first place. Could she be harboring guilt of concealing romantic feelings for him too?

I'm lame and needy.

I want all of her attention.

My face flushes with embarrassment that I'm jealous of my own brother and the realization that we'd both go to war over *her*, hits me.

CHAPTER
TWENTY-FOUR

Today was invigorating. Even if it felt like I was clenching the detonator to two ticking time bombs. Holding a brush is as exhilarating for me as driving a race car is for a Formula One driver. Not knowing the outcome of a piece, the steady wave of images as my hand works swiftly trying to create alongside my brain's impulses. That feeling is magical. Painting is soothing and something I haven't had the opportunity to do much since our move, despite Bea's and Russell's best efforts.

They've tried to sign me up for every hobby under the sun. I should have painted something long before today just to get them off my back and to stop their persistent hounding to find a pastime. I just haven't been in the mood or relaxed enough to feel like creating. After this morning, I'm already itching to paint again. For the first time in a long while I feel like I can breathe.

The animosity is so palpable in the vehicle, the moment Trice slides the gearshift into park, everyone is scrambling to open their doors and scurry out of his mom's SUV. This feud between Trice and Crew isn't only taxing to them. I could even see annoyance on Lonnie and Aiden's face when Trice refused to stop for ice cream on the ride home. Trice appeared desperate to get back home. What those two need is a round table in a neutral zone. They need to talk about the boating accident, Matt's memory, and where they stand with one another.

Crew takes my canvas when we pull into the driveway, claiming it as his own. It's a simple landscape of an ocean view with pink, purple, and orange tones fading into the sunset with white birds in the sky and a small palm tree perched on the sand.

Lonnie and Aiden, with their paintings in tow, head toward the clubhouse. They both want to hang their master-pieces in there. I understand them both wanting the space to feel more like their own since it once belonged to the older boys. Putting their own stamp on it is understandable.

"I'll see you later, Crew," I lean forward and give him a one-armed hug. "That paint will take days to fully dry so be careful if you lean it against something." I don't want him to feel dismissed, but he knows that Trice and I need to talk without an audience. A look of sadness passes over his solid features. Biting my lip, I add. "I'll text you in a little while, okay?" He nods and heads toward the gate to the backyard.

"Trice, can we go inside and talk?"

"What's left to talk about? You're obviously dating my brother or doing whatever it is you're doing with him behind my back." Like a dragon breathing fire, anger flares from his mouth.

It was never my goal to hurt him. It wasn't even my intention to fall for his brother. For months, I tried with all my might not to. It was a losing battle after all the time I spent being hot and then cold toward him and finally giving in to my desire for Crew Jordan. I should have seen him coming from miles away. He weaseled his way into my heart despite my best efforts to keep him out. He's like a light-house, luring me in and beckoning my heart toward safer shores.

I turn on my heels, unlock the front door, and purposely leave it open. If Trice wants to have an honest conversation, I'm leaving the ball in his court.

We're three hearts bound by love and lies and as amiable as I want to be with Trice, because I do care about him, he has to accept what is going on between his brother and me. He's the best friend I've ever had. In a few short months, he broke through my hard exterior and helped remind me that I am a teenager and I'm not unlikable like the world taught me I was.

He made me step out of my comfort zone and have fun, even when I had forgotten what it was like to act my age. He gave me driving lessons and didn't chastise me when I knocked his headlight out. He helped me stop looking over my shoulder and provided me a safe place to be myself. To find out who Aurora Elyse Bradshaw is without danger lurking behind every corner.

Without his persistent jokes and presence, I'd probably still hate my life and this town. Somewhere between senior year starting and now, Trice's friendship helped heal me in ways that I can't even understand myself. I just don't know if I can have it in the way that I need it now, if it means jeopardizing his happiness. I won't be that selfish. Even with his cosmic smile and the way he puts me at ease, if being with Crew means that Trice is in constant torment, I know I'll have to choose one. It's almost impossible because both make me feel treasured in entirely different ways. From the boisterous laughter that Trice easily drags out of me to the myriad of feelings Crew makes me feel.

I don't know if I *can* choose.

Trice's face is haunted as he rounds the corner into the kitchen where I'm sitting at the island. The arctic blue of his eyes bore into mine and I know I've crushed him. It's written on his face.

"Let me get you a drink," he doesn't respond as I open the refrigerator and grab a bottle of water. I hold it out for him, and he takes it without as much as a thank you. His silence speaks volumes, and it puts me on edge. "Thank you for taking us painting. It means a lot to me. It felt so good to paint again."

"He didn't even know you liked to paint. Why would you want to be with someone who doesn't know you like I do?"

I want to tell him that Crew has been trying to get to know me for months, but I've shot him down every time. I don't think it will help matters so I lead with, "I didn't know how *you* felt about me fully until I saw your face when we kissed. I mean, I did maybe a little. I wasn't really sure, and now…I don't know what to say." I bite my lip until I feel it pulsate.

My heart is thumping with an unsteady beat in my chest as our friendship starts to crumble in front of me.

"How could you not have known, Rory?" His face drains of color. The guy standing in front of me is a shell of my once exuberant best friend. "I've been pining after you for months. You never saw me though. It's always been him. I see that now." The anger and hurt in his voice squeezes my heart until it feels as if there is no more blood left in it to pump through my body.

I climb off my stool and reach for him. Trice moves backward, shrugging me off, and I feel like I've been burned. Not by his touch. By his callousness.

"I care about you so much," I tell him. "You're my best friend and you helped me see that I matter to people. Your friendship brought me back from a dark place and showed me that my past doesn't define me. You never said anything about liking me until now."

"Are you hearing yourself? I didn't think I had to spell it out for you. You're a smart girl, Rory, and playing dumb isn't a good look. We've been hanging out for *months.* I drive you to and from school every day and walk you to your classes. We watch movies and share a blanket in my basement on a regular basis. Hell, we've held hands numerous times. Apparently, I needed a marker to write my feelings across my damn forehead for you to notice. Tell me you're not that naïve."

"I can't lose you over this. I can feel you pulling away. I'm so sorry, Trice. You've been so good to me, and I need you in my life."

He scoffs, "Apparently not as much as you need Crew."

"I never meant for this to happen. Crew just grew on me. I couldn't even admit how I felt about him to myself for weeks. Let alone confide in you." Tears well in my eyes. "We just decided to give it a try and see where it goes last night."

"You both can go to hell." His voice, full of wrath, sends chills down my spine. Fear twists in my gut because I know I've lost him.

Panic sets in.

"Don't do this." Anger invades my words, making them come out harsh. "I care about you both. Why can't we remain friends? Why do I have to choose between you both? This isn't fair, and you know it."

"I don't want to be your friend, Rory. I want you. All of you. He doesn't deserve you. And you're right, I broke down your walls. I showed you how it feels to be cared about and cherished. Where was Crew then? Probably screwing Della. What I want doesn't matter because you've obviously already been claimed by my brother, so forgive me if I need a little space."

With tears pricking the backs of my eyes, I swallow my pain and put Trice's needs first. "If that's what you need. I understand. I'll give you space." He turns and takes a full step toward the back door. With his hand on the handle, he offers me one last look. "I'm not going anywhere," I say. "Whenever you're ready to mend, this...us...I'll be waiting."

"Don't hold your breath." His words strike my soul like a lightning bolt.

I have to remind myself that he doesn't mean what he's saying because his eyes are the key to his soul, and although icy and brimmed with torment, he holds my gaze long enough for me to see that he's speaking from a place of anger. I have faith that he will come around. I just have to be patient enough to wait it out.

After he slams the back door, I storm into the living room and toss myself onto the couch. Tears roll down my cheeks before I even have a chance to get situated.

I cry for my friend who I hurt unintentionally, and I cry for myself when I realize that I'm not broken. For years, I held in my tears afraid that they showed my weaknesses.

I'm not weak now.

Trice helped me see that.

After what seems like forever, I wipe the last tear away and grab a book from the table I left there yesterday. I need to get lost in someone else's problems for a little while and forget about my own.

Lonnie and Aiden are still outside in the clubhouse. They'll be there for hours or until one of them gets hungry or thirsty. Their friendship is inspiring. Being bounced around from different homes when I was younger, I never had a friendship that survived the constant moves. So much has changed in that department.

I'm lost in my book when the back door swings open. Figuring that it is one of the boys, I slide a bookmark at the page where I stopped and close it. It didn't take long for them to come in demanding a snack. Glancing up, I see the shadow of someone much larger than Lonnie or Aiden shutting the door.

"What are you doing here?"

"Trice came storming in guns blazing all Clint Eastwood style ten minutes ago and went straight to his room. You didn't text me. I figured that conversation went well. So, I thought you might want some company."

I hold the book up in the air from my position on the couch. With a few quick strides, Crew is settling onto the couch beside me. "Since you have your fictional characters keeping you company, I'll just sit here and let *you* keep *me* company." He nestles into the couch and grabs the throw blanket off the back unfolding it in a frenzy and then covering himself up. "I didn't peg you as a big reader."

I cross my arms and wrinkle my nose. "What does that mean? I love to read."

"It wasn't anything negative. Trust me. Reading is sexy. I just didn't know you were so creative. Your love for art and painting and now reading. It gives me a different perspective of you."

"Do you like this perspective?" Scooting toward him, I lift the blanket and settle in by Crew's side. His arm slides behind my back and he gives me a gentle squeeze.

"I more than like it."

Opening my book, I slide my hand in and remove my bookmark. "You know each time you read a book, a tree smiles knowing that there is life after death."

"Now that's sexy." His last word is smothered by my lips. I savor the feeling of raging passion that his kiss stirs in me. I could get used to this. Crew and I relaxing on a Saturday and enjoying one another's company. It almost seems surreal in a sense. "As much as I want nothing more than to kiss you senseless. I want to know how the convo with Trice went."

Half sitting up, half leaning on his chest, I ask. "You'd really rather talk about your brother than kiss me?"

"When you put it like that, no. Absolutely not." He lets out a low, throaty sound. "But I told you I wanted to get to know more than your mouth. So here I am, asking questions. Now I want answers."

"A little cuddle session isn't going to charm me into talking ya know?"

"If you think this is me being charming, you have no idea what you're in for. You may even be impressed when you let me take you out on a real date."

"You once said you'd make a good boyfriend if you wanted to."

"You'll have to give me a learning curve because I'm a little behind in the dating department. Spill the gory details. Wait, should I make popcorn?"

"Stop. That's so mean." Sitting up, I cross my legs and face him. "I'm holding you to that 'real' date and, I'll cave. Apparently, Trice likes me. Like-likes me. Well, he did. He hates me now."

"You didn't know?"

The pit of my stomach churns. "I feel like garbage. He's always been so kind and always a gentleman. I just thought that was his personality. I mean I had an inkling. Now I feel even worse."

"Don't feel bad. It sounds like he's pulled the wool over your eyes. Honestly my brother is a dick most of the time. Now that he made it clear he has feelings for you, how do you feel about that?"

"Sorry for him and sad."

"Care to elaborate?" Crew grabs one foot and pulls my leg on top of his. He starts to knead at the soles of my feet with his knuckles. I melt with his every touch.

"I'm upset that he's hurt. He should have come clean and told me how he felt before. I would have told him that I cared about him. Strictly as a friend. And could have avoided this whole disaster of a day."

"Do you regret us?" He asks firmly.

My thoughts race. "No. Not at all. I do wish that we didn't spring this on him this morning. Especially now, knowing that he likes me. I can't imagine how much seeing us kiss this morning wounded him. I don't regret it. I think you had me from the first time we met, and you told me to get my eyes checked."

"My game is better than I showcased, I can promise you that." The tangible bond between us tightens. Resting our foreheads together, Crew sighs before his thumb climbs the outside of my throat, roaming deliciously up and down. "It's Trice's loss," he says.

The gentle massage of his hand sends a current of desire through me. I take his hand and place a kiss in the center of his palm before I lean forward and kiss his chin. His mouth swoops down and captures mine.

"I'm hanging on by a thread, and you're holding the lighter."

"I'm burning with you." Crew ravages my mouth, taking my breath away with the urgency of his kiss.

The back door swings open and Lonnie and Aiden stumble into the kitchen. "Eww!" Lonnie snorts.

Aiden laughs as he climbs onto the stool at the kitchen island. "Girls have cooties."

A flash of annoyance flickers on my face. "If girls have cooties, I guess I'll just sit here and read and let Crew make you guys lunch then."

CHAPTER
TWENTY-FIVE

Fall comes and goes, and we welcome the shortest season of the year, winter. Things between Aurora and I are going great. Being around her is easy. She makes me laugh, which is something that Della never did.

Sometimes it's hard to think about Aurora's past before she came to live with Russell and Bea. I'd do just about anything to erase any heartache she had before we met. Hell, I wish I could erase the pain of losing my brother as a friend too. At times, a part of me feels like she chose the wrong brother.

My therapist's voice sounds internally. *"The reason you self-sabotage is because it allows you to predict what is going to happen. Which gives you the illusion of self-control. You couldn't control the outcome of the boating accident. Just as much as you can't control getting a flat tire or catching the flu."*

Being with someone romantically and willingly handing them control not to break your heart is the ultimate act of trust. Although Aurora has tried to dismiss those thoughts repeatedly. Russell gave me a stern warning about our ages since she's not eighteen yet and I am, and Trice is still ignoring us both. He's perfected the cold shoulder. He might even be nominated for an Oscar for his behavior.

Aurora has been learning some new acting skills of her own, pretending like Trice's standoffishness doesn't bother her. Anyone can see that it does. She's been spending a lot of time with her friend Andrea. It's good for her to have friends that she can confide in, especially girlfriends. I'm thankful for her filling the void that Trice left in Aurora's heart. I wish Trice would get his head out of his ass and come to terms with her and I being together. Every time I've tried to talk to him, he storms off claiming he's late for practice or some other commitment that doesn't involve being around me. Deflection should be his middle name.

Knowing how much Lonnie means to Aurora, I've made a solid effort to rebuild my relationship with Aiden. We've gone to a couple college basketball games. I never paid attention to how much he loved basketball before. I figured he'd follow in Trice and my footsteps with football as our sport of choice. He's his own person, though, and it's endearing to see how much he loves basketball. Lonnie is a cool kid too. I can see why Aurora is enamored with him. He's honest to a fault.

Last week, I was eating dinner at Aurora's house, and he announced in front of everyone that I had a piece of asparagus in my teeth. A wave of humiliation came over me. Then I thought, what the hell, and put two spears in my mouth like a walrus. The table erupted in laughter and Aurora almost peed her pants.

These small moments, pockets of happiness, have been chiseling away at the pain left by Matt's death. I'm starting to feel more like myself. The version I was before the boating accident that sank the carefree guy I was. He's trying to claw his way back to the surface. She's the ray of hope that I desperately needed and is helping the full-of-life Crew come out again.

I can see her starting to open herself to the possibility of letting loose too. Despite the absence of friendship from Trice, she's becoming more than just my girlfriend. She's becoming my friend, too.

It's not lost on me what that means. I want to be her life jacket as much as she is mine. That's why this weekend, I have something special planned for her. Pete, my roommate on campus, flew back home to be with family over break so my dorm will be empty. She has no idea the extent I'll go to, if only to see her happy.

"You got permission from Russell and Bea for me to spend the night with you, alone in your dorm?"

"Sort of. I got permission to hang out with you. Then Andrea, and I, conspired for her to say you were staying the night at her house to exchange gifts. Since she's leaving to visit her family in Chicago on Christmas Eve."

"I've never slept with a guy before."

I lift my eyebrow. "Me either."

Her lips press into a white slash. "You doofus. You know what I meant. I've never stayed the night with a guy before. The other, well you know. I've done that."

Aurora and I finally had the exes talk. She admitted to doing some things she's not proud of. With her knowledge of Della, there really wasn't much for me to admit. She knows that I chose not to have sex and doesn't berate me for it. Even though she pushes my resolve on purpose, I know that tonight will be no exception. I want so badly to give into temptation. We keep inching closer and closer to crossing a line that will seal both of our fates evermore. Once it's crossed, she'll be mine forever.

"You're cute when you're embarrassed. Don't worry about

our sleeping arrangements. If you feel uncomfortable, you can take my bed and I'll crash on Pete's."

"I want to sleep with you," she blurts out. "Wait. Like sleep, sleep. Not, you know, more than sleep."

I wait, challenging her to finish. Rolling her eyes, she resists. "Let's just get to campus. I have food being delivered. You can see your surprise and then we'll see where the night takes us."

Thankful that my dad let me drive his truck. The light dusting of snow on the ground would be enough to send my car into a tailspin. It takes forty minutes before we arrive, and we pull into a parking spot. With a car or two here and there, the lot is almost empty. No one in their right mind stays on campus during winter break. It works in my favor since I long for privacy with Aurora. Since we've become an official couple, we haven't had much alone time. We've been hanging out at her house a lot, so she doesn't have a run in with Trice, who is still ignoring her. That means that Aiden has tagged along with me. We've played more board games, hide and seek, and video games than I have in years.

"Let me get your door." I open my door and step into the cold night air. It's frigid, and I regret not wearing a jacket over my hoodie. Grabbing her hand, I help her out of the truck and slide her backpack on my shoulder.

"Before I moved in with Russell and Bea, I lived not too far from here."

"I didn't know that. I mean I know you lived in the city. I didn't know it was close to campus." Sliding my key card from my pocket, I usher her through a set of locked double doors.

"Our paths could have crossed before that day in the corner store, and you may not have ever known." Her words are teasing, the meaning not so much. I break the ringing silence, by dropping her bag and pinning her against the brick wall.

"My heart could find yours in a sea of people. In this city. In this state. In the world. You're the missing puzzle piece I've been searching for. You make me feel whole for the first time in my life."

I watch as her smile stretches across her face. "I'd like to think that too. Crew, I… I..." Words wedge in her throat. "I need to pee. Can we hurry upstairs?"

Tucking away the thought that she was about to tell me she loves me, I hit the elevator to my floor and weave our hands together. "I'll lead the way." I wink when I catch her eye.

CHAPTER
TWENTY-SIX

RORY

My heart squeezes in alarm as I realize that I almost laid all my cards on the table. My tongue feels like an old newspaper, dry and dusty, by the time the elevator doors slide open. Irrational thoughts fill my head. My birthday is nearing in a few months, as is graduation. Spring comes with too many uncertainties. I can't tell Crew that I'm in love with him, only to pack my bags and leave just as quickly as I arrived.

He'd be distraught.

Not to mention how hard it was for him to break down the fortress around my heart. It took months of me pushing him away and him not once relenting. Even when I was a complete brat most of the time. Now that I have him, will I really be able to just walk away?

I hesitate to follow his lead as he opens his dorm room door. I'm torn by conflicting emotions. I want so badly to open myself up fully to him. I want to admit the truth and let it bleed from my mouth. I *want* Crew. How can I have all of him when I'm not willing to give him all of me?

I'm harboring my plans to flee, and the guilt is slowly smothering me.

"Welcome to my humble abode." He spreads his arms, inviting me into his room.

With a war of emotions raging inside, I cross the threshold and decide to bury my tumult for the evening. He's obviously gone out of his way to give me a surprise. I don't want tomorrow's worries to take away from tonight. I look around his room and try to comprehend what I'm seeing. "Did you...is that for me?"

His head swivels and he places my bag on the floor in front of his bed. "You were the happiest I've ever seen you that day when you were painting. I wanted to give you space to create, to paint again. Plus, it's not solely for you. Seeing you in your element did something for me too."

I take a step forward. Until we're toe to toe. "What did it do for you?"

"I shouldn't answer that honestly right now," he stammers. Gliding forward, I examine the easel with a work stool seated in front of it. The cost of this set up is not lost on me. "There's more. I wasn't sure what you preferred to paint with. I talked to Bea, and she told me when you guys went on a tour at the gallery in town you mentioned you'd love to have a set of acrylics."

"You didn't. Oh my gosh. You did!" I notice the paint set on his comforter. It's an Arteza acrylic set. One that costs too much for any college student to be able to afford.

"I did some research on oil versus acrylic. I read that a lot of artists nowadays are leaning toward acrylic because it's fast drying and easier to work with."

"This is too much. You shouldn't have spent this much money on me."

"It's nothing." He draws me in and covers my hands with his own.

"It is to me. I've loved painting for as long as I can remember. I've never been able to have a set up as nice as this. Money may not be an issue for you, but it certainly is for me. I'm still getting used to this lifestyle. It's going to take some time to be okay with being given something so generous. I really shouldn't accept this, but I know you're not going to give me a choice."

Crew's fingers flutter to the back of my neck and hold me in place. Our eyes say what our mouths can't. Feeling as if my breath has been restricted, silence looms between us as thick as a heavy mist. All the tension from earlier fades with his thoughtful act. I don't want to think about my future or turning eighteen and what that will mean for me and Lonnie. I want to experience life in the now. With Crew by my side. I swallow with effort and find my voice. "I heart you."

"You heart me? What exactly does that mean, Aurora?"

Nervously, I comb my hand through my hair and then throw my hands over my face in embarrassment.

"Don't hide from me. I just want you to explain what that means because I know how I feel and what it would mean to me to say that. I want to hear it from you."

Wrinkling my nose, I steal a slanted look at him and turn around quickly with my dignity somewhat intact. Crew shuffles in front of me and cradles my face in his hands. He smiles benignly, like he's dealing with a temperamental child. "Open that pretty little mouth and talk."

I feel my flesh change colors. My reaction seems to amuse Crew. "I just care about you a lot. I don't know what it means. I just felt it, so I said it."

"You do know what it means, and when you're ready, I'll be waiting to hear it again." Giving him a resigned sigh, I walk toward his twin-sized mattress and run my hand over the paint set. "They're yours. Open them."

Without hesitation, I start to tear and rip at the packaging in a frenzy. Feeling as if my smile will be permanently etched onto my face, I can't hide my excitement as I open my kit. No one has ever gifted me anything more unique or meaningful in my entire life. Sure, Bea and Russell gave me a cell phone and laptop. That doesn't come close in comparison to what Crew has just gifted me. This easel and paint set is a treasure. An outlet. A way to project my energy and escape. "Are you sure you don't mind if I just sit here and paint?"

"Hell no. That's why I brought you here. I want to watch you. Food should be here shortly. Get started and when it arrives, we'll take a break."

The clock hits ten at night and I notice my back aches from sitting in the same position for so long. We take a short break and eat Chinese food that he had delivered to his dorm. I don't know how he knew that crab Rangoon was my favorite, but he ordered me my own order. That's love and it makes him even more attractive, in my opinion.

"I think I'm done for the night."

Crew climbs off the bed where he had been watching me and opens the bottom drawer on his dresser. He turns and starts to unbutton his jeans and then slides them off and puts on a pair of sweatpants. I know I should turn away and stop gawking, but the message isn't making its way to my frontal lobe. Sitting on my chair, I swivel so that I'm facing his back. He slides off his shirt and tosses it to the floor while facing his dresser, oblivious to my longing.

I marvel at the breadth of his shoulders. There is so much ink tattooed onto his flawless skin, I get lost trying to take it all in. The magnetism of his body is potent, and my view makes my pulse leap with excitement. He turns, and I'm caught like a deer in headlights.

"Aurora, you're playing a dangerous game." The way my name drips from his lips sends me into a frenzy. I swallow tightly as the base of my throat keeps a steady beat with my heart. Heat rises from an unusual place on my body.

"I didn't mean to ogle you."

"I don't give a deep-fried pickle if you stare at me." He

motions to his abs that are on clear display since he hasn't put a shirt on yet. "I just want to reciprocate the feeling." He tosses a T-shirt at me from his dresser drawer. "I'm sure you packed night clothes but wear mine. I want to see you in my shirt." It's a command.

I implore Crew with my eyes. He may not be ready to hand over his virginity anytime soon, but I'm not a saint, and I'm not going to start acting like one now. Especially since we're finally alone. We don't have to stop mid-make out session because Lonnie wants to play a game with us. A shudder passes through me as I muster up the courage to take off my shirt and slide the material over my head and toss it to the side next to his discarded clothes.

Standing in just my leggings and bra, I glance up to see Crew's eyes searing a path from my neck to my navel. I slide on his shirt and without hesitation roll my leggings off until they're in a pool on the floor. His shirt falls to my knees, covering my bottom.

"I hope you have a spare pair of sweatpants in that dresser."

"My pants will swallow you whole."

I give a demure smile before saying, "Come on, Jordan, it's a little drafty in here."

He opens a drawer and pulls out a pair of pants and then takes a small step toward me, holding them out in front of him. The bulky material forms a barrier between us. "I know you're trying to chisel away at my decision to stay a virgin."

Shoving past him, I pull back his comforter and settle into his bed. "Is it working?" With fiery determination, he jumps on the bed and nestles himself between my legs. We're clothed and alone. A throaty growl escapes his lips and makes me feel like I'm chipping away at his steadfastness. Precariously, I test his limits once more by tilting my hips up to meet his frame.

"You're trying hard, aren't you?" There's a peculiar tone in his voice that leads me to believe that even he is questioning his motive to stay celibate.

"Did you say hard?" I taunt and then solicit another tongue-thrusting kiss. His breath is irregular as his lips part and let me in. We exchange open-mouthed, scintillating kisses for what seems like an hour before our molten-hot moment comes to a halt.

"I think I should take Pete's bed tonight." In a subtle move, he shifts his weight so that he's no longer above me, but beside me. His breath fans my skin.

A familiar wave of being unwanted engulfs me. I'm dragged under and discarded. I've never been *enough* for anyone. Not my birth parents or the countless foster parents I've had in my lifetime. I wasn't even good enough of a friend for Trice to want to fight for me. He just gave up and tossed me aside like our friendship was meaningless.

"I need to use the restroom." I quickly hop over Crew, slide on my shoes, and exit his room in a hurry. I don't even wait for a response as I shut the door and lean against it. The ridiculous notation that he doesn't even want me eats at me as I take a step down the deserted hallway to the restroom.

I don't know how long I'm gone until the sound of a door creaking on its hinges, tears my attention away from my self-loathing as I stand in front of the dimly lit mirror.

"Aurora, are you in here?"

After I consider hiding behind a shower curtain, I shove down my pride and answer. "Yes."

"Are you okay? What happened?" He inches into the bathroom, apprehension on his face. "Bones."

Did he just on the grave me?

Impassively, I shrug. It's not like I can lie now. He just declared bones. The concern on his face pulls at my heart-strings. "If you don't want to have sex with me, just be honest and tell me."

"That's why you froze up on me?"

I lean against the white porcelain sink when my eyes finally meet his. I consider his question for a moment, feeling all of two inches tall. The concern in his tone jars me. But my self-deprecation has a strong hold. I've been conditioned for too many years that I'm not good enough. "I just want the truth. Am I not good enough for you? Sexy enough? Wealthy enough? What is it?"

"Are you that naïve, woman?" His large hand cups my check, and he positions my face so I'm looking directly at him. "*You* are too good for me. I'm not good enough for you. You're so much better suited for my brother. He aspires to have a career in football, has goals, and a future ahead of him. I don't know what tomorrow looks like for me, much else the next year. I'm a year behind in college, have a criminal record thanks to Trice, and am so unworthy of your heart that it actually makes me sick thinking about it. I don't have much to offer you other than a promise. And *you're* standing here thinking that *you're* not enough. Turn around and look in the mirror, Aurora. You're more than enough. It's me that has this delirious notion that somehow, you'll see past all my flaws and love *me*."

His aggressive declaration leaves my mind reeling and my heart beating in a harsh, uneven rhythm. I yank on the hem of his shirt and pull him toward me, almost violently. "I said I heart you and I meant it. You're the most real thing I've ever had in my life, and I get to call you mine. My flaws run deep. I've had to steal just to eat. I'm a habitual liar because not telling the truth to my social workers became second nature. I had sex with someone twice my age just so I had a couch to sleep on once. If anyone should have reservations about this relationship, it's you."

The expression on Crew's face changes from cold fury to a pained tolerance quicker than I can wipe away the tear that slides down my cheek. The darkness in his eyes I saw when we first met is back. His jaw sets in a vicious hold and I hold my breath in expectation of what he might say to my truth.

"Bones," I gulp.

"I'm only going to say this once," Crew's voice is deep, husky, and the chocolate of his eyes turns to a burnt char. I think I may have pushed him too far. "You are worthy of love. You've been dehumanized by men and the foster care system. Your truth wounds me. The fact that you think I don't want to sleep with you hurts me to my core, Aurora. It's all I want.

"If you knew how many times I've had to take a cold shower since meeting you, you'd understand. You're an angel. If I didn't know any better, I'd say Matt sent you to save me. I don't want to have sex because the first time..." His voice drifts into a hushed whisper. "When I lay you down and slide into you, claiming you, marking you, it will mean *forever*. When you turn eighteen and you're ready for that, you just let me know."

CHAPTER
TWENTY-SEVEN

CREW

've lived in a constant state of purgatory since the accident. Numb and disassociated from the world. I was waiting for a fire to light my soul. Kissing Aurora is like a life worth of prayers being answered with a single peck. She's the passion that I summoned. Without warning, she's become my reason for…everything. I don't know what I've done to deserve her. I'm just glad that she's mine.

That night at my dorm, I was as honest as I've ever been in my life. I'd say the same for her. Hearing her bare her soul and spill its secrets and then finally letting me in. That trust is the best gift I've ever received. We ended up crashing as soon as we got back to my room. Emotionally spent. Holding one another like our lives depended on it.

We've been inseparable since.

On Christmas Eve, my mom hosted a small get together for a couple families in our neighborhood. She loves playing hostess and creating fancy hors d'oeuvres and cocktails. After the party, Aiden and Lonnie made reindeer food, and then we sprinkled it in both of our front yards so that Santa and his reindeer could stop and have a treat. The light in Aurora's eyes was unmistakable. It was pure delight. Happiness radiated from her in that moment, and I wanted to bottle it up. Store it forever. We parted ways and texted early into Christmas morning. Even though we dove into our relationship headfirst, we're still getting to know one another. We decided to backtrack a bit and do it the right way.

Me: Favorite food

*Aurora: *pizza emoji**

Aurora: Favorite vacation spot

Me: Hard toss-up between Hawaii and Colorado. Luv to ski and surf

Aurora: Go figure. I've never left KY

Me: You will. I'll see to it

Aurora: <3

Aurora: Favorite memory?

Me: The day I finally had the balls to wakeboard. Matt had been trying to teach me for two summers.

Me: Why did you get moved from your last placement and move in with B and R?

Aurora: That's an in-person convo

Me: Noted. What's your biggest fear?

Aurora: I've lived them. There's nothing else to be scared of

Aurora: This is too deep. Rom-coms or horror movies?

Me: Horror all the way

Me: How many guys have you slept with?

Aurora: …

Me: No judging. I'm curious how many you're going to compare me to one day

Aurora: Shut up. You have something they don't

Me: ?

Aurora: My heart

Me: Get some rest. Santa won't come unless you're sleeping

I drift off dreaming of Aurora in a bathing suit, windswept hair, lying on the beach with a book in her hand.

In the morning, Aiden's excited squeals wake me from a deep sleep.

"It snowed!" The pads of his feet echo in the hallway as he races down the stairs.

Sliding on a pair of red, checkered pants mom insisted we all wear to bed last night, I make my way downstairs taking the steps two by two. A white Christmas surprises us all when we gather in the living room and dad pulls open the curtain. A blanket of snow lays untouched in our yard. The clubhouse, situated in the center of our yards looks small with a mound of snow weighing on its metal roof. I slide open my phone and fire off a text to Aurora.

Me: *Merry Christmas. The best gift in the world is being your boyfriend*

The cheese factor is off the charts with that one. It's true though. Nothing under our tree can compete with the gift of being hers and she being mine.

Aiden is over the moon about golfing lessons that dad bought him along with the tiniest set of golf clubs I've ever seen. Ripping the box to shreds, he holds up a club grinning from ear to ear.

I gifted dad a gift card to *TopGolf.* Which incidentally pairs well with Aiden's gift and gave my mom a pair of earrings. Trice is still giving me the cold shoulder. Regardless of his hateful attitude, I gave him a new pair of headphones. He didn't get me anything. Not that I expected him to. Christmas is about giving, not receiving. A simple hello or thank you would have sufficed though. As much as I try to act like it doesn't bother me, the distance between us leaves me with a strange twinge of frustration.

I won't stop trying to win him back because, I'm the one who pushed him away after the boating accident. I was furious that he didn't even have the guts to acknowledge that I willingly took the fall and punishment for his actions. I did it to spare him.

It's not the fact that I took responsibility and paid the price. I'd do that again in a heartbeat if it meant that he wouldn't feel the animosity that the residents of this town tormented me with. It's more the fact that he didn't appreciate what I did for him, and now he's upset that I chose my happiness over his for once. I chose Aurora, and he's behaving like a child who didn't get his way. I hope one day he'll come around and accept our relationship for what it is. It's doubtful.

After we finish opening presents, dad cooks breakfast and then mom shoos us away to get showered and presentable for company. My parents usually host this holiday. Our house will be filled to the brim with cousins and aunts and uncles.

Knowing this is the first Christmas that Aurora and Lonnie have probably had where they're showered with gifts, I try to only send a few messages to her, not wanting to intrude on this day. If I know Bea like I think I do, she went overboard. I was always so envious of Matt. Him being an only child meant that he got more toys than my brothers and I put together. Our parents are strict on the want, need, wear, read rule. I can still hear my dad saying he doesn't want us to grow up to be entitled little assholes as I slide into my bathroom and turn on the shower.

The Greenwells and my family have always spent Christmas evening together. After the chaos of the day and seeing our extended families, we usually play games and snack on leftover food well into the night. Even after Matt's death, we continued the tradition. This year will be no different.

Aurora: *Merry Christmas to you too <3*

Smiling from ear to ear, I step into the shower and immediately turn the temperature knob toward cold. Aurora has that effect on me.

By the time seven o'clock rolls around, I'm bouncing on my heels with anticipation of seeing my girl. As soon as the doorbell rings, I hop over the back of the couch and rush to answer the door.

"Merry Christmas!" Lonnie shouts with glee as the door swings open. His arms are stacked with presents.

"You too, buddy." I rustle the tight curls on his head and wave everyone inside.

Aurora is the last to enter. Just the sight of her makes me weak in the knees. She's wearing a cream sweater dress that hugs her body in all the right places and knee-high brown boots that accentuate her slender legs. Her blonde hair is woven into a long braid that is draped over her shoulder. And her lips. They're painted a deep red, and instantly I'm shifting in my pants with images of her giving me a mouth hug. I don't know how much longer I can hold off. She's tenacious and has made her intentions clear.

Most of the time the only thing that is intimate about sex is the actual aspect of doing it. I don't care what anyone says, virginity is cool. My choice to remain a virgin is solely based on the fact that I need a deeper connection with someone and hadn't found that until Aurora. Getting to know her more, what she likes to do in her spare time, learning about her past, and her love of painting; it's pulling me under, and I know I won't be able to resist her for much longer. Matt died a virgin and I'm not about to go out that way.

"You look beautiful." I embrace her in a hug.

Still wearing my dress pants and white button down from earlier, her eyes roam over my body. "Not so bad yourself, Jordan."

"Get your butts in here." My mom shouts from the living room, eager to get the present opening underway. When families are as close as ours, you can bet that we exchange gifts too. That didn't change after Matt's passing. We had time to mourn his death and each of us did it differently. Russell and

Bea didn't push our family away like one might think after such a tragedy. If anything, it pulled our families together and made us closer.

The next hour is spent unwrapping gifts, tossing wrapping paper at one another, and laughter that is so rich, I'm sure that the sound will be ingrained in the walls for generations to come.

When it's time for Aurora and me to exchange gifts, the room grows quiet. Trice claims that he feels a migraine coming on and excuses himself to his room for the rest of the evening. Disappointment is evident on Aurora's face, but I plan to replace it with my gift. I'm sure she thought the paint set I got her was all she was getting this year. She's wrong. If she'll let me, I plan to shower her and show her how much I care about her for years to come.

When she gave Trice his present before he stormed off, I could tell how proud she was. Her smile quickly faded as he gave her a measly thanks and leaned it against the wall, not appreciating her talent. Like pouring salt into a wound, he didn't even hide his attempt to crush her spirit. The canvas with his football jersey painted on it and his number is a sight to see. Aurora is blind to her own talent. Knowing how much the sport means to him, she dug deep and created something magical only to be rejected by his idiocy. It's safe to say he's digging a hole that I don't think he's ever going to be able to climb out of.

"Don't let him get to you. Not today. Here, open yours." I slide a large, thin box in front of her.

"What's this? You already gave me too much with my art supplies. I can't accept whatever this is." She holds the package wrapped in golden paper.

"I can't return it, so you have no option but to open it." A faint light twinkles in her eyes. I know she's not used to receiving gifts. I haven't gotten her alone yet to ask her how Christmas morning went at her house. I want to know about every gift she received and how opening them made her feel. Anticipation nips at me as she carefully unwraps the package. Taking her sweet time, I reach over and rip the last shred of wrapping paper from the box.

"Crew Jordan!" My mom chastises me from her seat on the couch where she's holding what she claims is hot tea in her Santa mug.

From our spot on the floor, I match her smile. "What? I'm excited and she's going too slow. Come on, baby." As soon as the term of endearment leaves my mouth, I instantly regret it.

"Baby," Aiden coos. "Gross!"

"K-I-S-S." Lonnie adds, his joke causing Aiden to fall onto the floor into a fit of laughter.

"Just wait until you guys start to date. I'm going to torture you both for this." Aurora watches me. "Open the box," I insist. She opens it and slides out the big frame. A look of confusion covers her delicate features.

"I had a star named after you. That's a picture of it and here are its coordinates." I point at the information printed on the frame. For a moment our families' presence fades, and I forget that they're all watching us. "My world was dark for a long time after Matt's death. Until you showed up and shook it up with your smart mouth and beauty. You lit up my life. Like a star. I just wanted you to know how much that meant...how much you mean to me."

She audibly gulps. "It's perfect. Thank you." She leans forward and kisses my cheek. "Now your turn." Handing me a box that is almost identical to mine in size and shape, she sits up and tucks her legs underneath of her.

"What is it?" I ask.

"Open it and find out, goof."

I unwrap it in record time and slide out a canvas. My breath catches in my throat as my eyes take in the image in front of me with somber curiosity. The colorful masterpiece is incredible. It's unique and on vibe with Aurora's style. It quickly becomes my most prized possession.

There is a skeleton painted on the canvas with the thoracic region being prominent. The ribcage, spine, and pelvis are painted a tannish color. The contrast of the bones shines in the Christmas lights twinkling on the tree beside us. Within the ribcage a plethora of flowers—amaryllis, lilies, and roses all in different stages of bloom—sprout, poking through each rib. Green stems and colorful flowers are interwoven and fill the voided spaces. The word *bones* is painted under the imagery. The fact that she painted this for me means more than I can describe.

She admitted to 'hearting me' a few weeks ago. This painting says more. Something clicks, and I know beyond the shadow of a doubt that I love Aurora Bradshaw.

I know I need to say something, but there are no words in my vocabulary that can compare to how her gift makes me feel. I capture this memory and hold it deep inside under lock and key to keep this moment pure and unsullied. Wishing that her family, my parents, and our brothers weren't privy to our exchange, I lean forward and wrap my arms around Aurora tightly.

She barreled into my life as unexpected as a rainstorm. The depth of my private admission is like a reckoning that I can't postpone for long. I want to shout it from the rooftop. Her jade eyes look at me hopefully, waiting for me to say something. Anything. So, I do. "You win Christmas."

CHAPTER
TWENTY-EIGHT

RORY

Trice and I still aren't on speaking terms. I've texted and pleaded for him to have a face-to-face discussion with me. He either flat out ignores me or claims to be too busy, which I know is a bald-faced lie. He's become a master deceiver. It's honestly a slap in the face. I don't know what I expected from him. It certainly isn't his childish behavior.

I consider that this is the *real* version of Trice. The one that I was too enamored to see from the start of our friendship. When he tricked me with his fluttering eyelashes and supportive nature. He's being petty, and at times downright hateful. It's a kick to the gut. Especially since he lives next door, and I'm dating his brother. I feel like we've been playing the longest game of hide and seek. Whether I'm picking Lonnie up from a playdate with Aiden or going to see Crew, if Trice is home I try to keep to the shadows.

Andrea has filled the Trice-shaped hole that he left in my life. She's been bringing me to and from school and puts up with my constant need to control every situation, including where we got a part-time job at. I suckered her into applying at the paint place, *Painting with a Twist*. I haven't really given her much backstory on my life, other than that Bea and Russell are my foster family and my plan for my eighteenth birthday is to adopt Lonnie. She didn't really offer an opinion when I laid out my idea—which, granted, isn't that well thought out—but she listened. It was the first time I ever told anyone other than Lonnie. It felt good to get it off my chest.

It's a heavy secret to keep.

Winter break came to an end quicker than I liked. I was hesitant to go back to school, still being on the outs with Trice. Having a scorned best friend is worse than having to put on a wet pair of pants.

The days pass and the more time that is spent with Trice snubbing me, the harder it's going to be for us to reconcile if he ever comes to his senses. By the second month of being back at school, I find a routine and some semblance of balance back in my life. Between working and trying to accumulate a nest egg in my first ever savings account, I've never been happier for a distraction.

Part of my newfound freedom comes from getting my driver's license. I'm thankful for the independence as I drive to the therapy center in town. I didn't mind being dropped off and picked up, but I finally broke down on my last session with Mina and cried tears that had been pent-up for years. It may be weird to some to lay their deepest, darkest secrets on the table for their boyfriend's mom, but she's actually very easy to talk to and never gives off the impression that she's judging me.

It was liberating to crack my stone-cold heart open the rest of the way and let its insides pour out. Things that I had bottled up for years poured from my mouth. So much so, when Bea arrived to pick me up, it wasn't hard to miss the mascara that had dried under my eyes. She started probing, and I shut down.

That was the last session I attended.

Getting my license came with one stipulation: I had to continue therapy.

I park the car and sit in silence for a while, gathering my thoughts. I smother a groan and swing open the door. I'm greeted as soon as I walk into the suite.

"I've got you signed in, Rory," the petite receptionist with fire engine red hair and black-rimmed glasses announces from behind her desk. I give her a simple nod before I find an empty chair and take a seat.

Within a few short minutes, the clacking sound of Mina's heels tap against the floor as she nears the waiting room. There is a familiar laugh that follows her footsteps. A laugh I remember so well, it pains me.

Trice appears behind his mom.

Instinctually, my eyes cast downward. I've tried time and time again to talk to him, but to no avail. I don't have the energy to try anymore. As they near me, I hear him tell his mom farewell as I keep my eyes averted.

"Rory," Trice says by way of greeting, causing my head to rise. He hasn't spoken to me in so long I almost forgot what his voice sounded like.

"Trice." I catch his gaze and openly study him. Unsure what else to say, my lips remain locked. I refuse to allow myself to beg for his friendship any longer. It's apparent by his stance that he only acknowledged me, so he didn't appear disrespectful in front of his mother.

Not wanting to make a scene either, I remain cordial. Even though I want to tell him how much of a royal dick he's been. A look of melancholy passes between us before he embraces his mom and walks toward the door without a backward glance.

"Are you ready?" Mina gestures toward her sanctuary of secrets (read: office).

As far as I'm concerned, therapy is like Alcoholics Anonymous for those of us privileged enough to have drawn the short end of life's stick and have deep-rooted traumas. I refused group therapy several times when my caseworker recommended it. Talking to Mina isn't half as bad as talking to a social services caseworker who has ten times as many cases as arms and smells like a stale hopelessness. Mina smells like lavender.

I take a seat on her brown leather chaise adjacent to the small chair she sits in. She slides off her high heels and pulls her legs underneath her. "How are you today, Rory?"

Should I tell her that although I'm dating her son, who is so thoughtful and kind, I still feel utterly unlovable at times? Or that I still find myself hoarding food, like granola bars, under my mattress because I'm so used to the cabinets being empty from years of foster parents' neglect? Even though, without a shadow of a doubt, I know that I'll never be in a position to starve again thanks to Russell and Bea.

The thing about trauma is that it lingers.

My smile sets the mood. It's one I've cultivated over the years like an actress who learns to cry at will. It says, "I'm fine," but doesn't quite reach my eyes. "I'm good. Really good."

"You're also really good at lying." Her face displays an expression that I'm keenly aware of. Her bullshit meter must be going crazy. "I think you've gotten away for years claiming that you're fine or you're good, just to pacify people. That doesn't work here, Rory. Because I know you're not fine. How could you be after everything you've been through?"

"Is that a rhetorical question?" Mina's analytical stare answers for her. "I really am fine. I'm happy. I'm getting good grades and you know things between Crew, and I are good. I don't know what else you want me to say."

"I want the truth. Not for my own good, but for yours. Do you want to talk about the night with Lloyd and what happened?"

"Not particularly."

"Okay. We have fifty minutes. What do you want to talk about?" she counters while opening her little maroon notebook and flipping to a page that is folded down in the top corner. She taps against the page with her pen.

"Why does Trice hate me?" The question spills from my mouth despite her being his mother.

"How about this? I'll answer your question if you answer mine." I debate brushing her off and moving on to another subject, but I want to know how to earn his friendship back. Even if I'm tired of trying and am scraping the bottom of a barrel.

Extending my legs, I cross my ankles and take a deep breath before I square my shoulders against the cushion and get ready to spill my guts. "That night, I heard Lonnie crying through the wall. At first, I thought it was a dream, but it got louder and then nothing. Dead silence. I remember that I sprung up from a deep sleep, even though I couldn't comprehend what was going on. I knew in my bones that it was bad. I opened Lonnie's door and Lloyd was standing there…" As I take a deep breath and swallow, it feels like a thousand shards of glass are caught in my throat.

"It's okay. Take your time. You've blocked this night out for so long that all the feelings you're experiencing right now are coming out in a rush. It's okay to be a little overwhelmed. Do you need to take a drink?"

"No. I want to say it and put it behind me and never repeat these words again for as long as I live." Anger has held me hostage my entire life. I won't let this world or Lloyd rob me of anything else ever again. "He had his pants around his legs. I know what he was going to do. He probably would have gotten away with it if I didn't wake up."

"What happened when he realized you were standing there?"

I draw my legs up on the cushion and hug them. "I don't know."

"Rory, if this is going to work, I need your complete honesty."

"I don't know what happened because all I saw was red. I went blind with fury. I don't even recall the look on Lonnie's face. It could have been relief that I had barged in and saved him or terror. I. Just. Saw. Red."

"You know that you broke Lloyd's nose, don't you?" I glance up, surprised that she would know that. "I read the police report."

"I should have killed him," I say. "I would have killed him if Lonnie didn't find Lloyd's cell phone on the floor and call the police. They didn't get there quick enough, though, because he started to wrestle Lonnie for the phone and broke his arm. I can still hear the snap of his tiny bone. A lot of bad shit has happened to me, and I've never wished anyone harm, much less death like I do toward Lloyd. I hope he gets what's coming to him in jail and that he rots in hell for his sins like the maggot that he is." I'm thankful that Lonnie and I did not have to testify in court about that night and face that bastard again.

Her voice is soft and gentle when she speaks. "You saved Lonnie's innocence that night."

"I can't save every kid in the world who's at the mercy of a vile adult." I say matter-of-factly.

Mina's tone is sincere as she responds. "You can't. None of us can. What you can do is acknowledge that you're stronger than you give yourself credit for. You saved Lonnie from a fate that's incomprehensible. You *both* survived. As soon as you let that sink in, you're going to feel so much lighter than you do carrying the burden of that night."

"I hear you and I understand what you're saying. But I don't think that burden is going anywhere any time soon."

Clasping my hands together, I change the subject. My vulnerability only goes so far. "Your turn."

Mina closes her notebook and takes a small sip of water from the bottle beside her. "Trice doesn't hate you, Rory. In fact, it's the exact opposite. I think that in his mind, he believes you were supposed to be *his*. As his mom, I would never betray his trust and tell you what he and I have discussed on the matter. As your therapist, I think you need to give him more time. He needs to grieve what he lost. You need to accept that the bitter battle between you two will fade in time. You should focus on this newfound relationship with Crew. Trice needs to acknowledge that his feelings for you were not reciprocated in a romantic way."

I shrug in resignation. And then my voice waivers as I admit, "I know about the accident, and that Crew wasn't the one driving the boat."

Mina's eyes flare, but only for a second. "I know he wasn't driving either."

My brain lurches madly in my head. If Russell and Bea know it wasn't Crew, and his own mother knows, why did he take the rap for something he didn't do? I don't have a chance to ask before Mina sighs and then says, "My sons were always competitive. I guess they got that from watching how Shawn and Russell interacted while they were growing up. Those two men are the most driven I've ever seen. From whom can bait a hook faster to who cooks the best rack of ribs. They're intolerable. That night, when we got to the dock and saw Crew, he had already confessed to driving." I can feel my eyebrows bunching together as she continues. "Trice was drunk and underage. Crew knew he'd go to jail. The accident killed a kid and not just someone, but Matt Greenwell. Our best friends' child. If Trice admitted the truth, he could have been charged with involuntary manslaughter, or worse, because he was underage and under the influence."

"Crew lost his football scholarship. He missed his first

year of college while he was on house arrest. His whole life transformed in an instant. How could you let one kid suffer to protect the other?" The question I've been thinking slips out before I have time to stop it.

"Shawn and I didn't force Crew to do anything. He was sober and said that he was driving and dropped his phone, and when he leaned down to get it, they wrecked, and Matt went overboard. He was charged with involuntary manslaughter. The judge sentenced him to a year of house arrest and community service."

I cross my arms. "Which he spent at church singing in the choir, right?"

"Indeed. It was in that first year when his father and I started to see a shift in his disposition. He withdrew from our family. Started smoking cigarettes. His temperament became hostile, and he cut Trice off completely. He wouldn't even take online courses. Crew became a shell of his former self, and I thought I'd never see the warmth in his eyes return."

"What changed?"

Her voice is tender as she says, "You moved to town."

My heart breaks for all that Crew gave up to keep his brother out of jail. It breaks for Bea and Russell who lost a child, and it breaks for me, too, because I didn't choose a life in the foster care system.

As Mina wraps up our time, I decide not to allow Lloyd and Jean to claim any space in my head or my life any longer. I refuse to allow those who neglected or berated me matter anymore.

Lloyd is dead to me, and so is the past.

CHAPTER
TWENTY-NINE

Time passes by in a blur and spring is on the horizon with its cherry blossoms dancing in the breeze and warmer temperatures. Along with the change of seasons comes the biggest spectacle in the horse racing world, the Kentucky Derby. Having been born and raised near the racetrack, I'm used to the pandemonium that happens in the city in the weeks leading up to the fastest two minutes in sports. From fireworks, parades, and boat races, there are dozens of events scheduled. That doesn't include the lines of limos that bring in an array of celebrities who make the city their home for the weekend.

Usually, I'd be working parking cars for ten-bucks an hour under the table and taking advantage of the fancy out-of-towners the Derby attracts. Thank goodness no one ever bothered to ask if I had a valid driver's license back then. Money and greed are green and there was nothing I loved more than accepting tips from strangers who felt sorry for me. I'm not stupid enough to turn down easy cash, no matter whose tailored khakis and ornamental wallet it comes from.

The hustle and bustle of it all makes living in the suburbs this year seem dull in comparison. I shouldn't have been as surprised to learn that people in suburbia, an hour away from the city, also love this time of year. The chance to cut loose, drink, and throw money down the drain betting on horses encourages people to do all sorts of crazy things. Like wearing fancy outfits and hats that *The Cat in the Hat* might wear. What's even odder this year is that I'm willingly participating in the shenanigans that the Derby has brought to our doorstep.

With Della's father not having a horse entered into the race this year, he's decided to throw a massive party. Russell graduated with Della's dad and that's our ticket in. Crew said that he heard there would be a DJ, a bookie for placing bets, and an ice sculpture of a horse. Nothing says "I'm rich" more than a freaking ice sculpture.

As for Della, she still detests me, and I still want to pour bleach on her cheerleading outfit. I'm eager to see how this party goes knowing the last one I attended at her house on Halloween came with truth serum as a party favor. Especially since she and Trice have been hanging out.

It's like fate decided to start a band and invited my enemies to audition. I know that they all hang in the same circle and were friends before I even moved here, but part of me still thinks that him spending more time with her is just to get under my skin. It has. I just refuse to admit it to anyone.

Andrea and I have even been eating at a separate table at lunch. I didn't force her to choose sides, but it's comforting to know that she has my back. I thought Trice did too. Although, lately, it feels like he's stabbing me in it.

"You don't think it's a bit too much?" I turn in front of the mirror, feeling self-conscious and glance behind me. Bea is nestled on my bed, busying herself with peeling the sticker off the bottom of the heels she insisted we get to match my outfit. I've seen the dresses girls wear to an event of this magnitude. I know that my ensemble is trendy, and I'll fit in perfectly. It's just not *me*. When did I turn into the girl who dresses up in sparkles and wears a fascinator?

"Too much? Rory, you look amazing." She lays the shoe on my comforter and walks up behind me. "Crew is going to go bonkers when he sees you. On second thought, maybe you should change." A laugh escapes her lips. "Who am I kidding? You'd be beautiful even in a potato sack. I'm sure your mother was equally as breathtaking."

It's not the first time she's mentioned my biological mother. I confided in her about my make-believe story of what happened to my birth parents and how I landed in foster care. Bea surprisingly admitted to doing the same thing when she was younger. We're alike in many ways. Because of that, our bond has strengthened.

"Della's just…" I space my words. "Awful."

"You can call it like you see it. She's an entitled little brat. Trust me. I know her Daddy doesn't tell her no. He never has and probably never will. William Astor created himself a little monster there. Don't let her ruin your fun before it even begins today. Who cares that this shindig is at her house. Let's go drink their drinks and eat their food and enjoy ourselves. It's the first time I've been off work and not on-call on Derby Day in years, and I plan to enjoy it. Even if Russell is working."

Still trying to calm my nerves, I nod. "Did you hear that there's going to be a wine fountain?"

"I wouldn't expect anything less from the Astor's." Her lips curl. "Finish getting ready. I'm going to check on Lonnie and make sure he's almost dressed and then go slip on my dress."

"Hey Bea," I call out. She leans against the door frame. "I appreciate you buying me this. The dress, the shoes," I wave to the feathery headband atop my head. "Thank you for making this year…special."

"No tears, Rory. Your makeup is too pretty today to go messing it up. You're welcome."

I shut the door behind her and take a deep breath trying to muster up the courage to go out into public in this dress. I'm not modest. I'm a woman, hear me roar and all that jazz. It's just that this fabric is so form fitting, it's basically painted on my skin. When I move, it moves. I'm also a little nervous about Crew seeing me, knowing that his gorgeous honey eyes are going to rake over my body taking in my outfit.

He's going to have a hard time trying to keep his hands off me. The anticipation of him pulling me in and kissing me makes me want to crawl into a hole and pull a boulder over top because while all that sounds mind-blowing, he's still holding out on me.

We've messed around a little bit here and there. I'm always the one who begs him for more and gets shot down every single time. I hope his man-sized chastity belt doesn't restrict movement, and I wish I held the key. Call me a sinner, because if he dropped his pants in front of me…

We haven't discussed our futures and where we stand with them, much less the idea of marriage. With my eighteenth birthday looming, I haven't wanted to divulge my plan to adopt Lonnie and move away, to start fresh without social workers or home visits, to hear a judge declare Lonnie as my only *real*, legal family member. I've patiently waited all year for May, only for the thought of turning eighteen to suddenly petrify the living crap out of me.

Can I actually go through with it and pull Lonnie away from this life?

What do I have to offer him other than unconditional love? He is the happiest I've ever seen him. Excelling in school and on the chess team for his grade. He loves living in the country and having a giant yard to play in.

What kind of monster would I be to drag him away from all of that and for what? To live in a one-bedroom apartment while I become a server at the Pancake Palace and barely have enough time to help him with his homework while I struggle to keep food on the table for the both of us. That's if any judge would even accept my petition for adoption. My part-time job at Painting with a Twist doesn't pay enough to afford rent and necessities.

"Pull it together for tonight, Rory," I murmur, trying to coax myself into a better mood. Sliding my cell phone out of my pocket, I decide to send Crew a sneak peek of my outfit. My phone chimes seconds after I hit send.

Crew: *Take it off*

Me: *What?*

Crew: *Take off that fabric you call a dress and put on some sweatpants. We're not going anywhere with you looking so SPICY*

Crew: *If I can't have you, no one can :P*

Me: *It's your fault you're suffering ya know?!*

Crew: *This I know*

Me: *See you in a few. I can't wait to see how SPICY you look*

I mock him and hit send. I sit on my bed and as I'm slipping on my heels, my phone chimes. I reach for it and my mouth gets dry. A picture of Crew with his shirt off lights up my screen. He's wearing black dress pants and a belt. The phone is angled down and pointed directly at his abs. Abs that put a washboard to shame. Abs that I've run my hands over so many times, I know every bump and freckle. Abs that beckon me to wet my glossed lips with my tongue. I need a plan to break through his reserve because he's going to physically kill me otherwise. Ten minutes later, a second text dings.

Crew: *My car won't start. I have to call AAA to jump me. I'll be late to the party*

I decide to call instead of text and make my way downstairs. "You can't be late," I say as soon as he answers. "Andrea and Geoff are already going to be late. You know with Trice on team Della now, I'll just be standing there. I'll have to eat my body weight in cocktail shrimp just to keep from dying of boredom."

"I'm sorry. My battery is dead. At least it will be that fancy, expensive shrimp that is deveined."

"Please don't turn this into a joke. You know Russell probably won't let me drive that far on the interstate to come get you alone. Why don't you just ask Trice if he'll pick you up on campus? Otherwise, I'll be miserable until you arrive."

"You're joking right?" He snorts. "He's spent the last couple of months hating us and you want me to casually call him up and ask him for a favor? Have you lost your mind? And no way are you driving here. You can barely get to school without hitting the curb with a tire. That's not an option either."

"First, off. Rude. The tires on Matt's old beater of a truck were already all scratched before me. Second, I back into a mailbox one time and you're going to judge my driving skills for the rest of my life? Thirdly," my rant leaves me breathless and annoyed. "I know things are still tense between you and Trice, but you're brothers. He'll agree. Trust me." I fire off a message to Trice despite the dreadful feeling that stirs in my gut.

Me: Hey. Have you left yet?
Trice: No. Y?
Me: Crew's battery is dead. He needs a ride
Trice: I care because...
Me: B/c I want to hang with you both

Three little dots appear and disappear several times before a message finally comes through.

Trice: Bones?

It's not a lie. I do want to hang out with them both. I've been the one trying to force us to reconcile for months. Trice has been the one dodging me like I have the plague.

"Please do not involve him." Crew pulls me back to our

conversation on the phone. "I'll find a ride. One that doesn't want to punch me in the face for stealing his best friend."

"I'm texting him right now. I'll ride with him. He won't mind."

Me: *Bones! Come pick me up. I'll ride with you*

"Aurora, I know he wouldn't *willingly* do anything for me."

"Shut up! It's fine. He's picking me up. I'll see you soon." I hang up before he can continue arguing.

"Where are you going?" Lonnie asks as I round the corner and walk to the front door. The sapphire of his eyes widens as he takes in my outfit and headwear.

"Trice is going to bring me to the Astor's. Will you tell Bea I'll meet you two there?"

"Sure." He hollers as I swing open the front door with my cell phone and white crossbody in tow.

I strut to the car as Trice pulls into the driveway. My heels hit the pavement and tiny rocks on the way to the passenger side door. Swinging it open, the odor of alcohol emanates from the small vehicle. "What the hell, Trice. Have you been drinking?" I ask bending forward from the doorframe waiting for his answer before I decide if I'm going to get in.

He gives me a dimpled grin. "Don't you trust me?"

"Of course, I trust you. I also trust my nose and you reek. I don't want to be a teenage statistic. You shouldn't be driving."

"How else will your precious Crew get to the party?"

"I don't know. Maybe he can find a cab."

"You think there's a vacant cab near campus on Derby Day?" he counters. "I'm fine. I promise. I had one whiskey and coke while I got ready. That's it. Come on before it starts raining."

Hesitantly, I climb into the passenger seat of Trice's souped-up car. My gut has never proved me wrong, but I give him the benefit of the doubt. If he says he's sober enough to drive, I believe him. The engine purrs and we speed out of our subdivision in a blur.

"You look amazing by the way." His eyes flutter my way. The car swerves, making me second-guess my decision to ask him for a ride.

"Eyes on the road, Casanova."

My hand clenches my seatbelt as we speed down the road. There is an earthy smell of topsoil and a subtle, sweet floral scent in the air that filters out the odor of alcohol. It indicates that spring has sprung. Forty minutes pass in a blur, and I send Crew a message letting him know that we'll be there shortly. Suddenly the car slows down, gravel stirs under the tires, and Trice veers toward the emergency lane on the side of the freeway.

"Why are we pulling over?"

"I have something I need to say." Rain pelts the windshield as he slides the gearshift into park and the car comes to a sudden halt. I give him a wary look. Unease fills my gut.

I realize he's not as sober as he claimed to be when he opens his mouth and mutters, "I love you."

"Okay. Wow. You're definitely drunk." I try to maintain my composure. He's been ignoring me for months and then drops this bomb on me while we're on the side of the damn freeway. Leave it to him to decide that this is the time to declare his feelings and hash things out. He's poured our friendship down the drain with three little words.

"Rory, look at me. I need to get this off my chest." Liquid courage must be coursing through his veins. I fire off a text to Andrea asking her to come and get me. There's no way in hell I'm letting him drive any further. He's clearly lost his mind.

"I think you're the most beautiful girl I've ever laid eyes on. Inside and out. I know we're young and you have this whole independent crusade you're on but… seeing you in *this* dress." He glances down at my exposed thigh. "I can't *not* tell you how I feel about you anymore. You look, amazing. I've been dying inside since I saw you kiss Crew. I shouldn't have ignored you, but seeing you killed me. There *was* something growing between us, and I'm not going to deny my feelings anymore. I can't stay in the friend zone with you. I'm losing my mind keeping my feelings reigned in."

"You *were* my best friend and I'm dating *your* brother." Honestly spills from my glossy lips. "We're on our way to go get him and you think that this is the most opportune time to tell me something so…so—"

"Honest?" He interrupts. "Has Crew told you he loves you? Has your little lover boy had the balls to declare how he really feels? He hasn't. I know it. Because he's weak. He couldn't save Matt, and I'd bet my life's savings that he hasn't even fucked you yet. Claimed you. He hasn't, has he?"

"Trice," I whisper as a plea to stop his hateful slurs. But instead of stopping, he takes me sighing his name as an invitation. Leaning over the console, he grabs both sides of my face and leans in. I'm momentarily shocked. My brain stops sending messages to my body to talk or move. He nudges himself closer and his tongue dives into my mouth. This is so, so very wrong.

"Stop!" My voice is hoarse as I pull back, my brain finally catching up. My eyes are wide with terror at not only Trice's expression but at the giant truck sliding across the road behind us.

Squealing tires.

The crunch of glass.

Time stops.

Or maybe it's the world that stops spinning on its axis.

Images of Lonnie on Christmas float in front of me. I can almost reach out and touch the memory like a ribbon. His laughter echoes as I watch him in a fit of laughter as Russell opens a pair of socks with Bea's face on them that we helped him create.

The next flashback is of me and Crew. We're at his parents'

house exchanging our gifts. I never felt as treasured and adored as I did when I unwrapped a framed picture of a star and coordinates that he had named after me. He said that I was prettier than all the stars in the sky. I know he meant it because I could feel his words penetrating deep into my bones. They splintered in my soul, and in that moment, I knew I loved him.

My memories grow distant. I hold on to them with all my might, but it feels as if they're slipping away and as hard as I try to grasp them…they're gone and there is nothing left but darkness.

"She's breathing." A voice I recognize shouts. My head feels as heavy as a sack of potatoes. The voice echoes against each throb in my skull. "There's a pulse."

"Tri—" My throat constricts as I call out for Trice.

"Just breathe. Don't talk. We're going to get you cut out as fast as we can. Hang in there, Rory," is all I hear before darkness consumes me.

CHAPTER
THIRTY

CREW

The sound of my fist slamming against the wooden double doors can probably be heard all the way in the hospital's cafeteria in the basement. My hand aches, but it's nothing compared to the pain in my core while I wait and wonder about Aurora's condition.

When Russell called me and told me he came upon a crash and it was Trice and Aurora, I honestly think I blacked out. Here I stand in my black trousers and dress shoes wearing a hole in the linoleum of the floor as I pace back and forth. "You better let me through that door, or I swear to God I'm going to—."

"Calm down, son." A tight grip on my shoulder grounds me. I want to yank it off and pummel through the door in search of Aurora and my brother. "Let the doctors do their jobs. Bea should be here any minute along with your parents." Russell's voice hits me full force. Being a police officer, I know he's been trained to remain calm in any situation that he encounters. His practiced tone is grating on my nerves. I feel like I could crawl out of my skin.

"I can't lose her. I just got her," my legs give out and I sink to my knees on the waiting room floor. The fabric of my pants under my knees are thin against the cool floor. I welcome the chill to feel anything other than rage in this moment. "Fuck and Trice. I already lost… Matt. I can't go through that again. I won't make it this time."

"You won't lose her. Rory is tough and Trice is strong. *This* is much different." Russell answers, his voice calm. Damn him and his special training. "Tough times don't last. Tough people do."

I school my features as he helps me up and over to a chair in the lobby, while I wish I could trade places with them both.

I love Aurora Bradshaw and I never told her.

Those three little words have been on the tip of my tongue for months. I had plenty of chances. I don't even know what stopped me. Now I might never get the opportunity to tell her, and it will be no one's fault but my own.

Fear and irritation knot in my stomach. My mind is a mix of panic and optimism. When Matt passed, I was either shoved away by friends and the community and labeled as a murderer or I pushed those who cared about me away. Being alone felt better than being hated. With nostrils flaring, I slide out my phone and send a mass text to all our friends.

We need a village.

We need prayers, lots of them, and if that means sucking up my pride, I'll do it. I'll make a billboard if I must.

Russell is gone for what seems like eternity even though it's only been a few minutes. I see him at the nurse's station with a serious look on his face. Being Aurora's foster dad allows him to gain information about her condition, but they won't let anyone see her until she's stable. Regardless of kin.

I struggle with the silence as I wait for answers. For any news. Any shred of hope. I just need to know that she's alive. Even if they won't let Russell go back until Aurora is stable, surely, they'll allow Bea to see her. She's a doctor at this hospital.

Where is she?

Despite the badge he wears, the nurse shakes her head at Russell when he mentions my brother's name. She spouts off something about HIPAA and patient confidentiality before she moves on to the person waiting behind Russell. I feel so stupid about the distance I've allowed to grow between me and Trice. He's my brother. I should have fought harder for our relationship. I was so mad at him for getting drunk and crashing the boat that I let my fury blind me. Then I took responsibility and accepted the repercussions of the accident, and he didn't even offer a simple thank you. It seems so trivial and insignificant now.

Relief engulfs me as Bea's small stature finally comes into sight. She's in her Derby dress and tennis shoes. I imagine she slid them on in her car before she sped here. I hop out of the chair and run to her side, the sound of my shoes clicking with every step.

I grab her before she reaches Russell. "Please, please go see how she is. Tell me she's okay. I need her to be okay. I love her." Panic hangs on the edge of my voice.

Long gone is the resigned expression of a veteran emergency room physician. Bea isn't in doctor mode. She's in full-blown mother mode. Russell and she collide as tears slide down her cheeks, and she weeps in worry.

"I'm going to give you two minutes, Bernadette." Russell says as he holds the back of her head, her face buried in his chest. "Let it out. Then I need you to pull yourself together and go check on our girl." Her body shakes as she sobs into Russell's chest. I nearly crumple, recognizing the sound from the night of the boating accident when she was told her son was dead.

The reason they were parked on the side of the road is unclear. Russell said a cruiser is still on the scene trying to piece it together and figure out why the semi plowed into them. They think it was a blown tire, but that's yet to be determined.

Bea pulls away from Russell's embrace, takes a deep breath in and then uses her hospital ID to enter the locked double doors. I fall back into the ugly green chair and wait. I glare at the clock on the wall with hostility. I count each second as the hand ticks in order to occupy my mind. If I don't, I'm afraid the hospital won't have any furniture that's left unscathed.

Time ceases. I rub my eyes so many times my vision is blurred. Bea finally bursts through the wooden doors, wearing a white lab coat over her dress. Blood spatter is evident on the sleeves. *Is that Aurora's blood?* I feel ill.

Determination is etched across her face as she nears Russell.

"She's alive and alert? They said she was alive. But they wouldn't let me back to see her." Russell barks. "Tell me she's okay, Bea."

"She's going to be okay." Russell holds Bea in a tight embrace.

Her eyes find mine over his shoulder. "Where are your parents?" she asks.

"I… I don't know. I didn't call them. I was so worried about Rory. I didn't think to call them about Trice—" I choke on his name. My heart pounds so fiercely I fear it may beat out of my chest cavity.

"I called them," Russell adds. "They're on their way. They must have hit traffic. I know they had to drop Aiden off at a friend's house."

"Trice needs blood. He needs blood right now." Bea repeats.

Russell's eyes fill with understanding. "Okay. Let me see what I can do to get Mina and Shawn here faster." He speaks into the radio strapped onto his chest, asking for assistance to locate my parents and expedite their arrival at the hospital.

"I'll donate. I'm not afraid of needles. I have a full back piece of tattoos. Show me where to go." I move toward Bea and Russell, but they don't budge. Instead, they share a look, which leaves me confused. Why isn't she ushering me through the locked doors and jabbing an I.V. in my arm? "I said I'll donate. Come on." I grab the loose white sleeve on her arm and tug gently. "Let me through."

"Crew, honey." Her soft eyes travel over my face. There is a double meaning in her gaze. I just don't know what it is.

"Baby." My mom's voice comes from behind me. Sheer terror is etched onto her flawless features. I've seen that pain in a mother's eyes before. Last time it was Bea who wore that expression, paired with a soul-crushing scream that I'll never forget. It's been on replay in my nightmares for two years. Why my mother is wearing the same painful countenance is beyond me.

"You can't donate blood to save Trice." She clutches her hand to her chest as my dad rushes in behind her. He and Bea pass through the locked doors leaving me confused and staring at my mom.

"Why? I'm perfectly willing to. I haven't showed you, but when Matt died, I started getting tattooed. My entire back is covered, Mom. I'm not afraid of needles. Please let me help him." She pointedly looks away. "Did you hear me? What's the problem? Look at me." I must've stepped into a time warp, or I've lost my voice. There's got to be an explanation as to why no one is answering me. My lips thin with irritation as I boil over and shout. "Fucking answer me!" Any resolve I've held onto crumbles to the linoleum floor beneath my feet.

"Your blood type doesn't match Trice's. Your father and I had the pediatrician tell us just in case something like this ever happened. You can't donate, Crew. You're adopted." I pale as the words slip from her mouth. The enormity of her statement leaves me deflated. My body sags with her crushing truth.

I'm adopted?

My throat aches with unspoken words as I swallow them whole. I take a step back from my mom…her…this lady in front of me. I eye her up and down, dangerously slow. In a cocoon of anguish, I let out a choked, desperate laugh. "This is…this can't be happening right now."

She takes a step forward.

I retreat by taking a step back.

"Crew." Her voice is a whisper. Her eyes swell with tears as I hold up my hand, preventing her from coming closer.

"Don't." Torment gnaws at my insides and all the blood in my body rushes to my heart. It feels like it's about to explode. Her eyes close and tears fall down her cheeks streaking her make-up in their path.

Someone grab a defibrillator because I'm going down any second.

Her marine-blue eyes bore into my dark ones. Their differences now make sense. "Please, let me explain," she begs. "I love you, son. Please sit down and let me explain. It's about time you knew the truth. But I need to check on Trice first. Stay here, and I'll be back."

"Go on, Mina." Russell puts his hand on her shoulder. "He needs time to process, and Trice needs you. It's serious."

Trice needs them.

His condition is serious.

He's always the one who they run toward.

Now I know why.

Momentarily disoriented, I stumble through the emergency room doors. The spring air fills my lungs as I lean forward, placing my hands on my knees and I try taking in as much air as possible. My mouth is dry and it's hard to swallow.

Sirens echo off the tall buildings surrounding the hospital

in the middle of this bustling metropolis. The sound grows dim as I stagger zombielike toward the parking lot in search of Pete's truck.

Like a puzzle missing its final piece, I can't make sense of the news that I was adopted.

Was I an infant? Was I in foster care like Aurora and Lonnie? Why didn't my birth parents want me?

Confusion fogs my brain making it hard to think clearly. My thoughts fade from the forefront as I absentmindedly slide Pete's key into the ignition. When Russell called and said he was at a scene and it was Trice and Aurora in the car, I just took his keys without asking permission and sped to the hospital. I knew I had to get to her. To make sure she was okay. To tell her I loved her. I didn't do any of those things.

I can't keep myself afloat the terror of thoughts in my mind. They threaten to take me under like a riptide.

Self-deprecation eats away at my broken heart. I wasn't strong enough to save Matt. He went overboard before I could catch him. I dove in, but it was too dark. I couldn't see him, let alone reach him.

I'm not *related* to Trice by blood to save him.

I don't know how I can endure losing another person that I love, but I don't have the strength to stay and see how things unfold. Not when my mom…Mina… just turned my whole world upside down. Shook me up and then discarded me like a broken vase before rushing off to her beloved Trice. I've been second-best my entire life. It all makes sense. The stark differences in our appearances. Never feeling like I truly fit in with my family.

The weight of this news is too much to carry. So, I'll do what I do best: shut down and run away from my problems.

I drive straight to the tattoo studio and empty my wallet knowing that the pain of a thousand needles piercing my skin is better than the stabbing that constricts my chest with every breath I take.

CHAPTER
THIRTY-ONE

RORY

My head feels as if it was put into a blender and turned on high. My eyes slowly open into slits. My thoughts are haywire, much like my vision. Everything is blurry.

Memories of the crash fall like hail, small shards pinging against my brain. I remember Trice pulling over and then bam, everything gets muddled. I struggle to clear my mind and focus.

A godawful beeping sound radiates from the machine above my bed. I pry open my eyes. The lights are off. Bea's small form is folded into a chair next to my bed as the moon shines on her face. I can see she's wearing pale blue scrubs, not the casual business attire she leaves the house in each morning.

How long have I been asleep? Judging by the darkness coming from underneath the door to my room, it must be the middle of the night. Hospitals usually dim the lights in the evening trying to promote rest and healing. My attempt to sit up is as shaky as a baby fawn. The sheet rustles with my movement, and I huff in frustration as a bolt of pain shoots through my core.

"You're awake." Even sounding sleepy and hoarse, the exhilaration in Bea's voice is apparent. I take in her disheveled appearance. Her hair is in a messy pile atop her head instead of her usual neat braid rolled into a low bun at the nape of her neck. Mascara is smudged under her eye, and she's wearing the red-rimmed glasses that she only wears at night or while she's reading.

She startles me as she jumps up and shoves the chair she used as a makeshift bed out of the way. Her small hands start pressing buttons on my bed, and within a couple of minutes, the door to my room swings open and several nurses parade inside.

"Her vitals are stable. Page the on-call," Bea instructs, her tone bossy. It's easy to forget that she's a physician when we're at home. When she's playing soccer with Lonnie, running around the yard like a crazed lunatic, or baking homemade bread in the kitchen. Life with Bea has been so normal. It's easy to forget about her day job. Within these walls, she's a well-respected doctor with her clipped tone and tolerant expression.

"What's your pain level, Rory?" My answer falls flat as I wince trying to sit up once again. "Stop moving around. You're just as bad as Russell that time he broke his rib wakeboarding on vacation."

"I broke a rib." It comes out as a statement instead of a question.

"A rib, your right arm and you have a concussion. You've been in and out of it since the ambulance brought you in earlier today."

With as much energy as I can muster, I say, "Trice," while trying to pull myself up by the rails on the bed with my free hand. A piercing sting shoots through my chest and I shriek in pain.

Through clenched teeth Bea asks, "Are you all going to just watch her suffer? Someone get her another push of morphine." She turns her attention to me, grasping my left hand and holding it in hers. "Trice is alive. He's young and strong-willed. We're all rallying behind him."

Tears well in my eyes. "What does that mean?"

"A tractor-trailer blew a tire and hit you. The impact pushed Trice's car through the concrete median. Thank goodness the driver was already trying to slow down to pull off onto the median or it would have been worse. That's all we know right now. Trice's legs…his left leg is shattered. His femur is broken and his right foot. The most concerning injuries are a collapsed lung and ruptured spleen. His team put him in a medically induced coma due to the swelling on his brain also. It could have been a lot worse, Rory. You both must have someone upstairs rooting for you."

Tears pour from my eyes. I try to hold my arm over my stomach because with each sob my ribcage feels like it's going to come through the wall of my chest. My right arm is in a black cast from my shoulder to my hand. "I want to see him."

"Not tonight. Visiting hours are long-over and he's in the ICU anyway. They'd see me wheeling you in there. Even being on staff here doesn't grant me superpowers, dear. He's not awake and you both need to rest. Your physician should be here shortly, and I'm sure in the morning they'll do a repeat head scan. Let's make sure you're healthy and on the road to recovery and then we can arrange for you to see Trice."

"Where's Lonnie at? Does he know I'm in the hospital?"

"He's with Miranda." At the sound of her name, I jolt upward. Gritting my teeth, I hold my ribcage with my left hand, tightly, and try and slide the bar on the side of the bed down with my heel. I've never been in as much pain as I am now. All of that is nothing compared to the hurt that Lonnie must be going through. If they called Miranda, he's undoubtedly confused. He probably thinks I broke my promise to always be there and to protect him. I need to get to him. I need to show him that I'm okay and I haven't deserted him.

"What the…where are you going? Sit down. Stop, Rory. You're going to hurt yourself." Bea's small grip tries to keep me seated. "He's fine. He's safe. You were just in a wreck, Aurora. Calm down." I notice the way she uses my full first name before I erupt. As sweet as Bea has been, nothing will stand between me checking on Lonnie.

"Get your hands off me! I need to get to him. He needs to know I wouldn't leave him. You don't understand!"

"Either you calm down and lay still or I'm going to have them sedate you. You're no good for Lonnie in this state."

She's got to be joking. "If you do that, I will never forgive you. Lonnie is my only family. I need to talk to him right now."

"He's not your only family anymore. You have people who care about you now, even if you refuse to see it. My only priority is to keep you safe. Having you *like* me is just a bonus." She nods and then I drift off before the nurse at my bedside removes her syringe from my IV port.

CHAPTER
THIRTY-TWO

RORY

The sound of birds chirping from the windowsill pulls me from my lethargy. I'm surprised I can even hear them through the thick glass that separates us. It's been two days since Bea betrayed my trust and had her team of assailants in scrubs give me medication against my will.

For forty-eight hours, I've been in and out of consciousness. I can hardly hold my head up from the dizziness I'm experiencing. Like fog, it's hard to push past the noise echoing in my skull. Once my eyes finally open wide enough to take in my hospital room, I grab the faded pink pitcher on my stand and pour some water into an empty cup. A task that should take mere seconds takes me a minute or more since my only good hand is my non-dominant one. The first sip of water cools my throat and I follow with a huge gulp.

The door creaks open, and I lie back down and close my eyes, pretending to be asleep so that I'm not medicated again. I hate the way pain medication makes me feel. Without an ounce of control, I've lain in this bed and been poked and prodded like a science experiment.

"She's still sleeping." Lonnie's tiny voice sounds like a cherub singing in my ear. "When is she going to get up?" A pair of footsteps thud against the floor and echo in my small room. "I thought you said Rory was coming home today?"

"Her nurse is doing the discharge paperwork, and she should be done shortly. Give her a little more time to rest. I'll pack up her room, and then we'll wake her up. Okay, Lonnie?"

I'm barely able to contain my elation at seeing my brother. "Hey, buddy," my voice is frail.

"Rory! She's up, Bea. She's finally up." I feel him climb onto my bedside. "I'm so happy. I missed you."

"Me, too, buddy. How are you?" Waiting for his answer has me holding my breath.

"I'm great. I wasn't in a car accident."

"I mean with Miranda. I'm so sorry." I take in the slight turn of Lonnie's head as he peers over his shoulder at Bea in confusion. She's stuffing a bag with what looks like my Derby dress.

"Miranda was nice. She took me to get a cheeseburger for dinner and we went to the arcade. Then Russell picked me up and we went home. We missed that horserace though."

A flicker of emotion passes through me as I remember texting Trice to give me a ride to Crew's dorm because his battery wouldn't start, and he needed a ride to Della's. Trice picked me up and we were almost to Crew's campus, but then he pulled over and...my mind goes blank. *Where is Crew? Has he been here? Is Trice awake?*

"Bea, is Crew outside in the hallway?"

She comes to my side and places the plastic bag of clothes on the foot of my bed. Her expression turns grim. "Crew's not here. He...he hasn't stopped by to see you."

I want to pinch myself to see if I'm awake. I could be dreaming. Pain medication will do that to you. What does she mean he hasn't been by to see me? Did Trice's condition decline and he's been at his brother's bedside? I'm at a loss for words. I stare blankly at her trying to make sense of what she's telling me.

"He received some news that he isn't dealing with very well. Let's get you up and dressed, and we can talk more when we get home. Sound like a plan?"

"No, it doesn't. I need to know what's going on. Is Trice dead?"

Clutching her chest she exhales, "Mercy, no. They were able to wean him off the sedative and the swelling in his brain has subsided quicker than his team and doctors anticipated. He's still groggy and will be out of commission for a while. His body has a lot of recovery to do, but he's alive and awake."

"Is Crew with his parents and Trice then?" I'm still groggy, but I'm also feeling more confused. Why is Bea being so vague. It's like she's walking on eggshells.

"Lonnie, can you step outside and ask the nurse if she can get you a cup of Jell-O?"

"Do you think they have more orange cups?" He springs up from his spot on the chair.

"Why don't you go check?"

As the door shuts, a heaviness threatens to drag me down and settle in my chest. "What's going on? I want the truth. Nothing is making sense."

"Honestly, we don't know where Crew is. No one has heard from him since the wreck two days ago."

Processing her words in empty silence, I try to reach for the bag of my belongings at the foot of my bed. I don't know if my phone is even in there. At this point, it's the only hope I have. "Is my phone in there?" Bea doesn't answer. Instead, she dumps the contents onto my bed. My torn dress is inside, one shoe, and my necklace. My phone is missing. "Can I use your phone?"

Sliding it out of her pocket, she hands it to me. Her face is void of all emotion. Why is she not worried as much as I am? If Crew isn't here, where is he, and why is no one in a panic to find him? I punch in his cell phone number hastily and hold the phone up to my ear. It doesn't ring, rather it goes straight to voicemail. I fume, causing my heart rate to spike along with the alarm on my monitor.

"You're still in rough shape, Rory. I'll tell you what's going on if you promise to remain calm."

"I'm cool as a cucumber. Talk, please."

Bea scoots a chair over to my bedside and sits down. "He was distraught when I got here. Russell pulled onto the scene and called me, and I assume he called Crew. Apparently, he stole his roommate's truck to get here and broke about five traffic laws in the process. I had to make arrangements for Lonnie. I very well couldn't leave him at the Astor's party. When I arrived, Crew was threatening the staff. He didn't even ask about Trice's wellbeing. He was hyper-focused on you.

"After I saw you and spoke to your doctors, I gave him an update on your condition and his brother's. Trice was in critical condition. They didn't know how invasive his brain swelling was, and he needed a blood transfusion. Since he was in the driver's seat he got pinned against the concrete median and the force from the hit crushed the whole left side of the car. It's a miracle you're not in worse shape." I listen absently until I hear her voice break. "Trice needed a blood transfusion. He lost a lot of blood on the scene. Crew wasn't a match. He couldn't donate his blood to save Trice. Their blood types don't match, and Mina told Crew that he is... adopted."

For a long moment, I feel like time stands still. The birds cease to chirp. The sound on my monitor stops beeping, and my heartbeat becomes shallow.

Crew is adopted.

Some of the things I'd noticed in passing rise to the forefront of my brain.

The blatant differences between Crew and his brothers with their icy white hair.

The rapport between Trice and Aiden.

The way Trice has the same dimple as his mother that Crew doesn't have.

It makes total sense.

"Crew is adopted." I say the words as if I'm testing the sound of them out loud in a noncommittal way.

"He is. Mina tried to get pregnant not long after she opened her therapy center. She always longed to be a mother. Even in high school, I can recall her being the responsible one. The one who always stayed sober and made sure we made it home safely. When I went backpacking in Spain, she made me text her every night with the address where I was staying in case of an emergency. She was always the mother-hen of our group.

"Her friendship is very valuable to me. So, when Russell and I got pregnant with Matt and she and Shawn had suffered their third miscarriage, I lied to her. I told her that my test was negative to spare my best friend's feelings. It was a month later that she and Shawn decided to adopt. If you know Mina, you know that she is nothing but a perfectionist. She had their home study approved and mounds of paperwork completed in less than two weeks and within three months they were matched with an expectant mother. It was a miracle that the birth mom was as far along as I was. When we finally came clean and told them we, too, were expecting. Mina was over the moon. I remember when Crew was born, she said that her womb didn't ache anymore. She had the child that God meant for her to have. It was the best feeling in the world watching my friend, who was like a sister to me, be granted a gift as magical as motherhood."

The corner of my lip twists inward and I bite it. Hearing

the endearing way Bea talks about Mina becoming a mother does something to me. I've never given much thought to having kids of my own. Other than Lonnie of course. My main goal has been to turn eighteen, adopt Lonnie and start our new lives free from the foster care system. After that, I never imagined what could happen.

Career aspirations? I had none.

Falling in love and settling down? Never even considered it.

That is until I met Crew Jordan. He once said that our grief attracted us to one another. It's evident that we have more similarities than I ever could have imagined. We were both orphans. The only difference is, he got his happily ever after.

He was adopted, and I was still a ward of the state.

CHAPTER
THIRTY-THREE

RORY

The last two weeks have been a whirlwind of both emotions and perseverance. After getting discharged from the hospital, Bea took medical leave to take care of me and the constant attention is giving me hives. This attentiveness is going to take some time getting used to.

Even Lonnie has been smothering me. Every so often, he peeks into my room. He claims he was checking to make sure I was still breathing. We've tried to assure him that I just have a broken arm like he did before and that there isn't anything he can do to speed up the healing of my broken rib. To a seven-year-old, I might as well have been talking to a wall.

Bea was able to get me a replacement cell phone. She's instructed me to text her anything I need from the comfort of my bed. The only time I caved to her incessant demands is when I couldn't get my bra unclasped. A girl must be in bad shape to cave and ask another woman for help to unfasten her bra.

With my phone resting on my stomach, I spin it around in a circle with my good arm. The other is held firmly in place with a cast that is starting to smell. How I'll make it the next six weeks wearing this monstrosity is beyond me. I want to reach out to Trice and see how he's doing. I don't know what has stopped me. Probably shame. If I would have pushed him harder and made amends before Derby, we never would have had to pull over and be in a predicament that left us vulnerable.

The crash could have been avoided. The news of Crew being adopted could have been prevented or rather not sprung on him like that. He's suffering and he's doing it alone because his cell phone is still off.

With Crew being an adult, there isn't much to be done. Bea said that Mina is giving him until the end of the week to come to his senses or she's sending Russell and his officers out to search for him. After two long weeks with no communication from him and no transactions on his credit cards, it's safe to say they're past being worried. I've never seen Mina so distraught. She's been in our kitchen every night crying to Bea about how she failed Crew and how she wishes she had told him sooner. Regardless, he should have the decency to contact his parents, or at least me, and tell us he's safe.

The distance, I understand. He needs time to process the surprise that uprooted his entire life as he knew it. He just doesn't need to go through it alone. He has people who care about him even if he feels like he doesn't. I just wish he'd return my call so I could tell him that.

Until Crew comes around, I need to muster up the courage to talk to the other Jordan brother. The one who is still bedridden and won't have an option to walk away from me. Holding my phone, I type with stiff fingers and hit send before I can talk myself out of it.

Me: Are you awake?

A second later my phone chimes.

Trice: This may be the Morphine talking...Are you really txt'n me?

Me: It's not the drugs. Although, that morphine should be illegal. It knocked me out for two solid days

Trice: I've been a zombie for 2 weeks. Who are you kiddin?

Trice: Do you h8 me?

Me: Not even a little bit

Trice: I am so sorry. So, so, so sorry

Me: All I care about is that you're okay. I've been so worried about u. How are you feeling?

Trice: Do you want an honest answer?

Me: Hit me with it

Trice: Like I just got hit by a fn semi

Me: No pun intended :P

Trice: We need to talk. In person. Do you think Bea will bring you to the hospital? Visiting hours are until 6pm

Me: She's been watching me like a hawk

Trice: It won't hurt to ask. I have some things I need to get off my chest. I want it to be in person

It didn't take as much convincing as I had thought it would. It took me longer to get out of bed and find a suitable outfit. One where I don't look like a scrub and still feel comfortable. Bea was surprisingly okay with getting me out of the house for a "little adventure" as she called it. She mentioned that seeing some friends might promote beneficial healing for Trice and agreed I needed to get some fresh air.

When we pull up to the hospital, she tells me what room Trice is in and then says that she and Lonnie are going to run some errands and she will be back to get me when visiting hours are over. Her relaxed demeanor has me on edge. Just this morning she was hovering over me, practically smothering me, now she's shooing me out of her vehicle like she's on a mission. I happily accept the freedom.

A sudden rush of emotion comes over me as I walk through the hospital doors. My thoughts immediately go from Bea and Russell learning I was in a car wreck, to Crew not only learning that his brother and I were in a wreck, but also the news of him being adopted all in the span of a few hours. It's a lot to take in at once. I can't fault him for fleeing. I just wish he'd come home or at least check in with someone. He's only been gone for two weeks, but it's felt like an eternity. Especially since I've been confined to my bedroom until today. My only visitor has been Andrea, who came barreling into my room with a gift basket full of candy and fresh gossip from school.

Hitting the button on the elevator for Trice's floor, I chew the inside of my cheek as I anticipate seeing him. Bea explained that his injuries were severe and that he'll have a long road to recovery before he can even walk independently again. Nothing compares to the sight of seeing your best friend lying in a hospital bed with his legs wrapped in bandages and steel rods coming out of each side. I'm not sure if he understands the depth of his own injuries because as I walk through the threshold of his door, he's smiling from ear to ear. It takes me off guard. The exuberant look on his face doesn't befit the guy whose athletic career is on indefinite hold.

"There's my girl." Trice deadpans. "Not *my* girl, my best girl. Damnit my best friend who just so happens to be female."

I don't care about anything else right now as I march forward and fling myself onto him. His once strong grip is gone. I'm caught off guard by his lowered voice. "Too tight, Rory."

"I'm so sorry." I stumble backwards and plop into the chair by his bedside before holding my ribcage as the discomfort flares from grabbing him so tightly. "You look…Are you okay?"

"I've been better. That's for sure. Won't this scar make me look more badass though?" He gestures to a line of stitches above his eyebrow. "Those airbags are a force to be reckoned with."

"I don't really remember much about what happened."

The blue of his eyes hold me in place. "I remember it all. Even though I wish I didn't."

Our bond is tangible. Not in the sense of Trice's unexpected admission about being in love with me. It's more the fact that we survived something that should have killed us both. Our scars will fade. The memory of this past Derby will too. However, our friendship never will. I won't allow that to happen again.

Trice beats me to it. "Look, I could give you the whole spiel I had prepared before you got here. After I woke up, there hasn't been much to do but relive that day over and over. The look on your face? It's burned into my memory. If I could go back, I obviously would never have put you or myself in danger by drinking and driving, and I shouldn't have dropped that bomb in your lap either. Being in here, limited to this bed has given me ample time to think. Not just about you, or the car wreck. About life and where I fit into this world. I've been seeing a…a therapist. His name is Carl. He's been coming once every couple days for a session. He works at my mom's practice, so my parents trust him. I told him."

I eye him, waiting for more. "What exactly did you tell him?"

"I told him that I was driving the boat the night that Crew, Matt, and I wrecked. I killed Matt, Rory. It wasn't Crew. It was me. I was drunk. We wrecked and he fell overboard. It was so dark, and I was so drunk that Crew wouldn't let me dive in to help find him. I sat on our boat, swaying with the water, and helplessly watched them both go under. Just like I was too intoxicated when I knowingly let you get inside my car on Derby Day." Trice fiddles with the hem of his white hospital blanket.

"All I do is gamble with peoples' lives. People I care about. You could have died. Matt did die. I need help. I'm weak, and I've been fighting so hard to live in Crew's shadow my entire life that I just wanted to stop feeling so…mediocre to him. So, I began to drink. A lot. It's been a few years now, and I've become good at hiding it. I came clean to Carl, and he sat with me while I confessed to my parents. I've agreed to continue with therapy. Well that along with rehab so I can walk again. Both are going to keep me fairly busy."

"I'm proud of you. It takes a strong person to admit something like that. You know that I do love you back, don't you? It's not in the same way that I—"

"Love Crew though." He finishes my thought. I've never said those words out loud. Although, I've thought them more times than I can count, especially this week. "I know that. I'm sorry for springing that on you. If we're being honest, I think I just wanted what he had. He's always been so tough. Independent to a fault and doesn't give a shit what people think of him. I envy him in that way."

"You both have a strange way of showing it. I'm not up to date on healthy family dynamics by any means, but you need to come clean. He needs to hear you say you're sorry. He took the blame for the accident to protect you. Crew selflessly did that because he loves you so much, and you've done nothing but spit in his face for years. The good thing is you're brothers. You're sort of stuck with one another for life. Love builds families, not blood. When we find him, you need to apologize and set the record straight. I think the truth will go a long way."

"Tell that to Crew. Our parents are worried sick and desperate to find him."

"I can imagine. One child in the hospital and one out on the lamb."

"He turned his phone off so they can't even ping his location. He always joked when we were younger and told me that the milk man dropped me off on the front porch. I would get so pissed off. I actually believed him. Our parents were always pining over Crew, their perfect first-born son. I can't imagine how he's feeling, and he's going through it alone. Who cares that he's adopted? It doesn't change anything as far as I'm concerned. I mean other than the fact that you didn't spend the last year obsessing over blood-related brothers or anything."

"Your fervent, misguided delusion is impressive."

"I am currently under construction. Thank you for your patience while I gather up the courage to do the actual work to be a better person."

"Even with a shattered...body, it's good to see your ego hasn't deflated."

"No but my skull almost did. That brain swelling is no joke. My head has been pounding for days."

"I can't with you. Seriously, though, no one has to do anything alone. I've had Lonnie. If I didn't, I would have lost my humanity in the world a long time ago. Then I met Bea and Russell, and they showered me with love that I didn't even know existed. I'm not their child by blood, yet they feed me, give me shelter, and without even trying they've both shown me what a doting family can be like. Your friendship helped heal me too."

"Is that your way of saying you love me back?" His voice is a comfort.

"I love you, Trice. You're my best friend in the entire world, and I don't want anything to ever come between us again." His gentle eyes show me he understands. "I love Crew. I want to be with him...forever. Wherever that love takes us, I'll go as long as it's with him. My only goal was to turn eighteen, now it's to find him and tell him that... wait, what day is it?"

If we crashed on Derby Day, and that was over two weeks ago then that means...

"Happy eighteenth birthday, Rory." The beginning of a wide grin tugs at the corners of Trice's lips.

"It can't be. It's May nineteenth already?" I can barely manage a reply.

Trice slides out his phone and pulls up the calendar app and holds it up for me to see.

"I'm eighteen? I've been waiting on this day for…forever." In a desperate attempt to resist screaming in elation, I chew my bottom lip. The importance of today is not lost on me. The feeling of my heart beating, hard and powerful against my ribcage is startling and uncomfortable.

I'm not ready to leave *home*.

I'm not ready to adopt Lonnie. I have so much I want to do and see and paint. I can't do all of that while trying to raise a child.

I'm not ready to say goodbye to Crew…or Trice.

I want this life I've built here.

With my *friends* and *family*.

"I bet it would make your birthday extra special this year to be able to spend it with Crew. My parents said they checked his dorm, Della's house…" Trice's smirk is cunning. It's good to see his physical impairment hasn't deadened his wit. "And the clubhouse. I think I have an idea where he might be though. If I tell you where you can find him, do you promise me that you'll bloom where you're planted, Rory?" His question is loaded.

Crew planted seeds of optimism in the depth of my soul the moment we ran into each other almost a year ago. Those seeds grew roots, stood firm against my cyclone of fears, and yet, they did not wither or die. My feelings toward him have only just begun to blossom and when I find him, nothing will extinguish how deeply Crew Jordan is planted in my heart. The excited gasp that leaves my lips in a rush gives Trice all the answer he needs before he rolls the tray table closer toward his bedside and scribbles down an address.

"Bones," I promise, before I exit his room and sprint to the nearest elevator.

CHAPTER
THIRTY-FOUR

CREW

Denial is a one-way street, and I'm plodding down it begrudgingly. As if the sole of my foot is made of metal, I hit the pedal and squeal tires until the open road of the freeway is in sight. Refusing to go back to my dorm after I leave the tattoo studio, there's only one other place I can go without having to use my credit card, which can be easily tracked.

I need space to process the revelation I was just bombarded with.

Aurora is going to unalive me when she wakes up and I'm not there. Even the thought of her wrath doesn't compare to the need to put some distance between me and my *parents*. The insufferable look in my mom's—Mina's—eyes when she told me I couldn't donate blood to Trice will forever be embedded in my mind. Confusion courses through me as the white and yellow lines of the freeway guide me to the only place left in this world where I can find seclusion.

The lake house has always brought me comfort. This place was our mecca, even as kids, Matt, Trice, and I loved spending our summers there. We swam until the last day of summer when the nights turned the water cooler, and our lips turned blue. Memories come back in a rush as I pull off the exit and onto the back road that leads to the house.

The house is as much the Jordan's as the Greenwell's. No family ever came without the other. Until the boat accident that is. Bea never could muster up the courage to face the lake house again. Even though it wasn't this lake that claimed Matt's life. Russell and my dad have taken Aiden fishing a time or two since then. It's not like I can blame them for not wanting to come too often either.

This place has more memories than a scrapbook inside. From the small hole in the wall that we hid with a painting after we were riding our scooters inside when we were told not to. To the time we spent Christmas here and dad almost cut his thumb off with a pocketknife while trying to cut the plastic off one of Aiden's toys. Blood spewed like an episode of *Grey's Anatomy.* Trice puked on the rug, and luckily Bea had her medical bag in the trunk and stitched dad up on the kitchen island.

I put Pete's truck in park and find the small lawn decoration that has a key hidden in a little compartment underneath it. I'm hit in the face with melancholy as I open the door. The smell is fresh. Not musty like I had expected it to be. Leave it to my mom to make sure that the place still gets cleaned on the regular and is ready for us whenever our wounds from losing Matt finally heal, and we're ready to visit again. I didn't know how much I missed this place until I walk inside and turn on the lights.

Losing Matt was like ripping my heart open, scooping out the insides like pumpkin seeds, and placing it back in my chest without the muscles that make it beat. Never in my life had I known a devastation like that. Now I'm here in the place that once held the best memories for me, and I still feel hollow.

And alone.

The sun dips below the horizon as I peer through the window above the sink. Having spent the last two weeks in solitude at the lake house, my hurt and anger are still going strong, and my wallet is empty. Running out of cash for groceries means that I'll have to use my card and take the chance of my parents seeing where I am or tuck my tail and go home.

"Coming here might not have been the best idea," I say out loud before I open the bar cabinet and pull out the last bottle of liquor from the shelf.

The best way to deal with misery is to drown it.

CHAPTER
THIRTY-FIVE

My bladder feels like it's going to burst by the time I pull into the Jordan's lake house driveway. With white knuckles, I followed my GPS all the way here silently thanking Trice for the driving lessons both he and Russell offered several months ago. I never had the use for a vehicle when I lived in the city.

Obtaining my driver's license at age seventeen, while slightly embarrassing being later than my classmates, proved necessary tonight. Russell agreed to let me take the highway and slid me Matt's old car keys, showing his support for my crusade to find Crew.

The entire ride my mind was preoccupied with thoughts of him not even being at the lake house paired with flashes of my wreck every time a semi passed me on the interstate. The combination made my stomach queasy as my foot found its rhythm on the accelerator. Finding the strength to turn the wheel with a healing rib was another hindrance. My body slouches against my seat as I pull into the driveway and cut the engine. I feel like I'm frozen in limbo between wanting to get out and rush inside to see if he's here or scanning the sight in front of me with hawklike eyes and appreciating the view.

The lawn is pristine. They must pay someone to keep the grounds up year-round. I thought it might look unkept since it's been vacant. That wouldn't give Mina Jordan the credit she deserves. In my head, I had conjured up a house that is modern like the one they reside in now, but I couldn't have been more wrong. From the lush green grass, flowers that are starting to bloom, and the warmth of the wooden planks that make up the log cabin, it's a truly magical site. I half expect a fairy to fly out of a window into the moonlight that spills over the prettiest little cottage I've ever seen in real life. The outside is immaculate. I can't wait to see what the inside looks like.

First things first. Trice said if Crew did escape here, he'd most likely be on the lake. It was their special place as children he said. This house had been their second home during their summer breaks. The water their safe heaven. Until it became their nightmare.

Nursing my broken rib is a feat as I exhale a breath and round the house, sauntering through the incandescent greenery at a turtle's pace. I make it to a wooden dock that resembles a long cross with the end perched over the water. There's a small shack at the end of the dock. I imagine that's where the boat gets stored between seasons. I've never been on a boat, so I could be totally wrong.

With my head held high, I head toward the dock and prepare myself for an argument. My pulse thrums and adrenaline lines my brow with a drop of sweat from overexerting myself on my mission. I understand Crew needed time to process the news about his adoption. But it's been a little over two weeks. Now it's time for him to float back down to reality and deal with the cards he's been dealt like an adult. Between him abandoning his brother during his recovery to him deserting me and missing my eighteenth birthday, I'm beyond livid.

Hesitation has never been my thing. I'm a get-to-the-point type of girl. Feeling a ripple of uncertainty sneak up my spine, I swing open the door to the building at the end of the dock. This is the whole point of my trip. To make sure Crew is alive and safe. And possibly to slap him for fleeing and dealing with his bullshit solo.

What's the point of having a girlfriend if you just retreat and deal with life's hurdles alone anyway?

After my two-week confinement to my bed and then seeing Trice, I fled house arrest and mustered up the strength to walk to the clubhouse. Trice had told me his parents already checked to see if Crew was holed up there. A part of me had to check for myself. The clubhouse had been his sanctuary once upon a time. He'd for sure be there, I thought. Except he wasn't. He had been at some time because the place I had cleaned and tidied for Lonnie and Aiden was trashed.

The final straw that pushed me from concerned girlfriend to furious lunatic was when I saw he had broken the two pictures I had printed and framed. One was the picture I found of him, Trice, and Matt. The other was one I printed of Lonnie and Aiden. He wasn't only destroying himself by retreating. He was now ruining the place that our brothers had to play and escape to.

It was Trice who suggested that the last place he could think Crew would go would be his parent's lake house. After Matt's boating accident, Shawn had their boat moved from the lake near their current home back to the lake house. I guess it was one of those out of sight out of mind things. There wasn't a need for the boat closer to home since it was rarely ever used anymore. Trice didn't give himself enough credit for knowing his brother, because as I step inside the small building, Crew sits in the boat with his head bent and his large hands encasing it.

I stand frozen in the doorway taking in his silhouette. If the look of defeat could embody an image it would be Crew Jordan right now. *Be strong, Rory.* Bunching my fist at my sides, I call out his name. He doesn't budge or acknowledge me. "Crew!" I yell again, louder this time as I inch forward. My body casts a shadow on the floor. That gets his attention. He pulls a pair of wireless ear buds from his ears. The shock of my presence is written across his pained face.

My instinct tells me to rush to him, hold him and kiss away his troubles. I want to save him, even if it's from himself. Knowing I can't do just that, I plant my feet firmly and try to control the trembling of my hands. Yes, he feels scorned. He has every right to be confused and hurt. But he doesn't have to do it alone. He has a tribe of people rooting for him. Even after Matt's death, he became a recluse and pushed everyone away. For some reason, he's conditioned himself to deal with things alone.

That ends tonight.

"Aurora, what are you doing here?" He looks like he's seen a ghost.

"I'd like to ask you that myself. It's been two weeks. Have you been here all along?"

"I don't have it in me to have this conversation right now."

Even with the tension that stretches between us, I refuse to cower or back down. Although he looks shocked to see me, this isn't the reaction I'd expected him to have. "Good thing I didn't ask your permission. Don't you even care that we've all been worried?"

"How people feel isn't my concern."

"What about how I feel?" I ask and allow his silence to fill the boat house around us. It speaks volumes. "Do you have room in your pity-party-boat for one more?"

His dark eyes reflect glimmers of light. "No reservations

are required." He gestures with his hand for me to join him on the boat. "Be my guest."

"It's nice to see my company is still wanted." He doesn't recognize my insult, or he doesn't care enough to bite back as I climb onto the boat and sit in the chair directly across from him. Biting the inside of my cheek, I swallow the throbbing ache in my chest that my simple movement causes.

Crew leans back in the captain's chair and rests his elbows on the surface behind him. His face resigned. Guarded. "How'd you find me?"

"You can thank your brother for that."

The gruff way he hisses tells me he's been chain-smoking. "My brother. You're joking right? I'm sure you heard the news. Trice isn't actually *my* brother. The fact that he told you where to find me means that he's alive. Unless you conjured up his spirit on an Ouija board and his ghost told you where to find me."

"He's alive." Is all I can convey without sounding like a complete bitch at his detachment toward his brother's well-being.

"I'm sure Mina and Shawn are over the moon that their golden boy survived."

Before I can respond, he reaches down, and brings a brown bottle to his lips, taking a gulp.

"I thought you said you didn't drink. Your smoking habit is bad enough. Now you're getting drunk too?"

He sits quietly pondering my question and then nods. "I figured why should Trice be the only one having all the fun. I mean he gets drunk and kills our best friend and doesn't even pay the price for it. Then he gets drunk and crashes again with you in the car. Since I am the bastard of the family, I might as well live up to my reputation and enjoy myself. Plus, nothing pairs better with a cigarette than bourbon. You want a sip?'

"No, thank you. I'm not staying here and watching you

drink yourself into oblivion. I'm glad I found you. I'll call your parents and let them know you're safe."

"My parents." The sound of his laugh sends a chill down my spine. "And who might those be? Because if you've met them, I'd really like to as well. I'd like to ask them why they abandoned their own flesh and blood."

"You know damn well who your parents are. Mina might not have given birth to you, but she's your mother. It's a disgrace to her love for you to even question that."

"I wouldn't have to question her love if I wasn't kept in the dark for the last nineteen years."

Heat rises from the soles of my feet to my ears like a pressure gauge ready to explode. "Poor pitiful, Crew. How awful is it that you were adopted by two loving parents who have literally given you the world? You said it yourself that you never had to want for anything. You're a picket-fence kid. Remember? You even admitted it."

"You think you know how I feel? Do you know what it's like to be lied to for your entire fucking life only to have stumbled upon the truth by accident when your brother needed a blood transfusion to save his life? Don't sit on your high horse and judge me. You don't know jack." His words, laced with venom, sting. Their bite starts to fester, and my anger rises. If I wasn't nursing a broken rib, I'd reach forward and smack his angular jawline so hard that my palm would itch from its impact.

"Have you forgotten who you're yelling at? I'm the poster child for messed up childhoods. My face should be on a billboard for as many foster homes as I've been placed in." I take a deep breath and hope that it's enough to oxygenate my body because right now it feels like spontaneous human combustion is real. "Do you know what it was like living with Lloyd and Jean last year? Sometimes I went to school in the same clothes because the water got shut off and I couldn't wash them at night. Or what about when Jean, my old foster mom, decided to buy cat food instead of my allergy pills, and I went a week with a chapped nose and blisters from blowing it so much. I won't even get into the night I found Lloyd standing over Lonnie's bed with his pants around his ankles. If you think the news of being adopted into a loving family is a bad thing, then you wouldn't survive a day in my shoes or even Lonnie's."

Crew winces at my confession. I don't let the hurt on his face derail my thoughts.

"Your parents longed for you. They wanted you and desired a child of their own. Do you know what adoptive families have to go through to be *allowed* to adopt a child? They must be approved by the state. A literal stranger prances around their homes and judges them. Is it nice enough? Is it safe enough for a child to reside in? While every other person on the planet can procreate without a care in the world. Adoptive parents are under a microscope with their histories on display and under scrutiny of a judge who can approve them or deny them of their dream of becoming a parent." I shake my head as I see Crew's glum face staring back at me.

"Can you imagine being deprived of the opportunity to be a father just because the fire extinguisher in your home was expired? How about being passed over to adopt because an expectant birth mother didn't notice your parents' adoption profile book and chose a different family instead? Mina didn't birth you, but she carried you. She carried the weight of home studies, and the mounds of paperwork they require like fingerprints and health exams and stress like you couldn't even fathom."

I light into him with a ferocity I've never experienced before. It's like all the pent-up anger and resentment for my own appalling life in the foster care system is directed at my ungrateful boyfriend, because despite his feelings on adoption, he was *chosen.* He was adopted. He was one of the lucky ones.

"I won't pretend to know the specifics about your whole situation and story. What I do know is that Mina couldn't get pregnant for whatever reason and your birth mother chose her to be your forever mom. They longed for a child, and you needed a home. The magnitude of that love on both parts is unfathomable. You think you drew the short end of the stick out of you and your brothers, when really, you won the fucking parent lottery." My mind flutters and I choke back an exasperated cry.

"It's so unbelievable that you don't see it and, honestly, it's a turn off because the guy that I fell for isn't a coward. He's resilient and brave. The Crew I grew to care for stood up against adversities and loss, and I know beyond the shadow of a doubt that he'd face this news—this unexpected, difficult news—head on, just like he tackled everything life threw his way."

Playing the martyr card, he asks, "You done reading me the riot act?"

"Yup. I guess so." I stand and carefully attempt to climb out of the boat with my aching rib, needing to put some distance between us. Grabbing hold of the door handle, I glance over my shoulder. "It's too late for me to drive home now. Russell made me promise that if it got dark, I wouldn't drive back tonight. Since it's apparent you're not done sulking yet or drinking yourself into a stupor, I'm going to go inside and get settled for the evening."

"You're staying the night? Here?"

"No, I'm pitching a tent in the yard. Duh. Where else would I stay…in Matt's truck?"

"Russell let you drive here?"

"A lot of things have happened since the accident that you'd be aware of if you didn't storm off without a second thought. I honestly can't stomach being under the same roof as you right now. But it's too late and unlike some people, when I make a promise, I keep them."

"What's that supposed to mean?"

"For starters, you left the hospital not even knowing my condition to go on a trip to wallow away. You promised you weren't a douchebag. You promised me I could trust you. When shit hit the fan, you ran. I woke up in a hospital bed and *you* weren't there. You promised me we'd celebrate my birthday together. I should be at home celebrating with Lonnie, Bea, and Russell. Yet here I am."

Triumph flickers through me when I see the realization of his actions set in. "Fuck. I'm sorry. I'm so sorry, Aurora."

"Don't be." The defiance in my tone hints at a subtle defeat. "I'm used to being let down by those I care about. I guess we have that in common, too, now, don't we?" My own brashness startles me as I hear a quick intake of Crew's breath. I look at his paling face and rejoice. Maybe, just maybe, I hit home enough to make him come to his senses.

To my surprise, he stills after a beat of silence. His mask falls back into place, and he shows no reaction. As I stare at him, with my heart pounding in my chest, I will Crew to come back to me. I long for his banter. For the sight of him when he gives a genuine smile that reaches his eyes that makes me feel like a thirteen-year-old girl talking to her first crush.

His appraisal is so cold, goosebumps break out over my exposed arms. He breathes out one last sentence. "Just leave."

And my mouth snaps shut along with my heart.

CHAPTER
THIRTY-SIX

RORY

'm standing at the sink with a towel over my shoulder, hand washing the dishes that I used in a feeble attempt to cook something without burning down the house. I don't know what time it is when Crew saunters in through the sliding glass doors into the kitchen. I can tell by the solemn look on his face that his inebriation has subsided some. Drunk Crew is my least favorite version to date.

He pulls out a chair at the kitchen island and plops down. "You made dinner?"

"There wasn't much in the refrigerator or cabinets. I scrounged up what I could. It's grilled cheese. Don't look too much into it. We're both stuck here and have to eat." Sliding a plate in front of him, he uses my proximity to whip his hand out and pull me close to his side.

"I'm truly sorry for what it's worth. I...I just needed some time to think and sort through everything going on up here." He taps his head. "Having that bomb dropped on me, while I was already so wound up and worried about you, it was a lot to deal with."

Even though his voice is full of torment, I stand like granite. I know if I don't, if I waiver and let his words pierce through my heart, I'll cave to his apology, and I'm not ready to do that just yet.

"I can't imagine how you felt when you woke up and I wasn't sitting beside you. It killed me to leave the hospital not knowing what condition you were in. I just couldn't stay there. Not being helpless like I was. Losing Matt almost broke me. Even the thought of losing you made me want to die. I couldn't survive losing you both."

I was wounded when I woke up and he wasn't at my bedside. For two grueling weeks, I waited by my phone like a lovestruck goon, hoping that he'd call. As the days passed and I realized he wasn't going to, a different level of disappointment planted roots inside me. Backing up from Crew's embrace, I put some distance between us and impose an iron will.

"It looks like you're dealing with it in a perfectly healthy way." I allude to the chain-smoking and alcohol consumption with the wave of my hand.

"How I deal isn't your concern...I'm sorry. I didn't mean that either. I'm just...upset and confused. I don't want to push you further away. Where do we stand? Are we still together? Do you hate me for leaving you when you needed me the most? God. I'm an idiot for leaving you. I know this. Can you understand how I felt though? Please say something. Why aren't you saying anything?"

The anguish in his tone should be accompanied by a sympathy of violins and a harp. It's that tragic. "I'm just listening. You've been cooped up here for two weeks without an outlet. I'm sure you need to get this all off your chest."

"I want to understand how someone could just give me away," he says. "Did my birth parents not love me enough to raise me themselves? I have so many questions. Sue me for rather being drunk and numb than having to think about it all sober."

As curses fall from his lips, tears well in my eyes. I'm on the brink of crumbling. Crew may have needed time and distance to diminish the pain he's dealing with but seeing him in this state, broken and vulnerable, is complete agony. The feelings I have for him are so intense that the sadness of his expression pulls on the strong, yet delicate thread that is woven between us.

"You're making it sound like you were bought on the black market. Your birth mother placed you for adoption," I say, trying to make him see a different perspective. "It's the most selfless act that a mother can do. Imagine how she felt placing her child in another woman's arms and walking away? That's the biggest gesture of love that there is. To admit that you cannot parent and willingly let another woman or family raise your child as their own. Whoever she was, she's fearless in my book. She could have been a teenager and wasn't old enough to provide for you. There are a thousand different scenarios you could conjure up and trust me I have. All that matters is that you grew up with a pair of parents who love you."

I hold open my arms, encompassing the room we're in. "Parents who bought a lake house where you created special memories of your childhood. I understand you have questions." My anguish for the boy who feels so lost is nearly overpowering my control to keep my distance. My pride is like a shield hiding the hurt from when he told me to leave earlier.

"The beauty of life is that you get to ask those questions and get those answers. You can't run from the truth if the truth is what you desire."

"Do you know what I desire?" His steady gaze bores into me as a swath of his dark hair falls onto his forehead. He reaches across the island to where I'm standing and wraps his finger around the hem of my sleeve.

"Listen, enough with the googly eyes. You can't charm your way out of being an imbecile and not being there for me when I needed you. I didn't come here to rekindle things with you. You left…abandoning me when I opened up to you… that anger I feel toward you just doesn't go away because you're batting those obnoxiously long eyelashes at me." My body is betraying my mind.

I don't want to *want*, Crew. I shouldn't feel turned on by his closeness. If anything, I should be repulsed by him. He abandoned me.

"You need to man up and contact Trice and your parents. He's got a long road ahead of him and he's going to need your support. His dreams of playing football again are practically gone. The best part is, he didn't even mention himself and what he's lost when I saw him. He was so absorbed with finding you that he sent me here."

Roughly, Crew tugs at his hair and his eyes grow wild with pent up irritation. "Oh, I'm sure he is worried. Learning I'm adopted was probably like winning a sweepstakes to him. He gets all the glory and the attention he's always needed and desired. I bet you he starts to lash out and make poor decisions. Then he'll use it to his advantage and blame it on the shock of *me* being adopted and Mina and Shawn will cater to his needs like they always do."

"You couldn't be further from the truth."

"What? Did he have a sudden epiphany? Did that crash knock enough sense into him to put others first for once? I know I wasn't there for you when you woke up. I will regret that decision for the rest of my life. You can hate me. You can slap me," he motions to his cheek, "if that would make you feel better. But I won't let you push me away. Not now when I just got you back."

"How fitting since you pushed everyone who loved you

away and you haven't gotten me back by a long shot. Just because I'm here, doesn't mean I forgive you. You hurt me. I allowed myself to let you in a little and you nudged yourself in the rest of the way, and then you left just as quickly as you came. I don't know how I feel about that. My heart surely hasn't forgotten."

"I don't know how to earn your forgiveness, Aurora. I promise you that I will spend every day trying. I don't deserve it for what I did. But I need it. I need you like I need air. Sure, I can survive without it for a couple minutes, but it's brutal. That's how these last two weeks have been. I ran away to think when I should have been running to you. You're the only thing that makes sense in my life."

"Bones," I say not even really understanding what I'm asking for him to swear on before the word slips from my mouth.

My thoughts skid to a halt as his demeanor changes. It's as if I've broken through his fragile control. "You want my truth, Aurora?"

The hurt of Crew's absence cut me deeper than anything I've been through before. Even the years of shuffling to different foster homes and fending for myself. Nothing compared to the pain of him not choosing me when I needed him most. When I look into his eyes, I can't deny how unnerved he makes me. I want his truth more than I want my next breath. My thoughts scamper through my mind and nervously, I nod, prepared for whatever truth he spills.

"I love you. You seeped into my soul at the darkest time in my life. You reminded me what it felt like to be cared for and to have a best friend. *You* are the best part of me. I was blinded by my own ignorance, and I pushed you away. I'm sorry."

Crew eyes me warily. His gaze roams up and down my body. He may still be drunk on liquor, but I'm drunk on his nearness. I take in his features and study the way his brows pull downward in despair. The way his strong arms now hang at his sides. My body longs to feel the warmth of his touch again. I know that if he swept me into his arms and encircled me in his warm embrace, I'd be done for.

His stare grows darker, his eyes never leave mine as he climbs off the chair at the island and stands in front of me. His fingers are still splayed over the hem of my long-sleeved tunic when he grabs my phone as if he's on a mission and scrolls for a second searching for something. "It's today," he blurts, as if he's just had an epiphany. "You're eighteenth birthday is today. We have ten more minutes to celebrate."

One second, he's engulfed in anger, the next he wants to throw a party. "My birthday is the least of my concerns right now. We need to get some sleep and get back to town early tomorrow so you can see your parents and brothers. We can talk about us—whatever we are or where we stand—later. I don't have the energy to do it tonight."

"You're my only concern right now. You're *eighteen*." He accentuates my age like his statement should mean something.

I don't have much time to deliberate what those thoughts mean before I inhale sharply at his nearness. Crew takes my response as an invitation, just like Trice had done. I shouldn't be so breathy if it gives off mixed signals.

As he leans in and takes my mouth, coaxing it open, the smoldering heat between us is enough to join metal. I stand on my tiptoes as our mouths explore one another's in a wild swirl of intimacy. We've had several make out sessions in our history. Nothing compares to this. With this kiss we succumb to one another—our minds, bodies, and spirits.

"I am...so...sorry." Between each word, he tenderly plants small kisses on my neck, shoulder, and forehead before grazing my earlobe with his teeth. "I don't care how much chaos surrounds us. You're my person. I was so used to warding off the world alone, that I'd forgotten what it was like to be a part of a team. Please forgive me, Aurora. Even if it's not tonight, I understand. We can work toward forgiveness together."

That is my undoing. I curve into his body, allowing my emotions to take over. My blood heats and courses through my veins, pulsing from my heart to my core with each caress of his hands against the contours of my body. I memorize every touch as his hands roam, branding me and leaving my skin ablaze.

"I love you, Aurora." He kisses the bridge of my nose. "I will make this right. We'll go home tomorrow, and I'll talk to everyone. My parents, Trice, and Russell. If he didn't pull you out of the car…I can't even think about it. I need something from you right now. I know I ran from you. It was stupid. You're the only person I should have clung to and found refuge. Now I'm running to you to save me and pull me from the depths of my own mind. I need to be numb and block out the world just a little bit longer."

"What do you need from me?" I ask, my face flushed.

"You." His admission is like peeling back the scab on a newly healed wound. It cuts through me and leaves me vulnerable. Something that I don't like to be. Especially not now as he stares at me with his honeycomb eyes that are breaking through my brittle control.

"I need you to help turn it all off. I need you…in my arms and in my bed."

I look up and take a slow, deep breath. "I thought you were saving your virginity?"

His warm breath fans over my cheek as he whispers in my ear, "I *was* waiting. For you, Aurora. I've been waiting to give this gift to you. Happy birthday, my love."

My senses feel drugged. The misery of the last two weeks vanishes into thin air as Crew peers at me with intention in his eyes. Long gone is the amber of his irises. They're black and filled with longing. My brain tells me to stay resilient and challenge his gentle touch as it reaches out to embrace me.

Abandoning all thoughts, Crew caresses my waist, his touch sends jolts through my body like a blast of electricity, and I leap with excitement that he's finally ready to have sex. Thoughts of how this will play out in my frail state drift to my forefront. Is it even safe to have sex while nursing a broken rib? What if the pain is too much? I know Crew would stop in an instant if I asked him to. I don't want to *have* to stop him now that he's finally made the decision to give into what he needs and I'm ready to oblige despite the fleeting worry that trickles down my spine.

His beautiful eyes, dark as black satin hold my glare as he studies my face carefully. All thoughts of painstaking notations vanish when the glow of his smile warms as his eyesight travels down my body. I reward him with my own softened smile and my mind is made up. I will muster up all the strength in the universe and welcome the temporary pain the melding our bodies causes if it means that I finally get to have him.

Fully. Wholly and without any barriers.

A delicious shudder heats my core as I lean toward Crew and offer him not only my body like a sacrifice, but also my heart once more.

I pray he doesn't shatter it this time.

CHAPTER
THIRTY-SEVEN

CREW

"Conforming to society's image of myself, I am rather impressed with how many times I was able to make you—"

"Do not finish that sentence." Aurora tosses a pillow at my head.

I've missed the sound of her laughter. Not knowing how she was doing after I left the hospital was like wearing my heart outside my body, and I never want to experience that again. I ran to avoid dealing with reality and pushed the only person I've ever loved away in the process. I'll spend eternity making it up to her.

"How do your ribs feel?"

"You think that highly of yourself, Jordan?"

"No, you fool. You said your rib isn't fully healed yet. I tried to be gentle the first time."

"It's fine." I can tell she's lying through her teeth. "How is your tattoo since my cast rubbed against it all night?" She looks up at me lazily through half-closed lids. "I still can't believe you got my caged thoracic rib painting tattooed on your chest."

"Why can't you believe it? As soon as I left the hospital, I went straight to Dean's studio. Having your art etched into my skin for life wasn't even a decision. Plus, I'm tough as steel. No damage was done by your cast. Don't forget about the word 'bones' that's written in cursive underneath. That's the best part."

"That little epithet still makes me laugh. I mean *bones*, really?" I swallow her laugh with a kiss.

"Yes, really. It meant something to Matt, Trice, and me, and now it means something to us."

"That's because it's tattooed on your chest forever." Her hand glides over my skin, softly.

"You were already tattooed on my heart with invisible ink long before Dean's gun permanently placed your drawing on my chest. Did it earn me any points in the forgiveness department?" The bedroom grows serious.

"Maybe a smidge," she admits. "I just didn't expect that from you. Leaving, that is. Despite everything. Even the news of your adoption. You abandoned me when I needed you. You could have stayed in *my* room and waited for *me* to wake up. We would have figured this all out together."

"There're so many things I wish I had done differently. *Sorry* is just a word. I know that. I promise you that my actions will speak for themselves moving forward. For now, let me apologize by showering you in kisses. I didn't hear you complaining through your whimpers last night."

"I hate you. Sex isn't a weapon at your disposal." She giggles before tossing the sheet over her face. "But it's a good start."

The truth is, I was holding onto my virginity like a shield. It was the one thing that our town and the hate they threw at me after Matt's death couldn't take. I could stoop to their level and play the bad guy role perfectly. It was all a front and holding onto my virginity was a reminder that I wasn't the philanderer or sleazeball that they painted me out to be. Deciding to make love to Aurora last night was as easy as breathing.

If Matt were here, I know he'd adore Aurora. Not only is she smart and kind, but she's funny as hell. The most attractive thing about a female is their sense of humor. She's also not too girly, in the way that Della was always too scared to get her hands dirty and mess up her perfect manicure. Aurora is more laid-back and has a go-with-the-flow attitude. She's a natural beauty and the epitome of the girl-next-door. Both literally and figuratively. I know right now if I asked her to meet me at the dock to fish, she'd be game.

That's how I know that she was the perfect girl for me to give myself to intimately. Deep in my heart, I've known for a while. With all the backlash from town that surrounded Matt's death, the last thing I needed was gossip about me having sex with an underage female. I'm not that much of a bonehead.

Last night was the definition of perfection. Not only was it her birthday, making her an adult who could offer permission to have consensual sex…lovemaking, but binding our souls as I slid into her was an awakening in many ways.

I had been emotionless since Matt's death. My heart grew cold and distant when I lost my best friend and took the blame for his death. Trice turning into a stranger was the final straw that sent my barrier up full force.

Aurora broke through it all, turning my barricade to ash with the outpouring of passion that bled into an emotional battlefield. No words were spoken. They weren't warranted other than me asking if she was okay a couple times. Even though I know she wasn't a virgin, it was still important for me to check on how she felt. She didn't have to answer. Her claw marks against my flesh told me enough.

We let our bodies do the talking and they spoke volumes to one another.

If I thought I loved her before we shared our bodies and fused our souls last night, the feelings I have for her now are multiplied by a thousand. It's almost pathetic how much she means to me. Because I know deep down, I screwed up and don't deserve her or her forgiveness. That won't stop me from trying to earn it. I'm selfish like that, and if the last couple years have taught me anything, it's to fight without ceasing for whatever brings you peace.

"I love you so fucking much it hurts. I'm sorry. I know I keep saying it. I'll prove it to you. I just need time." Another apology slips out of my mouth before my brain even recognizes I've said it.

"I'm not going anywhere. I love you, too, Crew Jordan. I don't fully forgive you. I won't lie and sugar coat that. But I do love you, and I'm not going anywhere. If the foster care system taught me anything, it's to be resilient," she says smoothly and without hesitation. "Do you know what else I love? It's a close second to you."

I inch closer to her and pull her body to mine in anticipation of her answer. The best part of being a virgin is that I practically have no refractory period. I'm like a stallion ready to go at every glance she tosses my way. "Pancakes. Do you think we can get showered and get some breakfast? I feel like I could eat a cow."

Leaning forward, I plant a kiss on her exposed shoulder. I could trace the soft, ivory flesh of her body for days and never grow tired of it. My touch makes her quiver in response and before we can discuss breakfast plans any further, we find a tempo that binds our bodies for the next few hours. I lay next to Aurora in a floodtide of ecstasy as she succumbs to sleep like a satisfied lover. Breakfast will have to wait.

Desperate for answers, I grab her cell phone and leave her upstairs to rest. I don't know how heated this conversation is going to get. The person I dial, picks up instantly. "Rory, was he there? What took you so long to call? Russell is livid. When you didn't check in, we all assumed you wrecked."

"She's here and she's fine." My voice is gravelly. "You can call off the search party."

"Crew?"

"Yup."

"Glad she found you, man. You know she hasn't had her license for long. That's why they wouldn't let her take one of their vehicles and come get you herself the day of the Derby. They knew the roads would be crowded, and she didn't have enough experience. I'm thankful she made it safely to the lake."

"Thanks for sending her. Can you tell Russell that she's fine, so he doesn't come storming through the door?"

"Hell, no. You can have the privilege of calling him yourself. He's pissed that she didn't text when she got there. I mean livid times a thousand, bro."

"Hold on, I'll shoot him a text." I fire off a text from Aurora's phone telling Russell that she is fine and is sleeping right now and apologize for her forgetfulness of texting him upon her arrival last night. While Trice goes on about the horrible hospital food he's been subjected to, I send a message to my mom as well. I'm not quite ready to deal with that whole mess, even though I know it's inevitable. With my attention now fully attuned to Trice, I swallow my pride and initiate another conversation that is long overdue.

It's almost an hour by the time Aurora strolls into the kitchen. Trice and I kept our conversation light. He said he'd rather talk to me in person about deeper shit when we get back. "There she is," I say while trying to cover the speaker of the phone.

"Wait, Rory's finally up? Put her on the phone," Trice demands.

"She's a little indisposed at the moment."

She slaps my arm while wearing nothing but my T-shirt. It's a good look on her. I envision her standing in our one-bedroom apartment, both of us refusing money from our parents while flipping pancakes on our little stove. The future doesn't seem as bleak as it did just a day ago.

"Don't tell her this. Bea had a surprise ready for her yesterday before she rushed off to save your ass. She ordered a cake and Lonnie and her hung streamers up. The whole shebang. Y'all need to get home. It's time to face reality. I'm here for you, bro. Whenever you're ready to talk to mom and dad about your...the adoption, just call me, and I'll be on the line with you while you're there. We've spent too long being enemies. It's time we fight for each other, not against one another."

Trice's words resonate with me the entire ride home. I'm following Aurora in Pete's truck, thankful that he didn't report it stolen and wasn't as mad as I thought he'd be when I sent him a text apologizing this morning. I hold my hand out the window, feeling the breeze rush over it and for once, feel free of the past that has kept me a prisoner for far too long.

I don't know how the conversation with my parents is going to go. It may get heated, and I may spout off things I'll regret. I do know for certain that Aurora will be with me, grounding me. She's had my back and never once strayed from me since we made it official. I owe her the decency of listening to what my parents have to say even if their truth hurts and brings more questions. Ones that I might never have the answers to.

Aurora is adamant that we stop by the hospital before we go home. I know that she and Trice made amends. I'm thankful for that because she wouldn't have known where to find me otherwise. After Trice and I hung up, Aurora and I sat at the kitchen island and ate the rest of the cereal and milk I had purchased before cleaning up the kitchen. She caught me up on his condition and told me that he admitted to her that he was driving the boat the night of Matt's accident.

It's a truth I never thought would see the light of day.

As we walk hand in hand through the hospital, memories from the day of their auto accident resurface. It's a somber reminder of what I could have lost.

"I'm going to give you guys some space and go get a coffee."

I give Aurora a quick peck on her cheek and then find my brother's room. The sight I see when I swing open his door feels like a kick in the nuts. All the breath leaves my lungs. Aurora had told me about the swelling in his skull and his broken femur and his legs. Seeing his face, the lingering yellow and purple bruises that haven't faded yet and the contraption that his legs dangle from leaves me in stunned silence.

"If you like what you see, take a picture. They last longer." Trice's voice is rich in sarcasm. I'm glad to see his sense of humor is still intact despite his appearance. "You should have seen me a couple weeks ago."

"Fuck, I'm glad to hear your voice."

"I talked to you this morning, dude."

"In person is what I meant, you jackass. I'm glad to see you." I inch closer to his hospital bed. "I'm sorry, man. I had so much going on in my head, and I just needed to take a beat. I needed time." Trice doesn't acknowledge my response. His emotions seem to be in control, whereas I feel like I'm on the verge of hysteria.

"I had no idea that my blood wouldn't match yours, and I flipped. I couldn't save Matt. I couldn't reach him. It was too dark. Knowing that I couldn't do anything to save you either. It cut me deep."

"Crew, look at me." Trice's eyes hold mine. "I'm not mad

at you for needing space. I'm mad because we haven't heard from you. We've all been anxiously wondering where you were and what was going on with you. All you had to do was call or text me, and I would have held mom and dad off. I could have bought you the time you needed to process things."

I draw my lips in thoughtfully. "I know."

"I don't think you do. You. Are. Not. Alone. You never have been. Even after the boating accident when you took the fall for *my* actions. You weren't alone then. I was there. I tried talking to you. Hell, I told mom and dad that it was me driving. I think they already knew because when you got in the back of that cop car, you were stone-cold sober. But I couldn't get through to you. Pushing people away is your specialty. You should have it trademarked. I never thought I'd see the day that you let anyone in again, and then Rory strolled into town. You finally opened up, and I knew that any chance I might have had with her was over after the night that you threatened to out me. I saw a spark in your eyes that had been missing. I screwed up by pushing you both away when I couldn't accept things."

"That's why you ignored us for months."

"Just because I couldn't be around her and not look at her in a way that would get my face rearranged. The day of the Derby, I was blitzed. I knew that I'd see you and her together. I couldn't face reality sober, so I took a bottle from dad's office. I shouldn't have let her get into my car that day. If anyone is sorry, bro, it's me."

The deceptive calm of his voice resonates with me. I believe every word he's saying.

"I put your girl in danger. Just like I did Matt. That's my burden to bear, and trust me, I feel his loss like a gaping hole in my chest. I'm sorry, for what it's worth. I know you may not believe me. But I am so sorry for everything. It should have been me who suffered the consequences. Not you. You lost your football scholarship because of me."

"What's done is done. We can't press rewind. Although, if we could, I'd love to see you up on the stage at church singing with your off-pitch voice." The tension between us starts to fade.

"That first day Rory went to church she was mesmerized by your performance. I kept looking at her from the corner of my eye, stealing glances. She was in a trance. I should have seen it then. It would have saved me a lot of embarrassment. It's been you all along. I'm sorry for…Matt, and I'm sorry for trying to steal your girl."

"I appreciate it, man." I nod. "I'm sorry for pushing you away. We both could have grieved together. Instead, we were knuckleheads. Can I ask you a question?"

I note the color of Trice's royal-blue eyes, so unlike mine. "Ask away."

"Did you know that I was adopted?" I ask, searching his face for a glimpse of truth.

"Honestly, no. Never in a million years would I have guessed that. Mom and dad told me about a week ago. They said they wouldn't allow any more secrets to plague our family. Does it really bother you that you're not blood related to us?"

I've asked myself that exact question a handful of times since I fled town. It's not the fact that I'm adopted that hurt so much. Being around Rory and Lonnie has taught me a lot about the foster care system. Not to mention that her come-to-Jesus moment with me yesterday left me with plenty to think about on my drive to the city today.

Gathering my bearings, I say, "It's the fact of being in the dark for so long and that I couldn't save you. I couldn't save Matt either and…it didn't sit well with me. I bolted. Aurora laid into me like I've never seen her before. She made a lot of valid points and hearing a little bit of her history in the foster care system was enough to turn my stomach. It made me think that maybe being adopted isn't such a bad thing after all."

"Someone was a match, though, Crew. Look at me. I'm thriving. Living my best life here. I think the nurse assistant who gave me last night's sponge bath and I might be hitting it off," he jokes. "I have nothing but time on my side. I'm going to need my big brother in the gym and at my physical therapy sessions. I'm glad you seem to have come to your senses, because you are as much a part of our family as I am. Blood doesn't mean anything to me, and if you ever hurt Rory again, just know that I'll be in a wheelchair for the foreseeable future ready to give her the ride of her life. You know of all the experience I've gained during your little crusade for purity."

"You're a perv."

"Hey, I'm not the one holding onto my virginity like a saint. Shit. Remind me to ask the doctor next time he comes in if my dick will still work."

I steal a quick glance at the door to make sure Aurora doesn't waltz through it before I spill my guts to my brother. Can you blame me? A man needs an outlet. "We had sex last night."

"You boned her in our parents' bed at the lake house, didn't you? You dirty dog. Hell yeah!" He raises his hand in the air, and I ignore his request for a high-five leaving him to slap his own hand with the other one.

Trice has always been flippant about his sexual encounters. If memory serves, he lost his virginity to some girl in our neighborhood when he was fourteen. He's had a slew of conquests since then. With his blonde hair, blue eyes, and southern twang, plenty of girls have fallen target to his spells.

The town nailed the wrong Jordan brother as a womanizer.

"Shut up. I'm not talking about this with you. Our intimate life is private."

"You're the one who brought it up, dude. You obviously want to talk about it. You finally punched your V card, and you want to skip out on sharing the details? Not happening. Spill."

With a stronger sense of protection and respect for Aurora, I'm not about to give him what he wants. "I'm not telling you anything. I shouldn't have brought it up. I just…we did it. A couple times and it was—"

"Worth the wait?"

"She was worth it. The first time I stumbled through the motions. By the third time, I found my groove. I've never felt more in tune with my body before I was in hers."

"I hope you used a rubber, and she doesn't become your baby mama."

"I'm not an idiot. Of course, we did." Satisfaction surges through my body. "I've been waiting for her my entire life. I love her, Trice. If I can ever earn her forgiveness for my little stunt and get back into her good graces, she'll be it for me. She's going to be my wife one day and maybe—far into the future—my baby mama."

"Damn. The sex was that good, huh?"

"You better wipe that smug look off your face and don't ever—" The creaking of the door stops me midsentence.

"Is it safe to come in?" Aurora asks.

"Come in," Trice answers. "We were just having a little chat about your evening. I hear it was *very* eventful."

"Crew, you didn't." Her eyes coolly accuse me of my indiscretion as she walks further into the room. "Tell me you guys aren't sitting here, casually talking about the fact that we made love last night."

"Well, if Crew didn't fess up. You sure in the hell just admitted to what went down."

Her glow of happiness appears to dim. "Trice, what would

happen if I took you on a wheelchair ride and left you near the infant nursery. Do you think you could yell for help louder than a room full of newborns?"

"You wound me," he winks when he catches her eye.

Holding up her cast, Aurora says, "I think we're even."

"Fair enough."

It's our cue to leave when the door opens and a nurse strolls in with a computer on wheels. We give Trice a quick goodbye and prepare for the next conversation that needs to be had.

CHAPTER
THIRTY-EIGHT

CREW

The sun's orange glow casts a shadow on Russell and Bea's house as we both pull into the driveway. I tell Aurora that I'm going to head home and get a quick shower. She refuses to see me off saying that we've spent enough time apart these past few weeks.

With my arm around her shoulder, I swing open the front door to her house and immediately want to backpedal. Russell looks like he wants to rearrange my face with his fist as he comes barreling into the foyer.

Aurora moves in front of me like a shield. "It's not his fault, Russell. I'm sorry. It completely slipped my mind that I was supposed to text you when I got there last night. I'm still not used to people being worried about my whereabouts. Don't blame him."

"I am blaming him. If he didn't run away, you wouldn't have had to chase him down, and I don't care that you're eighteen now, young lady. You could be thirty and Bea and I would still be concerned. It doesn't matter how old you are, you need to check in. And you," Russell juts a finger in my direction. "Your parents have been going out of their minds. Shawn is going to have to start dying his hair because of all the gray hairs that have sprouted. They're sick with worry. You need to talk to them and let them explain."

My irritation remerges, and I say gruffly, "They certainly owe me an explanation."

"You might have gotten one if you didn't storm off like a child before they had the chance to talk to you. You want to be a man? Then start acting like one."

Bea walks in and stands beside her husband. The foyer stills. "Come on now. Let's save the arguing until after dinner. Lonnie has been dying to have a slice of Rory's birthday cake. I'm going to call him up from the basement. Please wash up and go into the kitchen. We have a surprise for you." She and Russell turn and exit the foyer.

"We've had enough surprises for a lifetime. Come on," Aurora pulls my hand. "I'm going to eat my body weight in cake. Then we can go next door and talk to your parents. Then I'm going to sleep for like thirty days."

"Just sleep?" My eyes begin to undress her.

"You're insatiable."

"I'm nineteen. What do you expect?" I ask, Aurora's body stills beside me. It's good to know that she craves me just as much as I crave her.

We get situated at the kitchen table when Bea opens the basement door with Lonnie hot on her tail. "I was worried about you, Rory." He screeches and beelines for her chair.

"Inside voice," Bea scolds.

"You told me that we always need to say our feelings out loud," he responds. "This is me doing that. I was so scared that you got into another car wreck."

"I'm okay, buddy. See," Aurora motions to herself. "I just forgot to text Russell. It won't ever happen again, I promise."

That seems to satisfy him enough that he gives her a brief hug and then settles into a chair. Bea serves us dinner. Aurora and I both pile food on our plates like we haven't eaten in days.

Once we eat and sing to Aurora, Russell cuts the cake, and we devour our slices. We're spent for the evening. I know I need to get home and face my parents. Even though I dread hearing the truth, I need it. I need some type of closure.

"There's one more thing we have for you," Bea clasps her hands.

"Present time." Lonnie bounces in his chair.

Sliding a thin, manila folder in front of Aurora, Bea gives Russell a sidelong glance and they join hands.

"What is this?" Aurora asks.

"Open it please," Bea says in a low, controlled voice while gesturing to the folder.

A sharp intake of breath leaves Aurora as she opens the folder and slides out two separate documents.

"Adoption papers?"

"They're petition to adopt papers." Bea says, brushing her silver-blonde hair behind her ear in a show of nerves. "Russell and I would like to legally adopt Lonnie."

Confusion is written across Aurora's face. She looks like she's going to hurl. I grab her hand and grip it tightly, silently letting her know that I have her back. We made a vow that neither of us would ever have to face any hurdle alone again. I'm her tether in the storm and she is mine.

"Every child deserves a safe and loving home. To know that they are valuable and worthy of love. We know you just turned eighteen and you're officially an adult. You can make your own decisions and choices, but…we want to adopt you too." Bea's voice waivers. Like a ball of nerves is caught in her throat she pales and takes a deep breath. "We love you as our own, Rory, and want to legally be your forever family if you'll have us."

Joy bubbles in Aurora's laugh and a yelp of what I assume is excitement breaks from her lips. My only purpose in life is to hear that sound, over, and over again. Aurora endured more than any teenager or person should ever be forced to. She knows what it's like to be hungry, without shelter, or protection from this world.

When she stumbled into my life, I was lost. I was on a voyage without a map to an unknown destination. She became the destination for me. Filling the empty parts of me that Matt's death left in my heart, and then she pieced me back together without even trying. Aurora won me over effortlessly and although it took a little more convincing for her to love me back, she finally said it.

Aurora and I share a bond so deep, born from tragedy and adversities, we formed a union, that has etched its way permanently into our hearts. She owns my heart and soul.

And my future.

I glance over to see a single tear slide down my girl's face. Not giving her time to react or weigh in on Russell and Bea's plan to adopt her, I lean forward and brush her tear away with my lips.

"Don't get used to sharing their last name for an extended period," I whisper. "You won't have it for long."

CHAPTER
THIRTY-NINE

RORY

High school came to an end a few days after my birthday, and with that monumental day having finally passed, I've tried to envision a new plan for my life.

My goal of adopting Lonnie and fleeing the state is now moot since Bea and Russell are in the process of adopting him. It's bittersweet. Knowing I will legally be his sister, though, will forever be the best birthday present I've ever received. I can't, however, tell Crew that his star isn't my favorite anymore. He'll get bent out of shape and no one wants a whiny boyfriend.

Yes, I've decided to cut him some slack knowing that he was under astronomical stress and made a mistake. We're only human. Sometimes we need a little grace, and I hope if I ever need it, he'll extend the same to me.

It's only been a few days since we've been back in town and have established a new normal in both our household and with our neighbors. After Crew's conversation with his parents, he finally got the answers he wanted and desperately needed. All except the identities of his birth parents. The worry lines on his forehead seem to have slackened some. I think learning that he was wanted by a mom and dad who so desperately desired to be parents has soothed and healed him.

We've had a decent couple of days. Even though he's been exceptionally sneaky today. I texted him to ask if he wanted to watch a new release with me that Trice was raving about, but he blew me off, giving me some bogus excuse about not feeling well.

We were heading in the right direction with our relationship, until today. Now I don't know what to think. Uncertainty has raised its ugly head and made herself known.

I fire off a text to Trice to try and ease my nerves.

Me: Your brother is a dweeb

Trice: Try living with him. You could have picked the more superior Jordan (insert selfie of Trice)

Me: Stop! :P

Trice: Maybe one day if you guys get married I will. Nah. I'll still flirt with you even as his wife just to get under his skin

Me: I can't win with either of you. What's his deal today? He's moody

Trice: You'll see

Me: I'll see what?

Trice: What has my big bro's panties in a twist

Me: I need more info. Enacting friend code

Trice: Enacting bro code. You'll see soon enough

Me: You're being weird

As I lay my head back on my pillow a knock sounds at my door. "Come in," I call out.

"I'm going to say something that sounds very cryptic. I need you to go along with it." Bea stands with her hands behind her back holding onto a piece of paper and a mischievous smile stamped across her face. "I have a map to give you."

"A map for what?"

"If I give this to you, the only caveat is that you have to text me at every stop."

My brow furrows. "Why are you spouting off with a riddle?"

"Do you agree?" Bea edges closer to the foot of my bed and dangles the rolled piece of paper in my face, taunting me.

Curiosity killed the cat, but hey, cats have nine lives. I've survived foster care and a car wreck that should have killed me. Surely the instructions on a sheet of paper won't be what takes me out. "I agree. Gimme." I hold out my hand, and she places the rolled paper in my palm. "A map? You weren't kidding."

"It's a scavenger hunt. Get dressed. Keys are on the table in the foyer. Have fun and remember to text me at every stop so I know that you're safe. I'm taking Lonnie and Aiden to a birthday party at their friend's house." Before I have time to respond or ask why I'm going on a scavenger hunt, she leaves and shuts the door behind her, preventing me from getting any answers.

I get dressed like a mad woman on a mission. Like that game show where you can keep any item of clothing for free if you can put it on your body and wear it. Brushing my hands through my hair, I swing open my bedroom door and sprint down the steps. The first X written on the map appears to be at our town's cemetery. Although I can walk there, I decide to drive since I don't know where the other stops on the map will take me.

When I get to the cemetery, I jump out of Matt's old truck as my eyes roam over the plots all littered with flowers. Not one gravestone is missed. It's a picturesque sight.

"Over here," I hear, recognizing Andrea's voice. She steps out from behind a tree, and I beeline toward her.

"I have something for you," she says, placing a letter in my hand. "I've lived in this town my entire life. I've seen a lot of people get together, but I've never seen anyone find their soul mate here." She gives me a tight squeeze and a gentle slap on my rear before turning and heading toward her car.

"Thank you," I yell as she climbs inside and blows me a kiss before driving off.

I'm bemused by first Bea's exit and now Andrea's.

I fire off a text to Bea, letting her know that I arrived at my first destination, and then I unfold the paper Andrea handed me.

My eyes widen with the familiarity of the handwriting.

Dearest Aurora,

A little birdie told me that you felt sorry for the abandoned headstones. I can't imagine never visiting Matt's grave. Contrary to Trice's belief on the matter —which I came clean to him about—I've never come home from campus and NOT stopped at Matt's gravesite. Trice told me about the first day of school last year and how you stole flowers from a couple of plots to give to those who had none. As you can see today, no gravesite is empty. My only purpose is to make you happy and if that means coming by the cemetery weekly to place flowers on every single grave, I'll do it for you. I'm sorry for abandoning you when you needed me most. I vow to make it up to you. I hope by the end of the night, you'll see how sorry I am and just how much you mean to me.

See you soon,

Crew

I grew up feeling alone. Unloved and unwanted. I never knew that I could feel…contentment like this. Trice may have opened the door to my heart and showed me that I am likable and worthy of true friendship. But Crew swung it open and then removed it from its hinges. His love has healed me and brought me more joy than I can even explain as I stand and look across the field at each plot lined with flowers.

I glance over my shoulder to see that I'm alone before I gulp back a sob and hot tears glisten my cheeks. I weep happy tears and, for the first time in my eighteen years on this earth, my spirit is at peace.

The drive to the next stop seems to take forever, even though it's less than two miles. My knee won't stop bouncing as I drive, even with my persistent attempt to keep it settled. The X on the next stop appears to be at the lake located in the center of town. I follow the speed limit silently cursing and wishing I could go faster.

When I arrive, I anxiously sit in the truck and look around the area as I slip the gearshift into park. People go about their business, blissfully unaware of my anticipation to see what I'm going to discover next at this stop on my map. There's a couple walking their dog. A mom and her small child enjoying a picnic. And a guy with pale blond hair and eyes the color of the sky sitting in a wheelchair with both of his legs in casts.

Trice.

I jump out of the truck and jog over to him. "What's going on and don't lie to me? I don't like games and I'm… confused as to what this charade is all about." I rant as I approach him.

"What's there to be confused about, Rory? My brother is madly in love with you and is taking you on a journey that you won't ever forget. Don't ruin it with your need to know everything and be in control. Here," he reaches into the pocket of his hoodie. "I have something for you. Make sure you sit down over there on the bench and read it. The bench has the best view of the lake."

"The lake." *The one that Matt died in.* I refrain from asking, knowing the truth in my gut.

"The very one. See you later." Trice answers my question.

I'm getting pretty good at not being perturbed by sudden departures at this point. I watch as a woman in scrubs pushes

Trice's wheelchair back to a van and then helps load him inside of it before I pull my attention to my next letter.

Taking a deep breath, I open it.

Aurora,

Welcome to the spot that changed my life for the worst and the better. It occurred to me that I've never brought you here. In all honestly, I've avoided this part of town as much as possible. I figured if we're going to move forward together, we might as well do it with no burdens plaguing our past. This is the lake that took Matt from our world and left me an emotional Jenga puzzle. The water is just as much at fault as Trice is for wrecking, and me for letting him drive in the first place. I lost Matt that night along with a piece of myself. You helped to fill the void that his death left in my heart, Aurora. You were able to piece together my broken heart, and I hope that I can make amends for hurting yours.

See you soon,

Crew

Stunned into silence, I sit with my hands under my thighs and stare out at the water. I'm not sure where this night will bring me. I can only hope it's into Crew's waiting arms. This sharing and outpouring of love is enough to send me weeping to my knees. I'm wildly in love with Crew Jordan and when I see him, I'm going to kiss him like there's no tomorrow. I don't need a map to know that. He's the X that's already stamped upon my heart.

Taking one last glance at the lake, I stuff the letter into my back pocket and pull out the map. Freddy's Corner Store is the next stop on today's adventure. I think I know what this clue is about. It's where we first met. I decide to walk since it's less than a block away, leaving Matt's truck in the parking lot. I practically skip through town, high on adrenaline, only to find Lonnie holding hands with Russell near the front door of the store. The neon open sign is off. Bewilderment stuns me. "I thought you were with Bea?"

"We fooled her." Lonnie looks up at Russell with a cheesy smirk. "I told Crew I was a good actor."

"We have something to give you." I already know what Russell is going to give me before he holds out his hand and places a piece of paper in mine. "I'll text Bea and tell her you made it to your next stop. Go inside." He gestures to the door. "Don't go easy on him." The *him* he's referring to I assume is Crew. "Make him sweat for a while. He hurt you, and it's okay to forgive those we care about, but men are fools a lot of the time. More often than not."

"Thanks." I whisper, before he turns and he and Lonnie head down the sidewalk, away from where I'm planted.

"Let's see what door number three has in store shall we?" I say aloud to myself.

Stepping through the threshold of the store, tears fill my eyes.

There, resting in the aisle where we first met, is a giant stuffed teddy bear that towers over the shelves, holding a red balloon. I move as fast as lightning and grab the note attached to the bear.

Aurora,

I know you loathe cigarettes, but can you imagine if I wasn't here that day? I certainly can't. I'm sorry that I was so bullheaded, and we spent months bickering like fools when we could have used that time to get to know one another better. One thing is for sure, you said you didn't need a knight in shining armor that day, and you were right. Because in the end, you're the one who saved me.

There's one last stop on your map. I think I saved the best for last. I'll see you shortly.

I love you,

Crew

As sure as I am that automobiles *can't* fly, I am certain that Crew is the love of my life. No apprehension resides in my heart anymore. My posture wilts as I place a hand on the wall next to me and try to catch my breath. I don't know when he had the time to plan today's events, or how he managed to rope everyone in on his scheme, including Freddy, the store owner.

A part of me is beaming at his plan to win my forgiveness. It's safe to say that it's working because I don't care if the next stop is as ordinary as sitting and playing a game of chess. If Crew is there, and I'm in his arms, I'll be happy.

Swinging open the door to Freddy's store, I'm greeted on the street with patrons out and about. The sun illuminates the horizon and casts its shadow over the open field adjacent to the town square. With summer right around the corner, our little town is about to be teeming with tourists. It's wild to think just a year ago, I too, was a visitor to this town.

It feels like *home* now. Except home isn't a place. It's a person.

Crew.

Giving the map a quick look, I notice that the last X on my map has me walking less than a block away. Wanting to get to that spot before the sun fully sets, I hustle through the crowd on the sidewalk, brushing by them in a rush to find my boyfriend.

The building where I was instructed to go appears to be abandoned. There are no lights on in the storefront, much less a sign, and newspaper covers the inside of the large front window. I slide out my phone and shoot Crew a text, afraid to go inside, lest I meet a murderer lurking the depths of the dark storefront.

Me: *I'm at the last X. This can't be right*

Crew: *You're not lost. The door's unlocked. Come inside, babe*

It takes some might to push open the heavy door. I step inside the large rectangular room. My eyes are met with darkness that seems to swallow the entire area. The building is far longer than it is wide and has several metal poles throughout the space giving it an industrial feel. There is the faint rustling of the bush planted just outside the door, but no other sound can be heard within other than that of my footsteps and my nervous breathing. I take a step backward toward the door in order to stand in the weak light that is shining from the street-lamp outside.

"Crew?" I call out, my voice trembling. If this is his idea of a prank, the joke is about to be on him because I am not sticking around a second longer. I'm about to head for the door when his voice halts me in my tracks.

"Where do you think you're going?" Crew asks as the room grows bright enough for me to see. Turning around, I find Crew at the center of the room. Several strands of stringed bulbs hang above him from the rafters in the shape of another X. Their glow is enough to illuminate the other-wise dreary, empty space.

He's the real treasure on my map.

My breath catches as my line of vision travels from the strands of lights hanging above Crew's head to fully take him in. Dark wisps of hair frame his face. He's wearing his classic jeans and a black shirt in true Crew Jordan fashion. I could stand here and admire him forever. Pulling me from my stupor, he calls to me.

"Come over here, beautiful. I have your last letter."

Without missing a beat, I glide forward and into his awaiting arms. They're like cuddling into a warm blanket straight out of the dryer. "What is all of this about?"

"I was plotting how to earn your forgiveness. It took more time than I had originally anticipated. Plus, I had to gather some reinforcements. This is my grand apology."

"How did you get Trice out of the hospital, or do I even want to know?" I laugh, thinking about the lengths Crew has gone to for this surprise. "Thank you for all of this. I...I don't know what else to say. Other than where's the last letter I was promised?"

Clutching my hand, he guides me to an easel that is set up

in the middle of the room. He pulls out the stool and I take a seat while not so patiently waiting for my prize. I will cherish these handwritten letters forever. With a gentle tug, the material that was covering the image on the easel falls to the floor and my stomach with it.

In Crew's handwriting penned on the canvas, it reads:

You are the anchor that keeps me steady, floating above the current that threatens to pull me under.

You are the sliver of light in the dreary dusk that I cling to, avoiding the shadows of uncertainty in this life.

You are the beauty in chaos.

You are a Bradshaw-Greenwell.

Will you be a Jordan?

I look up, disoriented by his words and a commotion of sounds coming from a dark hallway. Confused, my eyes dart around the room as my family and friends appear and stand around Crew and I, forming a circle. My mouth falls open as I realize what is happening.

Too stunned to cry, I turn my head in search of Crew. His presence centers me just as much as I do to him, based upon his declaration on the canvas. When his gleaming honey-colored eyes find mine, we hold a stare that speaks without our mouths moving. Crew takes my hand. I'm thankful for his reassuring touch as the small crowd around us grows silent.

"I love you more than I've ever loved anything or anyone in this world. It's unusual, some might even say rushed, to fall in love so young and commit your life to another person. I say the world can go fuck itself. I'm tired of trying to please other people and be what society expects of me. All I care about is being good to you. Loyal. Protective. And respectful. I won't make you promises that I'll never screw up again, or that we're going to be happy every day for the rest of our lives. That's not real. Life is about embracing the chaos. I want to make the hard times easier. I want to give you the life you dreamed you'd have. *I* want to be your forever home. Not this town. Not even because we'll share a last name. *Me.* I want to be your refuge just as much as you are mine."

My heart squeezes as Crew's words float around me. They're full of promise, optimism, and redemption.

"Will you marry me, Aurora Elyse Bradshaw-Greenwell and make me the luckiest guy in the entire state of Kentucky? Hell, in the whole damn universe?"

His question hasn't garnered an answer before Lonnie is passing him a painted canvas with words sprawled across it. I'm not even sure when he had time to plan a proposal of this magnitude. It's evident by the wide smile cut onto his strong jawline and the amateur painting that he's holding in his hands. It looks like he took duct tape and spelled out the words will you marry me with a question mark and then splattered an array of colors on the canvas that spread out in different directions. My heart swells at the gesture.

Standing, I seize the painting from his hands and gesture for Lonnie to take it back and then nod. Crew arches a dark brow. He already knows my answer, but as stubborn as he is, he wants to hear it.

"Yes. Yes, I'll marry you. Under one condition though."

"I'm listening."

"We're framing these in our first place together. I want to remember this day for eternity."

"Facts." He treats me to a beautiful smile before his lips come down on mine. I bury my hands into the thickness of his hair as our entourage of onlookers clap and cheer, showing their outpouring of support.

Crew never got the closure he desired after we learned a few days ago that his adoptive parents wished to remain anonymous. He did, however, choose to accept that he is an adoptee. We both did. Because I allowed Russell and Bea to adopt me. It seems, though, that Crew has stolen their thunder, as the ink on their petition form is barely dry.

Despite all that, he just proposed with the most heartfelt declaration of love I've ever borne witness to.

The reality of all that's transpired this evening settles in, and I lean forward and kiss my fiancé's chin.

Crew Jordan is going to be my forever family.

EPILOGUE
ONE YEAR LATER...

RORY

It's been a cyclone of a year.

Trice remained in rehab for months and underwent several grueling surgeries. With his dreams of being a football star dashed, his only goal now is to be able to walk without assistance. Fear gnawed away at my once full-of-life friend, and he sunk deep into a depression as he grieved the lost mobility of his body. Justifiably so. Even with the support of his brother, who opted to take classes online so he could be at Trice's bedside and help aid in his recovery, Trice plummeted into a slump that not even Crew's presence or mine, could save him from.

Having your entire life turned upside down will do that to you. Trust me, I know a thing or two about tidal waves of life changing events.

Pain and happiness coincide and come in bunches, and sometimes, one outweighs the other. That's the beauty of life though. We can accept our realities and yield to the world allowing its pandemonium to numb us to our cores, or we can stand up and fight like hell for the lives we envision for ourselves. Breaking any generational curses along the way.

I chose to fight.

Crew chose to fight.

Trice has taken strides to fight for a future that doesn't confine him to a wheelchair. That's good enough for right now.

Crew and I have spent the last year falling deeper in love and have been absorbed in planning our small, intimate wedding since his shotgun proposal. With Crew finally declaring his major in college as business, his pursuit of obtaining his degree will help our future endeavors. The goal to open a small art studio has been heavy on my mind after learning that the building where we got engaged was vacant.

Bea and Russell—yes, I still call them by their first names, although Lonnie is smitten every time he calls out for his mom or dad—agreed that since we've kept the wedding costs low, they would like to gift us with a monetary present. And since we also declined Crew's parents offer of an extravagant honeymoon, we've opted to use that money to invest in our futures.

I'm not the kind of girl who daydreamed about what her future held. I'm a realist. The future was always bleak. Until I met Crew. He gave color to my world and made it beautiful. Since then, I haven't stopped dreaming. I want a place where people can come and gather to make art in any form they wish, where it won't cost a fortune either.

With Crew's business degree and my knack for art, we can create our own haven for artists. Our little version of the sacred clubhouse where you can choose from painting, molding clay, or just having a small sanctuary to read or write.

Luckily for me, my fiancé supports my dreams whole-heartedly.

That said, I'm proud to announce, we're the new owners

of an unoccupied building. An added bonus is that there's a small, open-floor-plan apartment upstairs that we plan to move into after the wedding.

The wedding that is happening today.

"Head out of the clouds, Rory." Andrea snaps her fingers in front of me with one hand, while the other holds her bouquet of flowers. "Are you having cold feet or something? I told you the only way this dress is coming off me tonight is if someone is peeling it off with their teeth."

Casting my eyes downward, I take a deep, steadying breath. "I'd be stupid to leave Crew Jordan at the altar. Plus, I missed prom. I can't miss this too." My joke falls flat.

"What's on your mind then, because I've been talking to you for a couple minutes and your head was in a haze?"

"Pinch me," I instruct my friend and hold out my arm.

"You're not kidding, are you?"

"Not even a little bit. Shut your face and pinch me." Every muscle in my body tenses as I await her fingers wrath.

"Ouch!"

"Don't go all bridezilla on me. You told me to pinch you. You should have specified how hard."

I whisper, "This isn't a dream."

"Of course, it's not, and it's not the time to ponder the enormity of this day. Your fiancé is waiting for you down that aisle out there, and Lonnie is chomping at the bit outside this door. He's going to wear a hole into the floor and fall through it if we don't hurry. Take a deep breath and let's go get you married to the love of your life."

"People are saying we're too young to get married, ya know? Crew's own grandparents refused our invitation to the ceremony. Maybe we need to wait and have a longer engagement."

Andrea's fingers grab either side of my face, and she tugs my jaw forward. "You've been engaged for a year already. Screw those snobby, old goons. Tell me this, are you in love with him, Rory? Because I've never seen you this happy. Does true love come with an age restriction? Who cares what people think. You and Crew have something rare and real. To have found it at our age is fates doing."

"That's a stupid question. I love him more than anything in this entire world." I bite my lip and take another deep breath trying to relax.

The truth is, I would have married Crew the night he asked me. We both agreed to wait a year at the discretion of our parents. I shake off my nerves and square my shoulders. "Okay. I'm ready for my happily ever after. I deserve *him*."

With Russell on one arm and the other looped with Lonnie's, I peek down the aisle at the altar. Crew stands with both hands in his pockets looking like the essence of sex appeal. I can't wait until he sees what I have for him on our wedding night.

The music plays, and as we inch forward, I finally take in our surroundings. Andrea stands to the left of the altar, and next to Crew, Trice sits in his wheelchair. It's still a sight to see him without any casts or metal on his legs. The contrast of his blonde hair and blue eyes against his navy suit makes him stand out in a crowd. I know one day he will make a woman proud to call him hers.

He doesn't do justice to the sight of his brother though. With his dark, russet hair and eyes as rich as honey, I know I've won the husband jackpot.

Russell guides me to the altar and the officiant gleams while asking who gives me away. The magnitude of this moment sinks in. The girl who strolled into town with nothing but a baseball cap and a trash bag with all her worldly belongings stored in it. Who had to steal allergy pills from the corner market, is now standing before her family and friends in a white dress.

I'm marrying my best friend and becoming a picket-fence woman.

As my fiancé takes my hand in his, he gently rubs his thumb along the top of my folded fingers. I'm lost in the depth of his eyes. Eyes that drew me in from the first glance and have held me captive under their watchful gaze since our initial encounter. As we prepare to say our vows, I look around nervously.

His gentle touch settles on my chin. "Look at me, Aurora. It's just us. You and me against the world. Focus on that."

The buzzing in my stomach calms with his words, and I recite my vows, repeating word for word after the officiant. When it's Crew's turn, he turns to face Trice, who slowly stands. My eyes water at the sight of my best friend standing on his own. I watch as his dad, Shawn, comes up beside him and offers his shoulder for support and then pushes his wheelchair out of the way.

"Just because you got the girl brother, doesn't mean I can't steal the show," Trice says, joking before handing Crew a folded piece of paper.

"Aurora," Crew reads, his voice gravelly and full of emotion. "Even though I know you're a force of your own and can weather any storm life throws at you because you're a complete badass—sorry, Mom." He pauses and turns to Mina, who waves him on from her seat in the front row. "I promise to keep you safe and to stand beside you like a beacon in the night, reminding you that home is wherever we are when we're together. I'll love you until my last breath, Aurora Elyse Jordan, and I can't wait to see where this journey takes us."

"Bones?" He knows the meaning and that I'm asking if he will take his vows to the grave.

Giving me a slow nod, Crew smiles. It's filled with affection and delight. Our guests fade into the background as he cups my chin in his hands, leans forward until our foreheads are touching and says, "Bones," in a whisper only I can hear.

Our mouths crash together in kiss that reminds me of our first so long ago.

I'm hypnotized by my husband's mouth as the faint sound of applause and our officiant's voice remind me that we're not alone. "I hadn't gotten there yet," the officiant says, "but since you skipped to the good part, let me now pronounce you husband and wife."

THE END

WILL YOU
MARRY
ME?

ACKNOWLEDGEMENTS

First and foremost, I want to thank God for so many things, including the ability to weave a story together. My writing, including my style, has changed a lot since my first novel was published in 2013, and for that I am relived. Honing one's craft takes time and dedication, and I have poured my heart and soul into this novel.

After an eight-year publishing hiatus, I think my husband, Vincent, had forgotten what it was like for me to dedicate so much time to writing again. Thank you for picking up when I slacked on chores and cooking dinner. I know my stomach and our son's is appreciative that you know your way around the kitchen.

I'd like to give a special thank you to my own therapist, Rebecca. After our arduous adoption journey, and the loss of my mom to Covid-19, I needed a healthy outlet. She quickly became a blessing in disguise. I am forever grateful to her for her words of wisdom in a dark time in my life.

To Jennifer Wolfel and Kerri Elizabeth, the first friends/beta readers to read *Beauty in Chaos*. Without your communication, trustworthiness, and criticism, this manuscript wouldn't be what it is today. You both have been amazing allies through my publishing journey, and I am so thankful to each of you for not only your time and dedication to my work, but also for your companionship. To the rest of my beta readers: Elle, and Courtney, your input and constructive criticism is very much valued.

I also want to thank Becca Manuel. She not only beta read for me on this book, but a couple of my publications before this. I will always remember her kindness and amazing hugs. She is a pillar in the book world, and she will be missed dearly. Fly high, my friend.

To Andrea Buisson, every blonde must have a brunette best friend. It's an unspoken rule. Not only is it rare that our sons have been best friends since they were both one years old, but that we are thick as thieves as well. Your friendship is invaluable to me. Some people come into our lives for a certain season. I'm just glad you came into mine and never left. Even if you're not a hugger, I think the completion of this novel deserves a big one!

To Holly Malgieri from Comma Sutra Editorial a special thanks for being the last set of eyes to read my manuscript and to my agent, Savannah Greenwell from Two Daisy Media for having my back in the weeks leading up to publishing and to Colleen Oppenheim and my team at The Next Step PR for being the best group of hype girls I've ever met.

If heaven had stairs, I'd climb them two-by-two like Crew did in the football stadium scene just to get to you, Mom. This book is dedicated to your memory. I wish you were here to read it. As I type this and tears fall down my cheeks, I am so appreciative that you showed me how to be an amazing mother. Thank you for raising me to have a good head on my shoulders, for teaching me how to be independent, and for believing in me and encouraging me to chase my dreams. Until we meet again. I love you.

Lastly, and certainly not least, thank you to whoever is reading this right now. If you're a new-to-me reader, thank you for purchasing my book and taking a chance on it. And if you're a faithful reader, thank you for allowing me distance during my publishing break. In that time, my husband and I welcomed our son into our lives, I graduated college with two degrees, and I found a spark that had dulled in me. It is because of you that I can take the chatter that goes on inside my head and make it come to life.

ABOUT THE AUTHOR

Nacole Stayton is thirty-something years young and resides in the Bourbon Capital of the World with her husband and son. Her debut novel, The Upside of Letting Go is an Amazon top 100 bestseller. She spends her days working in healthcare as a practice administrator and her evenings pinning away on her next novel. She can usually be found playing with monster trucks and dodging Nerf gun darts or enjoying an iced coffee poolside.

Join Nacole's reading group on Facebook, Nacole's Nation, for exclusive content, giveaways and more.

Visit www.nacolestaytonauthor.com
to purchase signed books, merchandise & swag.